Catherine McGregor is graduate of the Royal Military College Duntroon from which she was appointed to the Royal Australian Infantry. She was awarded the CEW Bean Scolarship for military history and undertook postgraduate study in Military History at Oxford University. Over four decades she held a range of operational and strategic policy postings including serving as speech writer to every Chief of Army from 1999 to 2014.

On Australia Day 2012 Catherine was awarded the Order of Australia for her exceptional service to the Australian Army. She has held senior political advisory roles and served to some of Australia's most significant political leaders including Bob Carr and Kim Beazley. Catherine is a senior cricket writer at News Limited and also an editorial writer and columnist for the *Daily Telegraph*. She has played cricket for over five decades and remains active as a player coach and selector.

An Indian Summer of Cricket

Reflections on Australia's Summer Game.

Catherine McGregor

ECHO BOOKS

First published in 2012 by Barrallier Books Pty Ltd. This second edition
published by Echo Books, an imprint of Barrallier Books Pty Ltd.
Registered office 35-37 Gordon Avenue, West Geelong, Victoria 3220 Australia
Copyright © Catherine McGregor
National Library of Australia cataloguing-in-publication entry:
McGregor, Catherine, 1956-.
Title: An Indian summer of cricket: reflections on Australia's summer game/
Catherine McGregor
ISBN: 9780995367784 (pbk)
Notes: Includes index.
Subjects: McGregor, Catherine, 1956-
Cricket--Australia--History.
Sportswriters--Australia--Biography.
Transgender people--Australia--Biography.
Life change events.

Book and cover design by Peter Gamble, Canberra
Typeset in Garamond Premier Pro 12/17 and Fragrance
www.echobooks.com.au
Cover photo: Mark Evans © Newspix.
Published by *The Daily Telegraph*, January 7, 2012.

Contents

To Tritia Evans. My greatest love.

Foreword

An Indian Summer of Cricket is a book as unique as its author. To the happy-go-lucky ship of fools of the Australian cricket press box, Malcolm McGregor was in 2011-12 a welcome addition—an alert, wordly outsider with a lyrical pen, a tender heart and a quicksilver intellect, just as likely to involve you in a conversation concerning counter terrorism or the American Civil War as about the off-break or forward press. His judgement was mellow, but his wit was quick: I remember envying a line of his about Michael Clarke needing his smooth edges roughened.

Little did we know that Malcolm harboured a secret, but then, perhaps, Malcolm was doing his best to avoid this secret's acknowledgement. It came out anyway, in his life, and in the concluding pages of his book, that Malcolm suffered acute gender dysphoria, and had at last resolved to face it. Deep as the wealth of cricket literature is, I would wager that no previous volume has contained a line as unanticipated as: 'By the time this book is launched I expect to be living permanently as a woman.'

Five years on, Catherine McGregor is a figure far better known, with a profile far outstripping the pressbox. But it affords me great pleasure that the friendship we formed in that season of the Border-Gavaskar Trophy has only strengthened. I have held her handbag at the Lodge. I have broken her foot with a straight drive. I have seen her in public and in private, in joy and facing challenge, and the experience has at every stage been enriching. That cricket brought us together, allowing for the establishment of a deeper bond, is in a way what *An Indian Summer* is all about. The love of cricket is not only about cricket; it is about love. For sure it's only a game, but a warm relationship with anything puts us in touch with our finer feelings. And it has, as Catherine likes to say, 'a rich, poetic heart.'

Glancing back over *An Indian Summer* rekindles many happy memories, and a few disappointing ones. The cricket was, at times, exasperatingly one-sided, a let-down, a chore. But sometimes so is life, which should make us cherish the good. Maybe that's why Catherine and I both cherish Test cricket, that it can press down on us like everyday existence, then every so often offer possibilities so delirious and kaleidoscopic as to carry us away. And it's hard to imagine that I'd have had the chance to get acquainted with Malcolm in the environs of a T20 series, in which case I'd never have come to count Catherine a friend. The gradual passing, the dawning awarenesses, the comings and goings, the dartings and divagations—Catherine unfolds cricket gently and lovingly, and reveals at last its potential as a vehicle of personal revelation.

GIDEON HAIGH
Melbourne
October 2016

Ricky Ponting helps Sachin Tendulkar during the third Test match of Australia's tour of India on 2 November 2008 at the Feroz Shah Kotla ground in New Delhi.
Picture by Graham Crouch Published: The Daily Telegraph, *November 3, 2008. (Graham Crouch © Newspix)*

Acknowledgements

This book is a tribute to a game which I love deeply and which. I feel has defined me and comforted me during my most challenging times. The book is dedicated to Tritia Evans my soul mate. As extravagant as my praise for her is it cannot convey the depth of what we shared.

Gideon Haigh has provided a foreword beside which my prose dims like Tavare following Sobers.

Beyond those whose kindness and inspiration first saved my life then imbued it with richness who are amply credited in the text, many of the complement of our rollicking ship of fools warrant special thanks. The camaraderie of the media contingent is deep, authentic and reflects the spirit of the game. All of these people have made indelible impacts on my life through their generous friendship. I am a better person and a vastly better writer for knowing them: Scyld Berry, Derek Pringle, Vic Marks, Ed Smith, Barney Ronay, Mike Selvey, Jonathan Agnew, Henry Blofeld, Peter Lalor, Will Swanton, Andrew Faulkner Wayne Smith, the incomparably funny George Dobell, Dan Brettig, Melinda Farrell, Roz Kelly, Greg Chappell, Russell Jackson, Dean Jones and Greg Matthews.

My publisher Ian Gordon conceived of this revised edition and had been patient and professional as always.

Since transition I have had no more stalwart friend than the brilliant beautiful and inspirational Ayla Holdom. The woman I knew before we even met.

I hope this work is worthy of all your grace and belief in me.

We all speak cricket.

Images

... Cowper's massive innings straddling the introduction of decimal currency in 1966 as a milestone in dissolving the cultural cringe.

1.   *An Indian Summer*
—cricket in the afternoon of life

Indian Summer (n):

1.   (Earth Sciences/Physical Geography) a period of unusually settled warm weather after the end of summer proper.

2.   A period of ease and tranquility or of renewed productivity towards the end of a person's life or of an epoch. See also Saint Martin's Summer.

'... the Australian summer, which incorporates Christmas and the long school vacations, is a time of optimism and restoration for most Australians, and ... Test cricket is the central, unifying ritual of this period.'

My spirit was soaring. Bus travel provides an opportunity for reflection. Moreover, it permits me to indulge in a vice that is the source of significant irritation to my wife and is therefore prohibited on long car journeys or in our home. As I have aged I have fallen in love with sixteenth and seventeenth century polyphony almost to the exclusion of other forms of music.

While I have long loved Gregorian chant and the music of the Renaissance church, finding it moving to the point of tears, it became something of an obsession through a spring and summer spent in Oxford in 2008. During that idyllic year I often visited college chapels and the Oxford Oratory to listen to their sung Vespers. It moved me deeply. Subtly over time I have almost lost the flavour of other forms of music, though occasionally I still pick up my guitar to strum along with Donovan singing *Catch the Wind* or some other anthem of my baby boomer youth.

On that winter day last year, as my coach wended its way to my home in Canberra, I was playing my very favourite piece of music over and over. This habit—or perhaps more accurately, defect of character—simply sends my wife Tritia spare. She loves music, including polyphony, but is more capable of moderation in all things than I. For me, abstinence is preferable to moderation. I either do something to excess, or refrain entirely. Moderation is impossible. Those capable of it tend to bemuse me. I neither envy nor pity them. But understand them? Never.

These days I accept my addictive nature with weary equanimity. If something makes me feel good then excess comes naturally and inevitably. I learnt this the hard way with alcohol more than two decades ago. These days it applies with equal measure to music and caffeine—and cricket. This may explain my vice of playing single passages of beautiful music repeatedly in pursuit of some form of transcendence. Others do not always enjoy the thirty-fifth consecutive repeat of Stile Antico's rendition of Clemens non Papa's *Ego flos campi* as much as they did the first.

Anyway, in my mind there will always be a link between this story and that piece of music. When I embarked on that bus journey, I had not planned to write about cricket. When I alit at the Jolimont Centre in wintry Canberra amid the gathering early dark, I was animated by a passion to write about India's forthcoming tour of Australia. The soaring cadences of Stile Antico had unlocked something inside me as my jaded Murrays coach, with its tired and torn upholstery, journeyed through an uncommonly lush winter landscape.

Some background is essential. Over the preceding weeks Tritia and I had been glued to television coverage of the Test series between England

and India. During a holiday at Port Douglas we had enjoyed access to live coverage of the Tests at Lord's and Trent Bridge. Pretty soon I was hooked and had watched almost every ball. Sleep? Moderation? See foregoing.

Surprisingly, the series also captivated Tritia. As Stuart Broad wrecked India in Nottingham I briefly feigned maturity and generosity to inquire, 'It's a pretty small room and I've been monopolising the telly a bit. Is this bothering you?' She looked up from her novel and said, 'No, I actually like the sound of the cricket. The low hum of the crowd is soothing. And the commentary is often radio at its best'.

Her response inspired this book in a way that neither of us was aware of on that hot August night in tropical Queensland. She enjoys cricket (though in moderation) and particularly enjoys the ritual of the first day of the New Year Test at the Sydney Cricket Ground. But she also had a long and successful career in broadcast journalism and her ear for what constitutes good radio is acute.

Tritia's comment reminded me that some of my earliest memories were of the sound of cricket on the radio either in the family car or my childhood home in Toowoomba. There was something deeply reassuring in the sound of those mellifluous voices describing play at exotic locations—Brisbane fitting that description to a kid in Toowoomba in 1962.

Although I have scattered memories of my very early childhood, attendance at school clearly demanded a level of consciousness hitherto absent. To a shy, somewhat sickly kid it also inflicted a trauma that makes my recollections of the events of 1962, my first year at school, surprisingly vivid. Ted Dexter led the Marylebone Cricket Club touring party to Australia and I gleaned from the rapt attention of my mother, father, older siblings and our neighbours that this was a matter of national importance. 'Have you heard a score?' seemed to be the ubiquitous initial greeting among adults that summer—preceding even the routine inquiry as to health and well-being. Invariably someone was able to provide an accurate answer, including the names of the not out batsmen.

Likewise, I learnt that the Poms were our natural enemies. The cognitive dissonance involved in maintaining this rage was lost on me at the time. The hatred of the English was kept within strict boundaries, namely their cricket team and their Rugby League team—unless they were playing New South Wales.

My parents had lived through the Bodyline tour and were still incensed by the English tactics. My mother in particular, confessed to a schoolgirl crush on Bill Woodfull and could be relied on—at least once every summer—to recount in lurid detail the incident in Adelaide where the English fast bowler Harold Larwood struck him over the heart.

The frequency with which this reminiscence was repeated escalated later in my mother's life with the arrival of the four-pronged West Indian pace attack. My parents were both staunch monarchists who regarded Winston Churchill as the foremost figure of the twentieth century. Neither had any truck with American popular culture and proudly considered themselves to be British subjects. The irony of their detestation of the English cricket team was not readily apparent to any of us at the time. Those were the days. The detested Poms toured under the grandiloquent title of the MCC—the Marylebone Cricket Club—sounding very grand in Toowoomba where clubs bore names like 'Diggers' and 'Past Brothers'.

In 1962–63, live television coverage of the cricket was confined to the final session of play, at best. Test cricket was synonymous with the radio and the molasses-dripping tones of Alan McGilvray. That MCC tour in 1962–63 entranced me. Fresh from memories of the charismatic West Indian team of 1960–61, the unimaginative play from both sides aroused virulent criticism.

Exhortations to play 'bright' cricket were reported to have emanated from 'The Don' himself. The English were accused of negative tactics and slow over rates. In the conclusion to the very first cricket book I owned—the official account of that tour, *with the M.C.C. in Australia 1962-3*—*The Sydney Morning Herald* journalist Tom Goodman warned that The Ashes had gone cold on account of the dour, directionless play of that series. He warned that Test cricket's future was precarious unless it produced more excitement. Indeed, Test cricket has been considered to be under almost constant siege ever since, though the persistent rumours of its demise have been exaggerated. Whether it can continue to defy such predictions is a theme to which I will return at intervals throughout this story.

Yet to a young child beginning to engage with the world outside the immediate family, that MCC tour assumed epic proportions. The names of the Australian team remain etched in my memory—Richie Benaud, Brian Booth, Norm O'Neill, Bob Simpson, Bill Lawry, Alan Davidson and Neil Harvey. Alongside these, the detested Poms—Colin Cowdrey, Ted Dexter, Ken Barrington, Fred Trueman, Brian Statham and Fred Titmus. The last named providing a reliable source of puerile amusement to my neighbourhood mates and I. You had to be there—it was the way we said it ...

Ever since then the sound of cricket on the radio has been one of the constants in my life, the backdrop for my significant passages. The South Africans were playing here in the summer of 1963 when the President of the United States was shot in Dallas, and that event began my active engagement with the wider world. From that day to this I have avidly read the newspapers and followed events in the world. While far short of maturity I was never completely a child again. That was assured by the death of my own father just a year later.

We were at home to Pakistan in a series that marked Ian Chappell's debut. I could barely pronounce any of the tourists' names, much less make pornographic puns at their expense. That summer passed like a waking dream amid my grief and disorientation. The last gifts my father had arranged for me were my first proper cricket bat and batting pads—each bearing the autograph of Queenslander Peter Burge. The thrill of this gift was lost amid a sea of grief. Despite his status as Queensland's favoured son, Burge was not high on my list of heroes. He was pudgy right-hander who seemed to be going prematurely bald. He was not enough of a cavalier for my youthful taste.

As a shy, fatherless boy I began my search for a hero and role model. In the summer of 1965–66 I found him—a tall left-hander from Victoria by the name of Bob Cowper. All of my mates settled on Doug Walters as the hero *du jour*. Walters had been dubbed another Bradman after consecutive centuries in his first two Tests, but he did not live up to that breathtaking debut. To me he never seemed to completely recover from the interruption to his career of a stint in the Army as a National Service conscript during the Vietnam War. On his day Walters was one of the great cavalier batsmen. There was enough hint of unorthodox genius leavened by technical imperfection to always have his admirers on the edge of their seats. Over the years Dougie thrilled and disappointed me in almost equal measure.

But Cowper was my hero. He was a left-hander as was I. I had suffered at the hands of a neurotic old nun who forcibly attempted to convert me into a right-hander. Only the aggressive intervention of my mother caused her to desist. So I was predisposed to like left-handers, whether at cricket or tennis, and I find myself unconsciously siding with them to this day.

The summer of 1965–66 saw me become a full-blown cricket fanatic. I was glued to the radio as the long series against Mike Smith's touring Englishmen unfolded. Men of a certain age will remember this as the summer when Australia's sons were rejoicing to the sounds of ninja star knives striking trees and the clash of improvised swords. The Japanese television series *The Samurai* had taken the nation by storm, simultaneously captivating most boys of my age while infuriating our parents whose memories of Kokoda and Changi were still all too fresh. This especially applied to my mother who attributed my father's death only a year before to the consequences of his service in New Guinea. Between scolding me for my risky attempts to jump off the garage roof in fond emulation of my hero Tombei The Mist, she would stare sadly at me over the dinner table, as though I was a particularly messy room that she had found just as she was about to sit down and watch *It Could be You* hosted by Tommy Hanlon Jr. In exasperation she would intone, 'Thank God your father never lived to see this'. My face would burn with shame at this reproach to my patriotism. Bill Clinton's presidency lay well in the future, beyond her life span, so I had not mastered what George F. Will later described as the language of 'exoneration and exculpation', otherwise I may have tactfully suggested that it was time for us all to 'Move On' from our resentment of the Japanese.

That was the summer when the seeds of this story were probably sown. It is both blurry and yet vivid by alternate measures. Too often we are unconscious of our own motivations and deepest urges. However I recall with some clarity the 'eureka' moment of creative spontaneity during my bus trip from Sydney to Canberra in August 2011 when it struck me that I wanted to write about cricket. And not just about the matches themselves, but a story that would help explain the place of cricket in our national culture by telling the story of a lifetime's love of the game.

The sensuous aspects of that summer resonate down the years—the sound of the surf and the aroma of suntan lotion blending with the salt air, and a crackly Astor transistor radio beside me on my towel inducing sleep through its gentle, humming ambience. Likewise, the radio would be sitting on the fence as my mates and I took turns bowling punishingly long spells at one another as we defended our improvised wicket until the light faded, or our parents insisted we come in for various scheduled meal breaks. Deciding that she would provide tea at the appropriate time for that adjournment in backyard matches, my mother clearly hoped to undermine the appeal of sword fighting and star throwing. Her carrot-and-stick approach was vindicated. Backyard cricket ultimately prevailed and eclipsed the 'way of the ninja' to provide the main form of entertainment among us until we all left school nearly a decade later.

Looking back, it is now apparent to me that we pioneered the modern rotation policy so loved by Cricket Australia. We would rotate seamlessly between ninja duties and backyard cricket the same way current Test players return to and from Twenty20 commitments. They are never dropped—merely rested. Or they return to their Big Bash responsibilities as though it was their intention to end up there all along. 'From little things big things grow', as the song proclaims. I would like to think that we were the pioneers of the modern system all those years ago in Toowoomba, though I think we probably showed more resilience than most of the current crop of Australian fast bowlers. My mates bowled long spells with neither complaint nor stress fractures. Perhaps we needed an agent or personal trainer to tell us how brittle we really were.

But it may be that such nostalgic musing is tainted by unreliability. My sense is that I did not miss much of the play throughout that series, from the rain-affected and abbreviated draw at the Gabba, to the final stalemate in Melbourne. While pundits criticised the lack of flair of both teams, I was convinced that any amount of dourness was permissible in defence of The Ashes. My idol, Robert Maskew Cowper, compiled a massive 307 in the final Test at the Melbourne Cricket Ground with that monumental innings straddling the introduction of decimal currency on the 14th of February 1966.

To kids imbued with the importance of all that pink on the map of the world, denoting the British Commonwealth, this was a seminal moment. In short order Britain announced that its military forces East of Suez would be withdrawn and the debate about entry to the Common Market got underway. Although more interested in accumulating the various denominations of the new currency than the geopolitics that it symbolised, I was aware through the discussions among my elders that the world was changing rapidly and ominously.

Through all this welter of change, the cricket, especially the ABC radio descriptions of play, seemed to provide an anchor—a soothing, predictable, immutable ritual each summer. Recollections of so many periods in my life conjure up that cicada-like hum. And as I have grown older, entering my own Indian summer in my mid-fifties, two things have occurred. I draw increased comfort from nostalgia, and I have rediscovered my love of language and writing. As the founder of analytical psychology Carl Jung once wrote:

> Thoroughly unprepared, we take the step into the afternoon of life. Worse still, we take this step with the false presupposition that our truths and our ideals will serve us as hitherto. But we cannot live the afternoon of life according to the program of life's morning, for what was great in the morning will be little at evening and what in the morning was true, at evening will have become a lie.

I have always loved writing and been moved by great prose, but most of my writing has been about Australian or American politics, or military strategy. For over a decade I have written keynote speeches for successive Chiefs of the Australian Army or articles for academic conferences and journals.

These topics continue to interest me, especially the historiography of the American Civil War about which, as I have noted, I also have never been able to read in moderation. Through my life I have accumulated thousands of books and articles on these topics and written many thousands of words on them as well—in turn, as a political columnist with both Fairfax and News Limited and more recently as the editor-in-chief of the *Australian Army Journal*. Professional interest can impose a creative straitjacket, especially when the topic is the changing character of war and one has a professional responsibility to the nation and one's friends to get ideas about war right.

Why cricket? Why this story? Why now? My passion for cricket is not purely nostalgic. Rather, in the afternoon of my life I have rediscovered my love for the aesthetic of the game, having lost interest in it for some years during the 1980s and 1990s when the turmoil in my own life dampened my enthusiasm for many things that had previously given me much joy. So, early this century I came home, like the prodigal son who awoke to return to the security of his father's house.

Once again cricket on the radio became the companionable backdrop to my summers. I focused obsessively on that marvellous series in India in 2001 when two magnificent teams produced some of the finest cricket ever played. But the real turning point came in the summer of 2008 in England. During one of the happiest and most stimulating periods of my life, I was a Visiting Fellow in the Changing Character of War Programme at the

University of Oxford under the guidance of the Chichele Professor of the History of War, Hew Strachan.

In the Changing Character of War Programme, scholars from law, ethics, theology, military history and international relations take a comprehensive approach to the understanding of war as a phenomenon. Most of the scholars and soldiers involved in the course have tended to be acolytes of the Prussian genius Carl von Clausewitz, hence most of us were sceptical of claims that the attacks on the United States in September 2001 heralded an epoch of unprecedented conflict, or that these attacks represented something innately different in the fundamental nature of contemporary warfare.

Connections made possible by technology, now commonly referred to simply as 'globalisation', have transformed the world system since the end of the Cold War. Politicians, diplomats and soldiers continue to try to make sense of its implications for war and conflict. Nor has cricket been able to resist the consequences of those seismic shifts in the global distribution of power and the insatiable demand for constant and immediate gratification that has become our habit after the information revolution. Without resorting to the overblown use of military metaphors to write about sport, it is clear that the same forces that are propelling India to major power status in the geopolitical sphere also have implications for the future of cricket.

Likewise, the proliferation of private military corporations—modern mercenaries—in direct competition with the traditional forces of the nation-state is redolent of the challenge to traditional Test cricket by Twenty20 franchises. Globalisation has empowered the universal and weakened the particular and the local. It has challenged traditional cultures and institutions. To some extent the rise of Islamic fundamentalism has been a response to this encroachment of the modern into some traditional societies. Test cricket, supported by the patriotic urges of the players and the fans, is something of an anomaly in the midst of the market state and the borderless corporation. The creature of this *Zeitgeist* is the Twenty20 franchise rather than the national Test cricket team, the private military corporation rather than the Anzac legend. 'I am a part of all that I have met', claimed Tennyson. Inevitably, my appreciation of cricket has been deeply influenced by my reading on war and statecraft. It is impossible for me to divorce my writing from it.

However, what Oxford also unexpectedly did was reignite my passion for attending live Test cricket. Initially I had merely decided to undertake a pilgrimage to Lord's, which had always loomed so large in my imagination. Ever since listening to the gravelly, claret-cured voice of John Arlott while lying in the winter darkness in 1968 and 1972 I had wanted to visit the home of cricket. Likewise, to my parochial ears the beautiful intonation of Brian Johnston and Christopher Martin-Jenkins carried hints of the faraway and sophisticated. A visit to Lord's had been on my 'bucket list' long before that term had been popularised. And of course, there had been the common boyhood fantasy of playing there in the 'baggy green'.

We booked well in advance to attend the first two days of the Test between England and New Zealand in May 2008. I actually had the tickets mailed to Australia before we had even left. Within minutes of our arrival Tritia and I were captivated. The atmosphere on a big match day there is superb. For this cricket romantic it produced tingling in the hairs on the arms and back of the neck. Lord's is a relatively small ground, which creates a real intimacy among the crowd, and in turn between the crowd and the players. On the second day the five-minute bell announcing the imminent commencement of play was rung by Neil Harvey, one of the 1948 Invincibles under Sir Donald Bradman.

The synchronicity of this touched me. Harvey played his final Test at the SCG in 1963 in the very first series that fired my boyish love of the game. And here he was, at the very first Test match that I had attended in over twenty years. According to T.S. Eliot, 'We shall not cease from exploration/And the end of all our exploring/Will be to arrive where we started/And know the place for the first time'. I felt at some level that I had come home—back to my father's house. Abandoning moderation I went to the ticket office and booked seats for every day of the England–South Africa Test in July and as many Middlesex home games as I could find.

The New Zealand Test was severely affected by rain and British journalist Andrew Miller scathingly observed that there was nothing on offer 'but frustration in the cold' for the 26,000 spectators at the ground and predicted (predictably) that 'Test cricket is in terminal decline'. But nothing could temper the luminous nature of the experience for me. Perhaps it was a case of seeing things not as they are, but as we are. And I was fulfilling a childhood dream. Through the gloom I could discern an aesthetic in the traditional game that had been obscured to me in my youth when I was obsessed with the results and the contest.

On the Sunday of the same match we were guests of an MCC member in the Friends of Members enclosure and watched Michael Vaughan compile a sound, if uninspiring century against a journeyman attack. That day confirmed my status as a born-again cricket nut. Lord's was chilly but bathed in beautiful spring light under which the outfield glistened, every blade of grass seemingly shining. Tritia and I each had one earphone from one of the tiny ground radios tuned to *Test Match Special* and delighted in the banter between Jonathan Agnew and Henry Blofeld. At one point Blofeld described in elaborate detail the passage of a KLM jet over the ground. We simultaneously looked up and realised that we could see it at the same moment he was describing it. In his cut-glass Etonian accent he dismissed it as, 'Possibly heading to America or somewhere like that'. We burst out laughing and, like a couple of school kids, simultaneously exclaimed, 'There it is!' Tritia also had childhood memories of listening to crackling radio broadcasts from England in the depth of the Australian winter evening and experienced the same wonderful sense of a pilgrimage completed that day. The sound of the broadcast also evoked deeper memories of other times and other places in her.

Nor apparently are we alone in this. Cautious about my impulsive burst of creativity on the bus trip, I discussed the idea of this story with a few friends to help me clarify my own thinking. In the process, two intuitions became the core hypotheses for this work. Firstly, that the Australian summer, which incorporates Christmas and the long school vacations, is a time of optimism and restoration for most Australians, and that Test cricket is the central, unifying ritual of this period. The Melbourne Boxing Day Test and the New Year Test in Sydney have become—like Melbourne Cup—great civic rituals embedded in the calendar. Secondly, central to our experience of the 'summer of cricket' is the ABC radio commentary, which is the pervasive sound of the Australian summer, though perhaps less so now than it was during my childhood. Then, my impression was that I was almost never out of earshot of the sound of the cricket on the radio from the end of the school year until well into the first term of the next year. If this was an illusion it was one that had also seduced many of my generation.

I was encouraged by two comments among my unscientifically assembled sample group as I sought to establish whether there might be interest in a nostalgic look at cricket through the prism of the forthcoming series against India. Firstly, nearly everyone could situate a significant event in their lives against the background of a Test cricket series. Men remembered sneaking out of a family wedding to listen to Lillee and Thommo scything through Mike Denness and his Englishmen in 1974–75, or the West Indians a year later. Others could conjure up David Hookes clubbing Tony Greig to the boundary off five successive deliveries in the Centenary Test in 1977. Others still insisted that they had listened to every ball of the final session when Ken 'Slasher' Mackay and Lindsay Kline defied the West Indies in Adelaide to permit Australia to snatch an unlikely draw in 1961.

Interestingly, women volunteered comments such as, 'I don't like cricket. But I love the sound of cricket on the radio'. Since our experience at Lord's, Tritia and I have developed a habit of listening to the lulling rhythm of cricket in bed as we drift into sleep, whether broadcast from England or South Africa. She is impressed at the sheer quality of the broadcasting with its whimsy, anecdotes and apparently irrelevant intimacies shared with the audience. She cannot be described as a cricket tragic, so if she understood what I was trying to say then perhaps a wider audience might also.

And so the idea of *An Indian Summer of Cricket* was born. Arguably though, its gestation began in 1962. Given how central to my enjoyment of cricket radio had been over the course of my life, I thought it might be prudent to test the concept with some of the current generation of ABC Grandstand presenters. Through an intermediary, Peter Longman, the head of ABC Radio Sport, I sought out Jim Maxwell the National Sports Editor and Executive Producer of the ABC commentary team.

Longman remembered my first and only book, which was a biography of former Wallaby captain Paul McLean. In Brisbane during the late 1970s and early 1980s when the Maroon Mean Machine under Bob Templeton was justifiably considered to be the best provincial rugby side in the world, Longman and some of the ABC team used to occasionally drink at the Officers' Mess of my infantry battalion. They were raucous occasions and

Longman enthralled these gatherings with his impressive mimicry of the mannerisms of leading Australian cricketers. He had Graeme Wood down absolutely pat and would go through an elaborate ritual of taking guard and marking his crease. It was amusing to the point of convulsion, especially after starting on the drink at the Breakfast Creek Hotel at lunch-time and coming home via Ballymore. Perhaps the limitless pleasure that Fred Titmus gave me at age seven convicts me as too easy an audience in these matters, but I rated Longman as a comic genius.

He generously put me in touch with Jim Maxwell, whom I believe deserves the accolade of best radio sports broadcaster in the country. He is certainly one of the most widely loved. While the majestic Alan McGilvray echoes down the years to me, Maxwell is as every bit as good. He has an authentic Australian voice and a style that creates an easy connection with the audience. Moreover, he exudes a deep love for the game and has an uncanny recall of statistics. This latter quality is absolutely vital to a cricket broadcaster. Much of the joy of listening to cricket on radio is the euphoric recall of past summers evoked by the constant references to obscure records and milestones. 'The first Australian to take five wickets in an innings on debut since ... The first Australian to take a hat-trick on debut since ...' I have yet to encounter a cricket lover who does not salivate at this stuff. And Maxwell has it all at his fingertips, as he demonstrated as we reminisced over our early memories of cricket.

He generously listened to my ideas in the ABC cafeteria at Ultimo on one of those late winter days at which Sydney excels—brilliant sunshine, cloudless blue skies and the merest hint of a chill in the air. It would have been a perfect day for an England–New Zealand Test at Lord's. Maxwell thought that the summer of 2011–12 was innately worthy of being recorded. I am indebted to him for his description of it as 'the last of the summer wine,' reflecting his pessimism about the possible effects of the Big Bash format on Test cricket in coming years.

He detected that sentimentality and nostalgia were significant sources of my motivation for this story. 'You might be on to something this year. We may be drinking the last of the summer wine if the Big Bash thing goes where it might. We may not see the longer Test series as the centrepiece of the summer again.' I was inspired by those remarks. But even more importantly I was encouraged to glean that Jim thought that some of the themes I had raised were worthy of exploration. He continued to be a generous source of encouragement over the Indian summer.

At his suggestion I also approached his colleague Peter Roebuck who formed an integral part of the ABC commentary team in addition to having written beautifully about the game in the *Sydney Morning Herald* for many years. Despite my admiration for Roebuck, I approached him with some trepidation. I feared a rebuke; his reputation for being prickly had preceded him. None of my contacts from writing about politics at Fairfax had a phone number for him nor would the Fairfax switchboard forward any form of message to him. Emphatically, 'No we do not talk to him. You need to email him'. This I did with no particular confidence. What followed assumes some poignancy in the light of his subsequent death in South Africa.

Rather than being dismissive or remote, Roebuck replied with a veritable torrent of enthusiastic emails which I have preserved. Over a number of evenings I wrote to him and invariably found an ebullient reply the following morning. Like Maxwell he helped me clarify my thinking and steered me towards an insight that had hitherto eluded me. He suggested that I explore the symbolism of Cowper's massive innings straddling the introduction of decimal currency in 1966 as a milestone in dissolving the cultural cringe. So immersed was I in that event as vindication of my childhood hero Cowper, who had been dropped for the Adelaide Test of that series, that I had never examined it for any deeper significance. However, one can also be too theoretical about these matters. The failure of the 1999 republic referendum would suggest that Roebuck's optimism was misplaced. For me, the later deregulation of the Australian economy probably generated a much greater socio-political impact that ultimately also transformed cricket.

One thing that arose from our correspondence was Roebuck's puzzling alienation from the land of his birth, which may have inspired a certain amount of wishful thinking about the deeper significance of Cowper's innings. Two things emerged from our lively and cheerful correspondence. Firstly, I was probably more of a traditionalist than he was. This surprised me, but probably should not have. Secondly, he was generous in his support to this work, offering to introduce me to some of his friends in the Indian media, especially Harsha Bhogle. We agreed to have dinner on the night before the Gabba Test in Brisbane. His final email to me ended with a reference to a mutual friend whom we expected to see at the SCG Test, Noting its significance as the 100th such match at that signature ground, Roebuck closed with, 'No one is going to miss this one. Cheers P'. We now know that Roebuck did indeed miss it. This saddened me more than I could ever have imagined. We never did meet, and this book is the poorer for it. I can only imagine what he would have made of the socio-political significance of Michael Clarke's 329 not out in Sydney.

Peter Roebuck's death rocked the Australian cricket world and cast a pall over the coming summer. If the 'afternoon of life' implies facing our decline and mortality, then throughout the Indian summer of 2011–12 I was confronted with this inescapable reality more often than I liked.

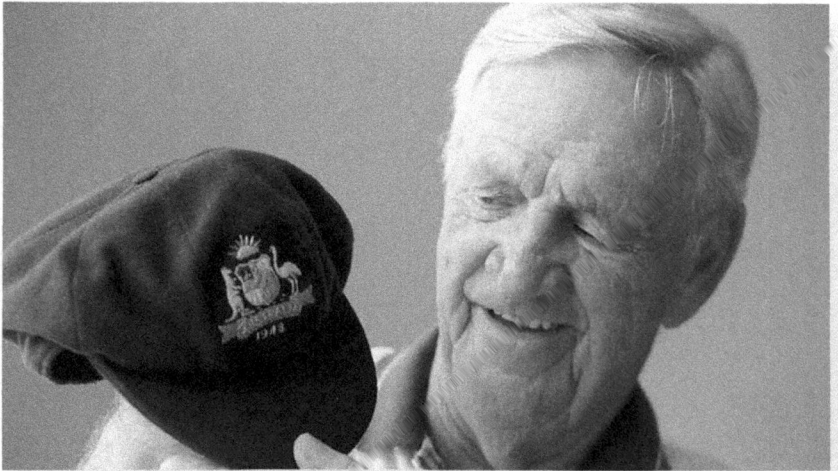

... we were informed that one of the grand old men of Australian cricket Sam Loxton, had died. ... one of Bradman's 1948 Invincibles ...

2. *The Gabba*
—four funerals and a Test match

... despite such rare exceptions, the start of the long summer vacation coincided with a Test match at the Gabba thereby investing the cricket with an aura of magic ...

Ultimately, the Gabba revealed more about the resurgence of Australian cricket than I was willing to concede at the time.

The repeated intimations of mortality contained in the deaths of Peter Roebuck, Arthur Beetson, Sam Loxton, and my mate Norman, clothed that time in Brisbane with a gloom that was reinforced by the drab surroundings of the Gabba.

Normally the opening Test match of the summer is a source of uncomplicated joy to me. For much of my life the opening Test of the Australian summer has been scheduled at the Brisbane Cricket Ground in Wolloongabba, known by that distinctively abbreviated Australian appellation 'the Gabba'. The lead up to the Gabba Test in Queensland always coincided with the lazy, petering out of the school year. Final exams, while stressful, normally entailed half days without formal teaching. It was always a beautiful time of the year with seemingly ubiquitous jacarandas in vibrant bloom. Summer holidays meant cricket, Christmas and beaches. Even now I can conjure the smell of barbecue smoke mingling with the fragrance of blossoms in our backyard as the twilight gathered. And now it appears an even more tranquil, more Tom Sawyerish idyll than it actually was.

The sequence of games for most Test series conforms to a familiar and comfortable pattern. Despite the breathless insistence of the television commentators, much of this is of recent advent. The 'traditional' Boxing Day Test is scarcely a tradition. The Melbourne Test was not routinely scheduled for Boxing Day until relatively recently and a Sheffield Shield match was played there around Christmas whenever Australian teams were on tour overseas. The custom of playing the opening Test of the home rubber in Brisbane actually has a more distinguished lineage, though even during my lifetime the practice has not always been adhered to. For instance, the first Indian touring team that I can recall, that led by the Nawab of Pataudi Jnr, played the third Test in Brisbane in January 1968. However, despite such rare exceptions, the start of the long summer vacation typically coincided with a Test match at the Gabba investing cricket with an aura of magic in my young mind. I have no recollection of the legendary tied Test there in 1960, though I used to listen enthralled as my stepfather would deliver his annual diatribe against England's Trevor Bailey on the Saturday of each Brisbane Test. Bailey had batted for more than a day in the Gabba Test of the 1958–59 Ashes series for a mere 68 runs. The punch-line delivered with a resigned shake of the head went: 'Bloody Bailey. All day for 50. And to think the next day Norman O'Neill just sparkled to get 71 in no time flat. And I didn't go because I had such a bugger of day the day before! Pommy mongrel.'

Fortunately, over the years the Gabba has provided me with far more satisfactory memories. I recall a beautiful controlled spell from Alan Connolly on the first day of the 1968–69 West Indies series to remove

Basil Butcher, Garfield Sobers and Clive Lloyd in quick succession as a powerful West Indies batting line-up crumpled for 296. However, a majestic second innings of 129 from Lloyd set up a West Indies win as Australia fell under the spinning spell of Sobers and Lance Gibbs in the final innings. There were some striking similarities between that West Indies series and the Indian tour of 2011–12. Both sides contained some wonderful champions who may have been making one tour too many. The Windies were resoundingly beaten, despite the presence of some real legends in their ranks. However, the Australian side that defeated them was cruelly exposed the following year in South Africa.

Then, in 1970, Keith Stackpole survived a run out appeal on 18 before savaging Ray Illingworth's Englishmen on the way to 207. Photographic evidence published the next day revealed the position of Stacky's bat as the wicket was broken, embarrassing even the most ardent Australian fan. As a kid I was an unabashed cricket patriot rather than a purist, so I was sanguine about this atrocity. To paraphrase Barry Goldwater, extremism in defence of The Ashes was no vice. I have since mellowed considerably, and after the rancorous Sydney Test against India in 2007–08, have not been so blindly ardent an Australian supporter. But I digress.

Back to the Gabba, and of course there was the inimitable Jeffrey Robert Thomson's sandshoe crusher delivered to Tony Greig in the opening test of the 1974–75 Ashes series. During that depressing Ashes series in 2010–11, as Australia's alleged quicks served up the juiciest of pies, I took solace in watching that clip of Thommo several hundred times on YouTube before crying myself to sleep. It was a ball as laden with portent for the outcome of that series as that from Shane Warne to Mike Gatting in 1993, or Steve Harmison's excruciating opening salvo in Brisbane when England came here to defend The Ashes in 2006–07. Thommo's menace loudly proclaimed the arrival of a golden age in Australian cricket when, for one crowded hour, he and Dennis Lillee routed every batting order that faced them. All of those Gabba Tests commenced on the opening day of my summer school holidays or later, at the end of my formal training period at Duntroon. 'Bliss was it in that dawn to be alive,/But to be young was very heaven!'

Yet the Indian summer of a man's life carries sober hints of mortality rather than the childish expectation of limitless possibility. And last summer, more than most, was punctuated by grief and loss.

I set out for Brisbane feeling ambivalent. Granted, I was elated to be embarking on my maiden summer as a cricket writer for *The Spectator Australia*, but my enthusiasm was tempered by the imminent deaths of two close friends, Norman Banks and Georgia. On the Saturday evening before I left I spent some time with my friend Norman who was gravely ill with cancer. We had known one another for around twenty years, but had only become really close over about the past decade when our lives intersected in an unexpected way. After I re-enlisted in the Australian Army we rekindled a friendship that had begun in 1989. He was an officer in the Royal Australian Navy and our paths often crossed at the Australian Defence Force Academy swimming pool where we each struggled to limit the advance of middle age by lap swimming. Norman was a vastly better swimmer than I and usually had more breath for chats when we towelled down after our showers. He was one person I was always happy to listen to. He exuded an appealing aura of calm and self-possession that he had exhibited in both his personal and professional life.

News of his serious illness had stunned me. He was diagnosed with stomach cancer not long after he turned fifty. He endured his illness with inspiring grace and courage and for a time had entered remission.

During his brief respite from cancer he returned to swimming. It meant a lot to him and I felt a constriction in my chest as I watched him purposefully gliding up and down the pool after his long lay off. His remission was cruelly brief. The cancer returned and in the middle of November he contacted me and requested that I come and visit him in the Duntroon hospital. He was calmly planning his funeral service and, to my surprise, he asked me to say some words. I was deeply moved by his request and acceded immediately. Over the next few days I was honoured to spend considerable time at his bedside. Whatever comfort I brought to Norman Banks paled beside his gift to me. He had been ravaged by his illness, but was almost transcendent in his serenity and acceptance of his imminent death. We even shared a few unexpected smiles. These were not the result of the awkward gallows humour of the variety that men generally use to mask their terror, rather they were warm reminiscences of fading memories. He was a man at peace with his life and death, calm and content with his lot. Quite simply, inspirational.

Before we parted for the last time I told him that I was heading away in a couple days to cover the cricket in Brisbane. 'Do you think you'll be here when I get back?' 'Definitely. It won't take three days to beat the Kiwis.' I embraced him and left, sharing neither his optimism about his own health, nor that of Australian cricket. My misgivings were well founded.

Whenever I look back on that Gabba Test I will recall the periods of silence preceding each day's play rather than much of the ensuing action. It was an unremarkable Test match and my gloom deepened over each of the four days. It was as far removed from the transcendent joy of Lord's or the Arcadian delights of my childhood summers as can be imagined.

On the very first morning of the match, Malcolm Conn of News Limited requested that the media contingent observe a minute of silence as a show of respect to our colleague Peter Roebuck, who had died in South Africa only three weeks before. His death affected me more than the death of a virtual stranger normally would. His previous email correspondence was filled with encouragement and enthusiasm; this and as his generous offer to meet before the Gabba Test imbued the moment with a deep sense of loss, not just for lost opportunity, but for the man himself. The beguiling intimacy imparted by his radio broadcasts made me feel I had known him for years.

One Sunday morning in November, my old friend and mentor Barrie Cassidy had called me with the news that Roebuck had jumped from the balcony of his hotel room the night before. Learning of Roebuck's suicide only moments before going on air with his Sunday morning ABC sports program *Offsiders*, he was scrambling to make sense of what had happened. Gideon Haigh, Australia's finest cricket writer and Roebuck's friend, was fortunately a guest on that morning's program.

It was Cassidy who had given me my crucial break into television in 1995 when he asked me to appear as a regular panelist on a new show called *The Last Shout* on Network Ten. The show's format had been inspired by his time in the United States where he had been impressed by the style of live political debates between columnists from opposite ends of the ideological spectrum. Ros Kelly, Bob Ellis and I rotated for the left and faced a combination of Piers Akerman, John Stone and David Barnett for the right. The show developed a late night cult following and convinced the ABC that there was sufficient interest in the format to justify scheduling it on Sunday mornings as *Insiders*. I joined Christine Wallace and Piers Akerman for its inaugural episode on the 15th of July 2001.

In any event, Roebuck's death devastated those who knew him. But then, in the immediate aftermath of his death, it emerged that seemingly no one *really* knew him. Even fewer were close to him. With hindsight, his estrangement from England struck me as odd. He had embraced Australia with the characteristic zeal of the convert, venturing in one email to me, 'One of Australia's most evocative and telling phrases springs to mind, 'Av a go (yer mug)!' Do you think the Poms could have come up with that?' It was my wife who had drawn my attention to his employment of 'we' when referring to Australia over the past few years. I did not find this entirely convincing. To me Roebuck was the epitome of a Victorian Englishman, lost in time rather than in space.

As I ventured in a tribute to him penned for *The Spectator Australia,* I could easily conjure the image of him commanding a column of Gurkhas on the North-West Frontier in the latter part of the nineteenth century. Downing schooners with David Boon? Never. The Editor of *The Spectator Australia*, Tom Switzer, was concerned that I had been too generous in my praise for Roebuck. Allegations about his exploitation of young men for sexual gratification seemed to warrant a reappraisal of the glowing tributes written on the morning after his death. For my part, I was content with what I had written about him and remain so. 'The evil that men do lives after them; the good is interred with their bones.'

On the first morning of the Gabba Test match we were also informed that Rugby League legend Arthur Beetson had died earlier on the Gold Coast. The mood in the media box had just started to lighten slightly after the Roebuck commemoration and play had got underway. The news of Big Artie's death cast a further pall over proceedings.

Arthur Beetson was a Rugby League immortal—large in stature, literally and metaphorically. He single-handedly imparted a mystique to the concept of the State of Origin series with his application of 'the biff' to his Parramatta team-mate Mick Cronin in the inaugural fixture at Lang Park on the

8th of July 1980. He was blessed with subtle ball skills seemingly incongruous in a man of such bulk. Yet Queenslanders knew that he had played in the 1965 Brisbane Grand Final as a centre for the Premiers, Redcliffe. Although he acquired the physique of a forward he never lost the hands and eyes of a back. His innate skills were enhanced by a deeply intuitive sense of the game manifested in his economical movements to arrive in the perfect place at the right time. That freakish football intelligence ensured that after his playing career he would excel as a coach and mentor to others.

On occasions he drank at the Kauri Hotel in Glebe on Sunday nights accompanied by his larrikin sidekick Tommy Raudonikis and a veteran of Cronulla's 1973 Grand Final team, Graham Bowen. They were all mates of the publican Barry Gilbert who presided over one of the few remaining bastions of proletarian culture amid the rapidly gentrifying inner city. Its exclusively hard-drinking, heavy-smoking, compulsively gambling, male clientele were vestiges of an Australia that has now vanished. I was incapable of moderation in any of these pursuits at the time. I was in good company though; I had even earned my own permanent position at the bar under the television set. I was *somebody* in the 1980s.

Hilarious profanities used to cascade from Tommy as the saloon bar patrons watched the Sunday night replay of the Rugby League match of the day. For his part Beetson, carried his massive frame and reputation lightly, smiling like a benign Buddha at Tommy's ribald antics. He was humble and exuded a sense of quiet comfort in his own skin befitting a man with nothing left to prove—always a compelling quality.

My most intimate dealings with my fellow human beings for most of the 1980s are best defined in Hemmingway's words—'We drank together'. Those occasional sessions at the Kauri Hotel confirmed the admiration from afar that I had felt for Beetson since watching his explosive, if abbreviated, Rugby League test debut against Great Britain in 1966. His play in that game unfairly earned him the slur 'Half a game Artie', and a reputation for extravagant talent and meagre fitness. He remedied this deficiency over time. While hardly a close friend, we enjoyed more than a nodding acquaintance, and his death likewise affected me.

He personified the Queensland of my youth with its strained race relations and burning insecurity about the apparent dominance of New South Wales at sport, especially Rugby League. Beetson was our avenging angel who came home to play for tribe and state. For years Rugby League fans 'north of the Tweed' had fantasised about seeing the 'real' Queensland team—all the champions who had gone to Sydney in pursuit of money generated by poker machines—play against New South Wales. State of Origin healed the wounds of all those lean years. For Queenslanders of my generation, clean sweeps over the Blues may become boring and unsatisfying sometime in the twenty-second century. We can recall those lopsided interstate series from 1962 to 1980 when Queensland won a mere handful of games—quite literally five, from memory. But Artie set all this to rights under the lights at Lang Park that chilly evening in July 1980. He meant even more to Indigenous Australians, regardless of their state allegiances. A sentimental connection to my youth died with the Big Man.

> The time you won your town the race
> We chaired you through the market-place;
> Man and boy stood cheering by,
> And home we brought you shoulder-high.
>
> To-day, the road all runners come,
> Shoulder-high we bring you home,
> And set you at your threshold down,
> Townsman of a stiller town.

Anyway back to the Gabba. Sliding into the seat beside me in the box on that opening morning was ABC commentator Kerry 'Skull' O'Keeffe. Notwithstanding his iconic status, he seemed hesitant, even slightly apologetic as he looked for a place to sit between his on-air commitments. Margie McDonald, a Brisbane-based reporter for *The Australian* who had been conscripted as a cricket writer for the Gabba Test, had just vacated the seat beside me. She is an accomplished and respected sports journalist of the old school, but was nervous about what she considered a lack of cricket credentials. As she plugged in her computer she told me that the last time she had covered cricket was in the 1980s. It was at the Gabba and Allan Border had been playing. I tried to reassure her that as long as I was around she would not be the least qualified person in the box. However, the death of Beetson had become the story of the day in Queensland and she was abruptly reassigned to cover it, vacating her prime space in the front row of the box.

Skull gingerly occupied her chair and asked me, 'Do you think she'll mind?' I told him that she would be gone all day on account of the Arthur Beetson story. This news had evidently eluded him and he asked, 'What Beetson story?'

'He just died, mate.'

'Oh no, 'Half a game Artie'', he sighed. We chatted about that deciding Rugby League Test in 1966 when Beetson left the field at half time having placed an indelible stamp on the game in the first forty minutes. Skull looked over my shoulder as I searched for images of the match on YouTube. We each knew that England had been awarded a penalty try, but could not settle on which player was involved.

While so engaged we were joined by Jim Maxwell who gave me a welcoming pat on the shoulder. 'Good to see you here.' I was delighted and relieved to be so anointed. Writing for a weekly publication with no background as a cricket writer, I was feeling very much an outsider among the seasoned media contingent arrayed along the long benches in the commentary box.His 'welcome aboard' meant more than he could have guessed.

'Can you remember which of the Englishmen was impeded before the award of the penalty try in that last test at the SCG in 1966 when Artie made his debut?' If our earlier chat at the Ultimo Centre had been any indication, Maxwell would know. 'Alan Hardisty.' No sooner had he uttered it than the grainy images on my computer corroborated his answer. We continued to reminisce about Angelo Crema, a one-test wonder from Queensland, who played in the first test of that series and John McDonald, a big fast centre from Toowoomba who enjoyed a more distinguished career for Australia. Maxwell named the entire Australian team. Before we had time to chart the remainder of Big Artie's career he and Skull departed to resume duties behind the microphone.

Such banter about sporting trivia was one of the highlights of the summer. Cricket nostalgia is one of my favourite pastimes and has become even more satisfying as I have grown to appreciate the richness of the game's history and culture. But any pretensions I had harboured as a trivia buff were ruthlessly extinguished during my time on the road over the Indian summer, especially when the Indian media contingent arrived later in the month. Most of the leading writers and commentators had unerringly reliable memories of an alarming range of obscure statistics and facts, some even dating back to the period BC (before Cowper).

Having spent the latter period of my journalistic career at News Limited I gravitated towards its group, which comprised Gideon Haigh, Peter Lalor, Malcolm Conn and Wayne Smith. They constituted an incredibly strong arsenal of cricket expertise, akin to the four-pronged West Indian pace attack of the 1980s. Appreciation of Gideon Haigh's intellect and insight preceded him. He is to my mind presently without peer as a cricket writer—and I mean on the world stage, not just in Australia. He has an acute appreciation of the game, which he expresses in beautiful witty prose. In fact, for my money he ranks favourably as a non-fiction writer in any category. Chatting with him over the following weeks was to be an engaging and educative experience.

Wayne Smith is a worthy heir to the redoubtable Frank O'Callaghan as the best rugby writer in Queensland. I remembered him fondly from the 1980s when I launched my biography of Paul McLean at Ballymore. He was a witty master of ceremonies and an engaging raconteur with an easy, unpretentious manner. Linking up with him further assuaged my new-kid-on-the-block anxieties.

Likewise, Peter Lalor and Malcolm Conn extended the hand of friendship to me on day one at the Gabba and over the course of the Test match I sought out their company during the intervals. Lalor and I shared a sympathy for discarded Test opening batsman, Simon Katich. As the New Zealand series unfolded, we shared knowing glances each time Phil Hughes obligingly edged the ball into the slip cordon. Remarkably, he was dismissed in the same manner in all four innings—caught Guptill, bowled Martin. Sadly our man Katich never returned from the wilderness and retired later in the summer. He was shabbily treated, still having a contribution to make to Australian cricket.

Both Lalor and Conn are prolific and shrewd analysts of the game who consistently and reliably recorded the events of the summer. They were also voluminous contributors to social media through Twitter, and because I had committed to covering only the Test matches I found myself missing the camaraderie of the box as they continued to 'tweet' from every venue at which the One Day Internationals were played. For his part Gideon Haigh did not attend the shorter forms of the game, maintaining a disdainful boycott.

Watching cricket in such esteemed and knowledgeable company, and from so privileged a position, was a dream come true and I was absolutely thrilled at the opportunity. The camaraderie of the media box was very engaging and made this summer one of the most pleasant I can recall. However, as panoramic as the view from the commentary box is, the soundproofing of the room makes the experience somewhat sterile. This was especially so at the Gabba, and later at the Sydney Cricket Ground. The smaller grounds in Perth and Adelaide were different. At each of these grounds it felt as though we were immersed in the action. Indeed, at the WACA ground the combination of searing heat and the improvised marquee accommodation created a distinct and very appealing Caribbean atmosphere.

In Brisbane it took me some time to realise how hermetically sealed our surroundings were. It occurred to me after a couple of days that I had not heard the crack of the bat on the ball or the murmur of the crowd, so I developed a habit of wandering around the ground at least once every session to savour the atmosphere.

These days the Gabba is unrecognisable as the ramshackle, charmingly seedy cricket ground of my childhood. The old wooden stands with corrugated iron roofs are long gone, as is the dog track which made a cameo appearance in the 1970s and 80s. In 1962, Johnnie Moyes noted that the late afternoon shadows encroached further on to the wicket in Brisbane than at any other Australian Test venue. They still do, notwithstanding the Soviet functionality of its current design.

In a fine piece for *The Spectator Australia*, Nick Bryant mourned the erosion of the charm of Australian cricket grounds under the pressure of commercialisation and to appease the football codes. As he wrote:

> The Gabba is an impressive modern stadium, with uninterrupted sight lines, the feel of being close to the action and some glass-fronted bars with balconies that look over the field of play. But again, much of the romance of the old ground has been sacrificed. During Australian cricket's unipolar phase, the ground became known as the 'Gabbatoire', because it was where visiting touring sides were slaughtered in the first Test of the summer. Now it also describes the heartless, industrial feel.

Whatever the merits of Bryant's argument, it was no small irony that he voiced it in a magazine that so conscientiously argues that the unregulated operation of market forces constitutes the best way to realise the common good. The same forces of globalisation that *The Spectator* repeatedly insists should not be curtailed by meddling governments have also inexorably commercialised sport. The tension between sport as business and entertainment, and sport as the manifestation of tribal and patriotic loyalties warrants deeper examination and is one of the recurring themes of this story. Bryant made an argument that resonated with me as an unabashed, sentimental traditionalist. Yet it was an argument lost long ago when the Australian Test team became a billboard for commercialism. Nor can that trend be understood without an appreciation of the globalisation of the Australian economy, which accelerated after the deregulation of currency markets in 1983. More on that later when I tell the story of the 100th test match at the SCG.

So, as I walked around the Gabba trying to savour the atmosphere of the crowd and to somehow connect to the sensuous pleasure of the cricket, I felt a twinge of sadness at the absence of the Moreton Bay figs of my youth and the grassy expanses from which I had watched Wally Grout and Peter Burge plying their craft. But if the ground had lost some of its charm, the characters I encountered had not. Wandering among the patrons at the Gabba I chanced upon some fascinating people who, in varying ways, contributed to the enjoyment of the cricket and the direction of this book.

The most memorable was a young woman who was studying Classics at university. Each day she regaled me with snippets of Pericles' funeral oration. 'If Athens shall appear great to you, consider then that her glories were purchased by valiant men, and men who learned their duty'. My youthful political hero, senator Robert F. Kennedy had inspired my interest in the Greeks. As he grappled with his private grief after Dallas he sought comfort and meaning in Aeschylus, Sophocles and Pericles, and their influence may be found in some of his most powerful speeches from his messianic presidential campaign of 1968. That eloquent funeral oration of Pericles' seemed unfortunately apt for the Gabba Test match of 2011. Although the cricket was eminently forgettable, those four days in Brisbane remain inscribed in my memory because of the deaths of four people whom I knew with varying degrees of intimacy. In the afternoon of life the bell tolls with immediacy—even when strangers die.

Just before play started on Saturday morning, the third day of the Test, the now familiar and morbid ritual of observing a minute's silence for another sporting legend was observed. This time we were informed that one of the grand old men of Australian cricket, Sam Loxton, had died.

He was one of Bradman's 1948 Invincibles who subsequently served in the Victorian parliament. I recalled his gentle, self-deprecating humour in the ABC documentary about the 1948 tour of England. He was like so many of those men he had served with in the war—in his case with a tank unit of the Second Australian Division—with the same marvellous sense of perspective about cricket as Keith Miller who famously noted that aerial combat was more demanding than Test cricket. He was of a type that no longer graces the international game—a man with significant achievement and life experience beyond cricket. He played both VFL football and Test cricket in the era when commercial pressures did not force talented men to choose between their summer and winter sports. In a nice obituary for *The Australian*, Mike Coward observed that Loxton usually finished his reminiscences by reciting, with great passion, the observation on the spirit of cricket by Lord Harris who, next to W.G. Grace, was perhaps the most famous figure in English cricket history:

> You do well to love it, for it is more free from anything sordid, anything dishonourable, than any game in the world. To play it keenly, honourably, generously, self-sacrificingly, is a moral lesson in itself, and the classroom is God's air and sunshine. Foster it, my brothers, so that it may attract all who can find time to play it; protect it from anything that would sully it, so that it may be in favour with all men.

Looking around the antiseptic coliseum of the modern Gabba and the one-dimensional professionals comprising our Test team, it was difficult not to conclude that the game that Loxton spoke of with such affection had predeceased him.

Then, on the morning of day four came the news that I been dreading for the past few weeks. Norman's wife contacted me with news of his death the night before. While not unexpected, this news saddened me greatly. The Kiwis had defied his predictions, forcing the match into a fourth day, even though the contest effectively ended in the first ten minutes of the first session when James Pattinson routed their flimsy top order in a venomous spell of fast bowling. In so doing, he became the thirty-second Australian bowler to claim five wickets on his debut in Test cricket. Despite the rarity of this achievement Pattinson was the third Australian to do this in 2011, joining offspinner Nathan Lyon and injured pace-man Pat Cummins who had collected their hauls against Sri Lanka and South Africa respectively. There was something of the great Dennis Lillee in his early years about Pattinson. He combined genuine pace with seething aggression towards the batsmen.

His spell on the fourth morning was devastating. He claimed three wickets in four balls to shatter the New Zealand top order. His dismissal of Martin Guptill was similar to Pat Cummins' removal of Jacques Kallis in Johannesburg a few weeks earlier. He got a ball up steeply off a good length to cramp the batsman into a self-preserving, ineffectual prod to short leg.

He generated genuine heat, but his real menace lay in his perfect length and late movement. From 4/17 and then 5/28 New Zealand were facing defeat by an innings before lunch. In quick succession after Guptill, he disposed of McCullum, Bracewell, Williamson and Taylor. The first-ball demise of their captain sounded the death-knell for the Kiwis and imposed the customary penalty on the wallets of members of the Primary Club, some of whose members were seated close to me. In his explosive spell Pattinson not only wrecked the Kiwi innings, he simultaneously killed any chance of a respectable crowd. There was no way of calculating how many fans turned around and went fishing after hearing of the carnage on the radio. But Jim Maxwell announced on ABC radio that at 11 am the crowd was slightly in excess of 2000—abysmal.

New Zealand cricket tours have never really fired the Australian imagination. However, I had ventured a prediction in my *Spectator* column that their team would pose a sterner test to Australia than most had envisaged. Moreover, despite a series win against Sri Lanka and a drawn rubber in South Africa, it seemed to me that Australia could be vulnerable, especially against an attack of honest medium-fast seamers. By the fourth day at the Gabba this judgement appeared to be the folly of a novice cricket writer who should have stuck to predicting elections. (I predicted Paul Keating would defeat John Howard in 1996.) However, the subsequent New Zealand victory in Hobart provided some welcome if belated vindication.

With hindsight, the Gabba Test match actually established patterns that were to be repeated later in the summer against the supposedly stronger Indian line-up. Michael Clarke and Ricky Ponting steadied the Australian innings at a critical juncture when New Zealand was beginning to probe their batting weaknesses. Even more importantly, the Australian pace attack exerted sustained pressure and developed cohesion. The whole was greater than the sum of the parts.

Peter Siddle who had taken a hat–trick against England on this ground in the Ashes series opener a year before, led the attack by virtue of his seniority. His returns were not as flattering as those of Pattinson, but he looked consistently hostile and to my mind contributed much to the success of his younger colleague through his relentless pressure on the batsmen. Until the summer of 2011–12 I had considered Siddle merely a brave journeyman, but as the series against India unfolded he emerged as a bowler of genuine Test calibre, matching his pace and aggression with a control and variation not hitherto evident.

Young Mitchell Starc did not impress as much as his more explosive fellow debutante, but already looked like a better prospect than the erratic and consistently disappointing Mitchell Johnson. Starc, however, continued to improve throughout the summer and produced some dangerous spells in the one-day series, which augurs well for his potential role in the Australian attack in England in 2013. By the end of the Gabba test many commentators were confidently asserting that Australia's fast bowling cup was running over. I was unconvinced at that time, but subsequent events lent credence to the claims of the optimists.

Ultimately, the Gabba revealed more about the resurgence of Australian cricket than I was willing to concede at the time. The ingredients of victory there constituted the foundations of the subsequent rout of India. My initial foray into the world of cricket writing had however been bitter-sweet. The repeated reminders of mortality presaged by the deaths of Peter Roebuck, Arthur Beetson, Sam Loxton, and my mate Norman, clothed that time in Brisbane with a gloom that was reinforced by the drab surroundings of the Gabba. My spirits lightened as my Virgin flight broke into bright sunshine on the journey home. But I still had a funeral oration to write.

He portrayed the nature of war as a violent struggle akin to a duel or a wrestling match, where each adversary seeks to impose its will on the other for a policy end.

Carl Philipp Gottfried von Clausewitz was a Prussian soldier and German military theorist.

3. *Clausewitz on Cricket*

Most notably, in cricket India has followed the trajectory that its strategic leaders aspire to in broader affairs.

It has been this way since Thermopylae. Clausewitz warned us that those who seek to evade this reality are unintentionally cruel, as well as stupid.

... cricket, like war, is a true chameleon.

'What do they know of cricket who only cricket know?' For that epigram from C.L.R. James I am indebted to my Indian friend Boria Majumdar, author of a superb history of Indian cricket titled *Twenty-Two Yards to Freedom: A Social History of Indian Cricket*. According to Boria, '... Indian cricket makes sense only when it is placed within the broader politico-economic context'. The same must surely be said of Australian cricket, which has not received the scholarly attention that it warrants given its significance to Australian identity. Here I seek to redress that to some extent by examining the rise of Australian cricket from the drubbing of England in 1989 and then through the era of Australian dominance of world cricket when it reigned in the manner of a superpower. This was the cricket equivalent of what the foreign policy specialists referred to as the unipolar moment when, for a brief period in the wake of the collapse of the Soviet Union, the United States was the sole global hegemon—a superpower. Some even called it the world's first 'hyperpower'. Regardless of the semantics, the United States lacked any credible peer competitor. The period of uncontested American hegemony and Australian cricket's undisputed dominance spanned roughly the same era.

While it may seem tendentious to draw too direct a connection between Australian cricketing supremacy and American global dominance, the roots of both sprouted during 1989 when the Berlin Wall fell and the vacuum left by the fall of the Soviet Empire radically transformed the global system. The forces of globalisation, given frenetic energy by the opening up of the former communist bloc, have since also radically transformed all major sports into sprawling global enterprises. Cricket has not been immune to this trend.

Meeting Boria Majumdar was one of the highlights of my Indian summer. He is a scholar of exceptional erudition with a seemingly innate Indian love of cricket. He has sought to examine the connections between globalisation and the commercialisation of all sports, especially the Olympics. Much of the analysis that follows treads in Boria's footsteps. I admire his dedication to the rigorous examination of the linkage between geopolitics and sport.

In the book co-edited with Fan Hong, *Modern Sport: The Global Obsession*, Boria argued that:

> Sport has become more than a simple physical expression or game—it now pervades all societies at all levels and has become bound up in nationalism, entertainment, patriotism and culture. Now a global obsession, sport has infiltrated into all areas of modern life and despite noble ideals that sport stands above politics, religion, class, gender and ideology, the reality is often very different.

Boria developed his theories about Indian cricket while reading towards his doctorate at Oxford. His college was St John's, just around the corner from my home in Oxford in the Beaumont Buildings behind the wonderful Ashmolean Museum. Unlike Boria though, I studied war at Oxford rather than sport. For much of 2008 I was a Visiting Fellow there in the Changing Character of War Programme under the direction of the Chichele Professor of the History of War, Hew Strachan. One of my favourite memories of that time was watching the filming of an episode of the television series *Lewis* starring Kevin Whately, the sequel to the wonderful *Inspector Morse* series set in Oxford. One drizzly evening the wall of St John's was illuminated for filming. Its beauty transfixed me as I huddled under the awning of the Randolph Hotel. Among the kaleidoscope of perfection of that spring and summer in Oxford, there was a stark beauty in that tableau that still excited me as I recounted it to Boria in the sweltering media box in Sydney on the second day of the Test match this January.

The Changing Character of War Programme, as its name suggests, was established to examine changes in the character of war, especially since the end of the Cold War. That title bears a significance easily lost on the uninitiated to whom discussions about war are immoral, disagreeably esoteric or simply boring. But among those with a professional or scholarly interest in war as a complex social phenomenon, the contention that, though the *character* of war may change, its *nature* is immutable is a genuflection to the seminal theorist of war Carl von Clausewitz.

Clausewitz is more often cited than read. Because his major work *On War* was effectively unfinished at the time of his death it is often opaque, if not downright contradictory. In common with Karl Marx,

John Stuart Mill and Charles Darwin, he perhaps has more to fear from misguided admirers than detractors. Yet *On War* deservedly ranks as one of the most influential works ever written and, along with *The Prince* by Niccolò Machiavelli, proffers enduring wisdom as to the nature of war, the security of the state and the brutal exercise of power among nations.

Some of Clausewitz's insights are now so commonplace they seem banal, yet they are profound. He portrayed the nature of war as a violent struggle akin to a duel or a wrestling match, where each adversary seeks to impose its will on the other for a policy end. In defining war as a rational act designed to achieve the ends of policy, Clausewitz left an enduring intellectual legacy, though one which generates criticism and controversy to this day.

Likewise, he described war as a 'true chameleon' that derives its hue from the prevailing *Zeitgeist*. The complex interplay of reason, passion and chance make war a violent, unpredictable tool for the prosecution of national interests. The complexion of war changes as it unfolds and adapts, manifesting the temper of the times and place in which it is waged.

These seemingly self-evident, yet enduring truths about the nature of war are at the core of the multidisciplinary team's work at Oxford, and I routinely revert to these first principles when I attempt to discern the defining elements in contemporary war and statecraft. To my mind, my friend Boria Majumdar is a Clausewitzian by instinct, if not profession. His analysis of the globalisation of sport, especially cricket, captures the complex interplay of forces that shape the changing character of sport as underlying socio-economic conditions shift.

Furthermore, Majumdar has an acute eye for the emergence of rising global powers. China is a rising power in both the strategic and sporting spheres. India has also started to realise the enormous potential of its demographic and strategic weight. Most notably, in cricket India has followed the trajectory that its strategic leaders aspire to in broader affairs. In wresting the right to host the 1987 Cricket World Cup from what Boria Majumdar describes as the 'Western lobby', India announced its arrival as a global cricketing force. It is now uniquely powerful on account of the prodigious money it generates through its massive media audience and the mountains of cash that percolate through all levels of the game there. As he argued persuasively in *Twenty-Two Yards to Freedom*:

> World cricket has undergone fundamental transformation in the years 1997–2003. India has been at the kernel of this process; to it goes the credit of placing the ICC [International Cricket Council] on a sound financial footing ... In India with sponsors eager to put their money into cricket, the BCCI [The Board of Control for Cricket in India] became the richest sports body in the country in the 1990s.

Indeed, the sums of money sponsors are prepared to lavish to reach the Indian market make the mind boggle. Sony Entertainment Network outlaid US$225 million to secure the television rights for India for the 2003 and 2007 World Cups and the three ICC Champions Trophies in 2002, 2004 and 2006, dwarfing Rupert Murdoch's STAR Sports bid for the 1999 event sevenfold.

Paradoxically, India manages to be both a status quo cricket power while still adopting the methods of a usurper in its challenge to some of the norms of the game. Perhaps this is a legacy of its roots; before independence cricket was often an expression of nationalist assertiveness against the colonial power. It may take a sustained period of dominance both on and off the field for the Indian cricket hierarchy to completely erase its sense of being outsiders.

It is tempting to overemphasise the similarities between the rise of great sporting powers and great strategic powers, and to overread the conspicuous impacts of globalisation on both the character of war and sport. Let me emphasise though that I am not seeking to resort to the gauche tabloid device of using the language of war and strategy to describe the most mundane elements of sporting contests. In his superb Bradman Oration, delivered at the Australian War Memorial in December 2011, former Indian captain Rahul Dravid eloquently rebuked the folly and immaturity of this practice. A following chapter will deal with that Bradman Oration in more detail, but his point that sports journalists insensitively resort to the language of war is well made. It is an infraction of which I have often been guilty, along with many of my colleagues in politics.

Nonetheless, there is an enticing coincidence between the fact that Australia's rise to global cricketing hegemony began in 1989 at the same time as the collapse of the Soviet Union, one of the truly seismic shifts in global geopolitics. In 1989 Australian cricket emerged from the doldrums. Between the retirement of Dennis Lillee, Greg Chappell and Rod Marsh at the end of the 1983–84 season and the recovery of The Ashes in England in 1989, Australia experienced a cricket famine of biblical proportions. The statistics are eloquent and uncompromisingly bleak. In those lean years between that Test and the Ashes series in 1989, Australia won just seven of its forty-six Tests. Series wins over New Zealand and Sri Lanka were the highlights, if such a description does not undermine the integrity of the English language. The mystique of the baggy green cap was debunked, at the time seemingly irrevocably. Humiliations at the hands of the predatory West Indians became routine, while the reviled Englishmen crushed us in emphatic fashion in England in 1985 and here in 1986.

When Allan Border's men embarked for England in 1989 they were widely condemned as the worst Australian team to have ever been sent there. Yet when David Boon, the very personification of the Australian revival of 1989, swept Nick Cook to the mid-wicket boundary at Old Trafford to recover the urn for Australia, a new golden age seemed to beckon. And so it came to pass. Over the next two decades Australia stood astride the cricketing world like a colossus. In the 1990s the hitherto impregnable West Indians were, in turn, tamed and then ruthlessly dismantled— dispatched to that nether world of self-doubt and introspection that had afflicted Australia from the inception of World Series Cricket in 1977. The West Indies has never completely recovered.

Although he did not endure to savour the accolades of the Australian resurgence, Allan Border was its architect. There was in him the ability to balance confidence with thoughtfulness that is exemplified by Rudyard Kipling when he advised, 'keep your head when all about you are losing theirs and blaming it on you'. Like an Old Testament prophet, Allan Border charted their course, assuaged their doubts and, through epic force of will and power of example, convinced them that a land of milk and honey was just over the horizon.

In that portentious prose at which Marxists excelled it may be said that it was 'no coincidence' that Australian cricket was in flux from 1977 until 1989. There was a revolution in the mode of production of Australian cricket, inspired primarily by Kerry Packer, that brash and brutish buccaneer, and his audacious coup to seize the marketing of the game from its sclerotic administration. The Packer revolution, in the guise of World Series Cricket, transformed cricket in ways that continue to define it to the present day. Befitting a media entrepreneur with an acute insight into the tastes and aspirations of most Australians, Packer changed the coverage and presentation of cricket irrevocably. His most beneficent legacy was the radical improvement in the quality of televised coverage of international cricket. The use of multiple camera angles, instant replays, and sophisticated technology to corroborate run outs and faint edges off the bat have all exponentially enhanced the entertainment value of televised cricket, as has the use of stadium lighting to enable day–night matches. But Packer also released the genie of commercialism, and it is now moot as to whether that genie serves cricket, or whether cricket serves the genie.

Cricket was a business before Packer launched his bid to control television coverage of Test matches though. And its transformation did not happen in isolation. The Australian economy that gathered pace in the aftermath of the float of the Australian dollar by the Hawke government in 1983, transformed Australian society radically making it more cosmopolitan and connected to the fluctuations in world affairs. The doyen of Australian political journalists, Paul Kelly, has provided the most insightful account of the realignment of the tectonic plates underpinning Australian life in the early 1980s in his majestic work *The End of Certainty*. As an interpreter of the meta-trends in Australia's social and political fabric, Kelly is simply without peer. He discerned in the Australia of the 1980s the dying embers of an established but declining order that he classified the 'Australian Settlement'. Its constituent elements—broadly the subject of bipartisan political consensus since Federation—were the White Australia policy, industry protection, and the conciliation and arbitration of wage and industrial disputes through a centralised system of quasi-judicial tribunals.

Although the White Australia policy had been abandoned in the 1960s, the Australian economy that Hawke inherited was highly regulated. Indeed, his career had been built on the adept manipulation of those levers of power that were indispensable to the operation of this system.

This corporate state model achieved its apotheosis at the National Economic Summit in early 1983. As the newly elected prime minister, Hawke presided over this forum like a benign monarch. Big business, organised labour and the academic elites, accurately branded the Industrial Relations Club by public intellectual Gerard Henderson, gathered to hammer out an accord, whereby the portion of gross domestic product accruing to labour would be increased through indirect increases to the social wage under the guise of Medicare and other social programmes, in return for a level of wage restraint that had eluded both Gough Whitlam and Malcolm Fraser.

With hindsight, it is difficult to conclude whether the defining characteristic of this model was its vaulting hubris or its naïveté. The float of the Australian dollar unleashed the forces of global competition on the Australian economy like a tsunami. The notion that a room full of business leaders grown rich and complacent behind tariff walls, and union leaders who had pimped their members to them for unsustainable wages, could ever again arbitrate the standard of living of Australia was soon exposed as a folly. Like genteel Edwardians blissfully incapable of conjuring the Western Front in even their darkest, most febrile nightmares, the participants in the National Economic Summit dispersed blissfully unaware that the cosy labour and capital cartel that they jointly administered was doomed.

> Those long uneven lines
> Standing as patiently
> As if they were stretched outside
> The Oval or Villa Park,
> The crowns of hats, the sun
> On moustached archaic faces
> Grinning as if it were all
> An August Bank Holiday lark; ...
>
> Never such innocence again.

After the float of the Australian dollar in 1983, the impossibility of insulating the non-traded goods sector and the Australian labour market against deregulated capital markets became glaringly, if belatedly, obvious. Whether Hawke and Keating had fully grasped this when they rolled the dice into the casino of international capitalism is impossible to determine with any assurance in the wake of their acrimonious and self-serving rationalisations for subsequent events. What followed though was a masterful, and at times inspired, improvisation as they struggled to protect their core constituency, while maintaining the confidence of global finance markets in their government. It demanded the unsentimental abandonment of some of Labor's most cherished shibboleths—steadily rising wages and public ownership. In particular, Keynesian deficit budgeting fell into disrepute. Privatisation, corporatisation, and user-pays systems replaced the universal provision and public ownership of the Australia in which I had thrived as a ninja. Emotive disputes over whether university students should make a co-contribution to their education, and whether the government should run airlines, banks or even jails were grist to the political mill during the 1980s and 1990s.

After the attacks on the United States in September 2001, such domestic debates appear remarkably civil, if not quaint. But then they generated a diffuse and intense backlash. The old Australia—overwhelmingly white, mono-cultural and traditional—was the main casualty of the emerging cosmopolitanism of the new Australia. The elites of the globally engaged cities, especially Sydney, but more recently the boom towns of Brisbane and Perth, flourished in this brave new world.

Those in regional Australia and on the urban fringes, who had derived their identity from the certainties of an era in which Australia reigned supreme at cricket and for whom large sections of the map of the world covered in the comforting pink of the motherland meant continuity and safety, felt insecure and often devalued. They sought champions such as Joh Bjelke-Petersen and later Pauline Hanson who were able to articulate their sense of bewildered grief at the passing of a country of which they had been fiercely proud, and which they felt had worked just fine. Their most strident advocate of late has been Bob Katter who recently wrote the book *An Incredible Race of People: A Passionate History of Australia*. He speaks for people like my parents and our neighbours from regional Queensland. His arguments were grist to the mill around our family dinner table where his admiration for the Queensland Labor hero 'Red Ted' Theodore was shared. My parents saw no contradiction in voting for Joh Bjelke-Petersen while mourning the dearth of 'real Labor men' like Jack Lang and Theodore.

But agrarian agitation never became violent in Australia. At more contested frontiers of modernity and antiquity, or tribalism and cosmopolitanism, conflicts have been violent. These clashes have been the stuff of the history that Francis Fukuyama told us had ended with the triumph of liberalism.

For a time, cricket was almost impervious to these influences. Through Packer's revolution it had entered the era of globalisation less vulnerable to external shock than much of the rest of Australian society. For a brief period of time the so-called Packer Circus had provided a private competitor to the official Australian Cricket Board monopoly. However, the rift had been healed well before the rest of the Australian economy felt the chill winds of privatisation and watched as iconic names such as Colonial Sugar Refineries, Trans Australia Airlines, Fletcher Jones and Bonds changed complexion or disappeared. In reality, the dispute between the Australian Cricket Board and the players who signed with

Packer can best be interpreted as a classic collective bargaining dispute of the type which was endemic in the 1960s and 1970s and through which Bob Hawke forged his reputation. It was the dying convulsion of the old centralised wage fixing system rather than the harbinger of the new deregulated labour market which is now familiar to modern day cricketers and which features fierce competition for Indian Premier League and even state contracts. And once the rift with Packer's mercenaries had been healed, the Australian team was restored to its rightful place as the premier sporting embodiment of the nation's aspirations.

Notwithstanding its indifferent performances from 1983 until the rout of England in 1989, the Australian Test team continued to command the affections and almost universal adulation of the nation. I remember how the tearful resignation of the Australian Test captain Kim Hughes, after an abject Australian defeat in Brisbane at the hands of the West Indies in 1984, transfixed the nation. Around the same time prime minister Bob Hawke had wept openly while talking about his daughter's struggles with heroin addiction. The nexus between the performances of the Test cricket team, the idealisation of Australian masculinity, and the overall health of the nation had perhaps not been as explicitly drawn since the Bodyline series. And just as Australian cricket was uncomfortably accommodating itself to the unaccustomed role of prey rather than predator, the nation was being warned it could become a 'banana republic' and the Argentina of the Antipodes. So parlous was the state of the cricket team that some argued that the coach of the Grand Slam-winning Wallabies rugby union team, Alan Jones, should be appointed the generalissimo of Australian cricket to restore our fortunes. As Australian cricket fought to adjust to a changing global order, so did the nation at large. It was a fractious, uncertain time.

Australia was not alone; fractures and uncertainty were the new reality of the global order. The changes to the Australian political, economic and social structure occurred when the global order was in the process of reconfiguring in a manner unimaginable since the end of the Second World War. In early 1989, the Soviet 40th Army limped across the border from Afghanistan, defeated and discredited. By the end of the same year, the Soviet Union had virtually collapsed, bringing to an effective end the Cold War and the tense bipolar stand off between the rival Soviet and Western blocs. For a time the new Eden beckoned. Foreign policy analysts such as Francis Fukuyama asserted that history had ended. Some American analysts such as Charles Krauthammer revelled in what they perceived to be a unipolar moment. The United States was about to realise its manifest, exceptional destiny—without the interference of a peer competitor. But history never takes a vacation.

The coherence and equilibrium provided by two nuclear-armed blocs throughout the Cold War unravelled. My friend and mentor, Colin Gray of the University of Reading, perspicaciously coined the term 'wars of the Soviet Succession' to explain the phenomenon of brushfire civil wars that spread though the newly unshackled constituent elements of the Soviet Empire. Nowhere was this nomenclature more accurate than in the brutal genocide that accompanied the disintegration of the former Yugoslavia.

For a time it seemed that the demise of Soviet power had created a vacuum, one that was soon filled by long-suppressed tribal and religious hatreds. In an attempt to understand and explain the resurgence of these conflicts of 'ancient hatreds', New War theorists, most convincingly represented by Mary Kaldor and Martin van Creveld, asserted that Clausewitz had been rendered obsolete by the fissiparous forces challenging the traditional state in the era of unprecedented globalisation. This rationale soon lost currency.

There were some disarmingly plausible elements in this theory though. Kaldor was correct in identifying the 'intensification of global interconnectedness—political, economic, military and cultural—and the changing character of political authority'. But I believe that caution needs to be exercised in not defining globalisation so broadly and imprecisely that the theory loses its explanatory force when applied to specific cases. While Kaldor in particular made a useful contribution in examining the nexus between criminal and insurgent networks and the propensity for combatants to finance themselves rather than relying on the state for their resources—including through plundering humanitarian aid—this is not necessarily novel. The theory seemed too amorphous to carry the burden of much of the low-tech fighting over traditional issues that often lurked under the enticing crust of 'new' causes.

However, it is clear that the incredible growth of information technology has led to one very significant change in the way war and conflict is waged. The instantaneous transmission of media images—the so-called CNN effect—has introduced a variable that commanders of previous eras did not need to consider. Of course the Boers waged an effective information and media campaign over British depredations against civilians in South Africa long before the invention of television, but in recent years the immediate access to television images of war by mass audiences has produced hitherto unforeseen effects. It is perhaps too early to gauge the full impact of this phenomenon.

The permeation of real-time images of conflict into homes poses questions not just for governments, but for society as a whole. Would Australian troops have been dispatched to East Timor in 1999 in the absence of poignant and immediate images of the suffering of the Timorese in the wake of the Independence plebiscite? The same question can be put for nearly every so-called humanitarian intervention from Somalia to Rwanda, or Kosovo to the Sudan. The list continues to grow, though the chastening effects of the inconclusive nation-building effort in Afghanistan may curtail Western enthusiasm for interventions beyond the most rigorously prescribed Realist case. However, the social media campaign demanding action against the Ugandan warlord Joseph Kony earlier this year suggests that the era of such interventions may not yet be over.

The immediacy of media images rapidly ramps up sentimentality among even sophisticated audiences, yet their passions tend to be ephemeral. The appetite for conflict recedes just as rapidly with images of death, even when it is that of the enemy. On the other hand, drone and satellite images render killing into a spectacle—sterile and far too clinical. Much of the population now has no link to their smaller professional armies. War has become a spectator sport.

To my mind this is the problem with the commercialised forms of cricket, especially the Twenty20 game. The teams are meaningless congregations of talented individuals, franchises in the banal euphemism *du jour*. Enthusiasm is transient; emotional investment minimal. Cricket is background noise and pleasing escapism. Yet I can barely recall the results of a single one-day fixture from any summer past. The odd innings, such as that explosive cameo by David Warner against South Africa in January 2009, springs to mind, but essentially I imbibe the short game in the same way I would a sugary opiate. Absent from this form of game is the sense of epic struggle which once engaged the nation and bound neighbours one to another. At no time since Australian forces have been at war in Afghanistan have I ever discussed this conflict with any of my neighbours, nor have we ever paused to exchange cricket scores. Thus is the effect of globalised media coverage on war and sport similar.

And in that respect at least, Mary Kaldor and the New War theorists did discern something genuinely new in the contemporary era. Of even less intellectual weight and a shorter life span was the so-called Revolution in Military Affairs, which seemed to promise an era of sterile, remote killing in which advanced nations would vanquish opponents using information technology and space-based weapons. Yet none of these theories were able to explain away the bloody realities of wars from Rwanda and the Congo through to Iraq, Afghanistan and Chechnya. The claims made for precision air strikes against the Serbian forces in 1999 aroused scepticism among soldiers at the time; claims that were soon comprehensively debunked by the character of fighting required against irregular enemies in a number of former Soviet Union republics and by the United States and its allies since 2001.

Returning then to Clausewitz, it seems to me that the prescient Prussian theorist of war and statecraft still has much to offer us in interpreting the contemporary world. Rather than either the end of history or the resumption of 'ancient hatreds', the 1990s saw a proliferation of limited wars over the distribution of resources and power—causes also known to Thucydides and Hannibal. Global interconnectedness has created a world where geographical frontiers mean less than they used to, which in my view has exacerbated resentment about the encroachment of an apparently decadent Western mono-culture in the Islamic world. Improved technology, especially the diffusion of cheap information technology, has democratised access to lethal weaponry. Hence the so-called non-state actors—groups outside the formal and legitimate state organisations—have been able to challenge sophisticated conventional military forces in a manner that is different in form rather than substance to those original *guerrilleros* who harried Napoleon in Spain.

What the end of the Cold War actually did was impart an even more frenetic pace to the process of globalisation. This has in turn, unleashed the gale of creative destruction described by Joseph Schumpeter with unmitigated ferocity. In an advanced democracy such as Australia, the tensions so created can be absorbed by a mature and sophisticated political system. The most serious casualties can be compensated through a taxpayer-funded welfare system. Even so, the dislocation to customs and to traditional institutions that occurred in Australia in the closing decade of the twentieth century strained the social fabric. While the centre ultimately held, the Australian Settlement was swept away. In its wake emerged a leaner, more competitive Australia. The concept of a job for life was one conspicuous casualty of this change. The pervasive pressure to corporatise every element of life transformed Australia.

Sport absorbed the dominant ideology of the market. Even rugby union—that resolute final redoubt of genteel amateurism—fell in 1995. Where once my mates and I would have died to wear the maroon of Queensland, the state team became a franchise known as the Reds, their ranks fleshed out by mercenaries from other places, including New South Wales. Where was my samurai sword when I needed it?

All the football codes became businesses. The sense of tribal affiliation based on family, neighbourhood and state was lost, or at least diluted, with the honourable exception of Rugby League's State of Origin competition. While caution in making sweeping generalisations about the tastes of a cosmopolitan nation must be exercised, I suspect that the Test cricket team has continued to be a unifying institution for the majority of Australians in this void, maintaining much of its patriotic hold over the Australian public's imagination.

Many of the world's nations were not able to manage the clash between the old and the new, the universal and the particular though. History did not benignly enter its twilight. Rather the ancient, the local and the religious violently rejected the modern, the secular and the universal. Much of the world decided to give war a chance.

In my professional life since 1999, I have tried to discern the defining characteristics of warfare in this epoch. Although I was tempted to agree with many analysts who believed they had seen a change in the nature of warfare in the wake of the Cold War's end, I no longer think that any of the modern theorists have discerned anything in post-Cold War warfare that would have vexed Clausewitz. War retains its essential nature as a duel—a violent, rational contest over policy. Granted, in the vicious hybrid wars that have raged from Somalia, Rwanda and the Congo, through the Balkans to Afghanistan, disrupted states seem to exhibit unique features to the uninitiated, just as the air war over Kosovo seemed to herald that long-sought nirvana of bloodless victory. But such appearances are misleading. As Nathan Bedford Forrest once famously observed, 'War means fighting, and fighting means killing'. It has been this way since Thermopylae. Clausewitz warned us that those who seek to evade this reality are unintentionally cruel, as well as stupid.

Since the attacks on the United States on 11 September 2001, we can now discern the predominant hue of Clausewitz's chameleon in its various guises. Perhaps the most distinctive aspect of contemporary war from the perspective of a soldier of a modern Western army is that the adversary is not likely to be another nation-state. Conventional state-on-state war has been in relative decline since Waterloo, though its comparative rarity is belied by the enormity of its scale and intensity when it does occur. But it is unlikely to have been of much comfort to a resident of Hiroshima to learn that they were at greater risk of an insurgent or terrorist attack.

I have wandered a long way from David Boon's winning sweep shot at Old Trafford in 1989 though. What does Clausewitz tell us about cricket? To me cricket, like war, is a true chameleon. Since 1989 it has increasingly conformed to the norms of the globalised sports market. Test cricket, as the pinnacle of the hierarchy of loyalty and prestige, along with the nation-state, is under challenge. In the modern world there is an even more intriguing confluence between the transformation of the global system and the commercialisation of cricket, with India playing a pivotal role in both. India is a rising global power by any definition. Its national team was able to defy Australia at the height of its mastery of the universe in 2001. While not as convincing abroad, the Indian cricket team has nonetheless shed its amiable, easy-beats status to win the most recent World Cup.

To borrow again from Clausewitz, the centre of gravity of the global game has shifted from the Long Room at Lord's to the subcontinent. And drawing the longest of bows, in the cricket domain India may be seen as a disruptive power that constitutes a threat to the traditional 'nation-state' teams through sponsorship of 'non-state actors', the Indian Premier League. None of this could have occurred but for the realignment in the global economy which started in 1989 with the fall of the Soviet Union. It is too early to forecast with confidence what the implications of this will be for cricket, especially Test cricket. However, it seems to me that national Test cricket teams will be only one among a cast of many with calls upon the loyalties of its citizens. The insatiable demands of the ubiquitous global media market will substitute its own commercial bids for time-honoured customs.

'His timing is so good that no matter how lightly he brushes the ball, it always runs faster than the chasing fieldsman.'
V.V.S. Laxman, whose initials ... stood for 'Very Very Special'.

4.   *The Indians in Canberra*

True humility—like class—speaks in whispers, but carries a broad blade.

'Sachin Tendulkar is not a person, he is an occurrence, a phenomenon whose uniqueness does not carry the rust of time ...'

Statham threw his hands to his mouth in anguish as The Don departed, along with a large segment of the crowd.

The omens for the Indian tour of Australia were not auspicious. Perhaps in retrospect the magnitude of their subsequent defeat conferred a greater bleakness on those December days than they actually exhibited. With the benefit of hindsight, it now seems the Indians started their quest for an inaugural series win in Australia in a lackadaisical, almost haphazard manner. It should have sounded alarm bells for me, but did not.

I had found Australia's performance against New Zealand unconvincing. Defeat at Bellerive in Hobart, especially the abject dismissal of Ricky Ponting, suggested that the fragility on display in Cape Town lingered just beneath the surface. Granted, India had been brittle in England and had betrayed a lack of fight when placed under even a modicum of pressure, yet there seemed to be enough gravitas in their batting to entitle them to favoured status. Nevertheless, there was an air of chaos and indifference around the side from its very arrival.

The tourists arrived by bus in the depth of night—3 am to be precise. Later, as I pondered when and where things went wrong for them, their extended stay in Canberra and the modest preparation they undertook while there brought to mind a line that Ulysses S. Grant once sagely applied to a fellow general, 'He got started wrong and just never got right'. Their almost stealthy arrival by bus amid miserable, unseasonable drizzle evoked another incident of the American Civil War era—Abraham Lincoln's surreptitious late night, unheralded arrival in Washington in disguise before his inauguration in the winter of 1861. Unlike the touring Indians though, Lincoln's underwhelming beginning did not establish the pattern for subsequent performance.

Like the man in the Simon and Garfunkel song, I turned my collar to the cold and damp and made my way to Manuka Oval for the first net session of the tour. I was hoping that I could exploit my home-ground advantage and steal a march on the mainstream media by gaining early access to the Indians and establishing connections to some of their media party. The big names in Australian cricket media did not turn out for the optimistically named Festival of Cricket in Canberra. In mid-December the Australian media was more concerned with the much-hyped Big Bash, Twenty20 competition and neither of the inconsequential fixtures scheduled for Manuka appeared especially appetising. If Canberra is ever to seriously press its claim to host a Test match, Cricket ACT will need to demonstrate more ability to promote big matches than it did last December.

During the preceding week I had enjoyed an almost private viewing of a Sheffield Shield match between New South Wales and Tasmania at Manuka. Notwithstanding the lack of atmosphere, the Shield match afforded the opportunity to view some candidates for Test selection, notably Ed Cowan and Ben Hilfenhaus. My assessment of the former was that he looked a very organised and complete cricketer, free of the crippling and seemingly intractable technical deficiencies that continued to beset Phil Hughes. On the other hand, I was unimpressed by Hilfenhaus, feeling that he looked listless, bordering on unfit. His subsequent performance in the Test series utterly discredited that judgement which I unfortunately committed to print at the time.

Canberra threatened rain for most of the day. The tourists arrived at Manuka amid clichéd subcontinental chaos, a leaden sky and a chilly breeze. They were scrutinised by a motley crew of local journalists and stringers rendered even more motley by the presence of yours truly. The media manager at Cricket ACT had advised me that the session would run from 2 pm until 5 pm. The timings seemed to become even more elastic upon my arrival. Could they have meant any time *between* 2 pm and 5 pm? But then of course, the only question that really mattered to the majority with little or no interest in cricket but had been dispatched to procure one particular image was:

'Is Sachin coming?'

'Quite possibly.'

'When?'

'Quite possibly later.'

Tim Gavel of ABC Radio—the resonant, reassuring voice of all sports in Canberra—confided, 'A half an hour ago they told me they would be here in ten minutes'. Then, just as the mood among the media pack was becoming mutinous, I noticed the troupe of imported teenage bowlers stand up and start stretching and running on the spot. Assuming that they knew something the rest of us did not, I moved closer to the nets. Nor was I disappointed. Sauntering down from the dressing rooms was the unmistakeable figure of V.V.S. Laxman, whose initials, according to the late Peter Roebuck, stood for 'Very Very Special'.

There is a chasm between great talent and rare genius. In any field of endeavour, champions announce their presence in subtle but telling ways. You can separate fighters by the way they move out of the ring. Seemingly innocuous, irrelevant movements and gestures provide tantalising hints of the uncanny skill that is carried unconsciously by those who play those sports in which hand-eye coordination and ball skills are paramount. In this, Laxman *is* Very Very Special. But even more special is his humility and grace. More on this later.

As he approached the wicket I importuned him for a photograph, just like a peddler at Kuta Beach. He acquiesced without complaint. I, however, managed to botch the operation of the borrowed digital camera, whose intricacies my wife had explained patiently (actually with mounting impatience) prior to my optimistic departure from home.

'The Army really did give you a weapon with live ammunition when you went overseas didn't they?' I no longer rise to that particular bait, preferring to file it away silently as evidence of spousal abuse for later Family Court proceedings.

If he was irritated by my incompetence, Laxman betrayed no sign of it. He waited patiently as I fumbled and trembled my way through a click, hoping that after my public humiliation I had actually turned the camera on. Thankfully I had.

The aspiring young bowlers drafted in for the session may not have provided the sternest test, but you know, you simply know, when you see a genuine champion. They ooze class from every pore, and seem to rhythmically inhale and exhale mastery of their art with each breath. Like Sachin Tendulkar, like Rahul Dravid, this man was in the Indian summer of a brilliant career, but he still exhibited that indefinable touch of class that is simply a birthright.

For me, truly graceful, effortless batting has equal elements of ballet and poetry. I explained the way in which music transports me towards ecstasy. The elegance of a genuine batting great moves the same part deep inside me. If I could describe it better they would give me a column in *Cleo*. Laxman was lavishly equipped at birth with the natural elements that define a champion with the willow. He makes it all look absurdly easy. And the power he generates defies rational explanation—so little exertion producing so much power. That uninterrupted hour-long private show will remain one of my treasured memories, not just of that summer, but of my life as a cricket watcher.

In brief, I would have cheerfully paid to watch V.V.S. Laxman, all wrists and nonchalance, easily deflecting the ball in that fading light, and climbed off my deathbed to do so. Well, I would have climbed off my deathbed if I did not have one of those drip things in my arm, and if my doctor thought some fresh air would be really good for me. Well, you get my drift. I was really glad I went to the nets to see this bloke up close.

Sadly, V.V.S. Laxman failed to play to his potential throughout the summer and left Australia with a dark cloud hovering over his Test cricket future. In Sydney he briefly provided a glimpse of his best when Michael Clarke allowed him the luxury of playing himself in against Nathan Lyon in India's second innings. He got away and lit up the Sydney Cricket Ground with some exquisite driving. It must have been an optical illusion, but one shot through the off side actually seemed to accelerate the further it got away from the bat. That piece of effortless execution brought audible exclamations of 'Shot!' from the Indian journalists near me in the media box, temporarily suspending any pretence of journalistic detachment on their part.

On another occasion he flicked the rampant Australian pace-man James Pattinson to the boundary with contemptuous ease.

On the Saturday afternoon of the Perth Test I enjoyed a companionable walk back from the WACA to my city hotel with Malcolm Knox who was covering the match for *The Sydney Morning Herald*. He is an elegant writer on any topic and has produced some very good cricket writing, though nowadays he primarily devotes his considerable talent to fiction. Like me he had been thrilled by Laxman's cameo in Sydney and had been as enthralled as I at an opportunity to watch him at close quarters in the nets. As he wrote in *The Sydney Morning Herald*:

> Laxman, who is my favourite batsman in world cricket, dominated the partnership with his twirls and clips. He is so compelling because after 130-odd Tests it's still impossible to work out how he gets so much energy into the very last instant of his shots. He practised hard in the nets this week, and I spent some time watching him without being any the wiser. He can be out of position, flat-footed, beaten in flight, and the next moment the ball is whistling towards the boundary because of some conjuring of his wrists that was faster than the observer's eye. His timing is so good that no matter how lightly he brushes the ball, it always runs faster than the chasing fieldsman.

We puzzled over the poor batting of the Indians, especially that of Laxman of whom we were both enthusiastic admirers. By that Saturday in Perth, Laxman's departure from the game was being widely canvassed among the Indian media. It saddened us both. Despite that tantalising glimmer of form at the SCG, there was nothing on this tour to rival his glorious 178 on the same ground in January 2004. His modest harvest seriously undermined India's middle order.

One of the reasons that I had wished him well was that I had enjoyed a brief chat to him on the evening of his arrival in Canberra, and consequently felt a personal connection to him for the duration of the tour. After the inaugural Indian net session I had again encountered him at the Australian War Memorial, with the remainder of the touring party, for the Bradman Oration. I approached him and Ishant Sharma in the stairwell leading to the dining hall while they were standing engrossed in conversation. I apologised for my earlier gaucherie with the camera. He gave a slight bow, 'It was my pleasure. It is okay'. True humility—like class—speaks in whispers, but carries a broad blade. I was a convert to his cause, and each successive failure left me inordinately disappointed.

Anyway, back to that Manuka net session where finally the murmurs and rustling gave way to a hush as the media pack parted like a biblical sea to permit the passage of Sachin Tendulkar. Seemingly, within minutes of his arrival at the crease a significant proportion of Canberra's taxi fleet was becalmed in a long silent line beside the Manuka Oval, their Punjabi drivers watching intently as the 'Little Master' practised. To me he was not as opulently beautiful to watch as Laxman, but as I saw the reactions among the Indian fans I was able to glean something of the impact he has on the people of his homeland and the crushing psychological burden this imposes on him. He seems to somehow generate an invisible force field around himself behind which he is oblivious to the adoration of the masses. Whether in the nets or in the middle of the SCG, he becomes the solitary occupant of a lonely, icy planet warmed only by his insatiable appetite for runs.

Sachin Tendulkar occupies a unique role in Indian life that has no equivalent in contemporary Australian cricket. Evidently Bradman achieved such status in Australia during the Great Depression and early postwar years. But Tendulkar dominates a modern complex nation of more than one billion people. His image is pervasive. He rapidly filled the vacuum left by the departure from the stage of Sunil Gavaskar, the first megastar of Indian cricket in the era of global media. Rohit Brijnath best summed up the Tendulkar phenomenon in a passage worthy of citation in full:

> For an entire generation of Indians, Sachin Tendulkar is not a person, he is an occurrence, a phenomenon whose uniqueness does not carry the rust of time: to watch him is akin to seeing the Northern Lights or taking a trip to Lourdes ... Watching Tendulkar goes beyond a cricketing experience for the mob, an occasion beyond the mere matter of the fine geometry of his strokes. It is almost more a religious occasion than it is an aesthetic experience. He is more saviour than artist ... Irrational passions define Indian cricket. The game is escape, it is identity, it is hope, it is national well being, and reason is not invited. Tendulkar, more than his predecessors, has embodied all this. India has never seen anything like [sic], and it will not either.

Every one of the visitors' net sessions attracted members of the Indian Diaspora as well as excited groups of young Indian travellers. The two meaningless Canberra fixtures involving the Indians were saved from embarrassingly low crowds only by the turnout of so many members of the Australian Indian community or travelling parties.

One group of young people that I met at Manuka watching the Indians at practice on the Saturday before the three-day Chairman's fixture told me that they aimed to attend every Test. Their passion for cricket was joyously infectious and they especially loved Tendulkar, but in a way that ran deeper than the usual teenage infatuation with rock stars. These were young, well-educated professionals from the finance and information technology sectors. Some of them had followed the team through England earlier that year and had yet to achieve their ambition of meeting Tendulkar, but he did not attend the nets that particular day, much to their disappointment. These dedicated followers were just heading off to Sydney and then on to Melbourne for the Boxing Day Test. One of them, Rabinder Singh, told me later by email that they had been fortunate in meeting some of the touring party back at their hotel before they headed off. I hoped they finally got lucky with the Little Master. They were a terrific group of people with the customary deep appreciation of cricket that seems to be hard-wired into Indians, regardless of age or gender.

The enthusiasm of the Indian fans provided one of the real joys of the summer. I was constantly amazed at the deep bonds of affection that Indians of all ages and from all walks of life felt for their team. Australians consider themselves serious about cricket, but nothing prepared me for the passion of the Indians, especially young Indian women, for the game. Any of the Indians with whom I chatted about cricket over the summer were incredibly knowledgeable, generally with a daunting volume of facts and statistics at their disposal. Cricket matters a great deal to them, and they approach their team with a mixture of pride and reverence that must be the envy of players from other countries. One incident from that first Indian practice session left an indelible impression on me though.

I sought the help of three amiable young Indian journalists—Sai, Karthik and Rohit—to identify those of the Indian team who were not already household names in Australia. They were gracious in sharing their knowledge of some of the less well-known Indian players, especially those whose faces were obscured by helmets. They enthused with me about the 1967–68 Australia–India series, in particular the courageous defiance of M.L. Jaisimha in Brisbane when India, chasing 395 to win, fell just 39 runs short.

Those were among my first memories of Indian cricketers. I still vividly recall walking in the Natural Bridge section of the Springbrook National Park in the Gold Coast hinterland with a crackling transistor radio glued to my ear as the gripping run chase unfolded at the Gabba. Occasionally the signal would drop out only to re-emerge with the Indians having edged closer to victory. They had struggled earlier in the series, especially against the pace of Graham McKenzie, but very nearly pulled off an improbable win in Brisbane on that hot January afternoon in 1968.

That summer is indelibly imprinted on my memory. Australian prime minister Harold Holt disappeared in the surf off Portsea on the 17th of December 1967. My summer obsession with cricket was matched by a burgeoning interest in the machinations within the federal coalition as a replacement for Holt was sought. As I have already mentioned, the traditional Boxing Day Test was not yet a tradition and the Melbourne Test actually started on the 30th of December of that tumultuous year, and ran into the New Year.

As a kid in an Australian country town, I was riveted by that series, conducted as it was against a backdrop of political intrigue. From my juvenile perspective the Indians were exotic, mysterious creatures straight from the novels of W.E. Johns—their team led by the Nawab of Pataudi Jnr. no less. Had they turned up to play on bejewelled elephants, I would not have blinked.

My young friends 'remembered' Pataudi's fine innings of 75 out of a modest Indian total of 173 at Melbourne. Their infectious love of cricket and startling recall of statistics from Test matches played when they were aged 'minus twenty', as they jokingly informed me, put me in a more positive frame of mind to attend the Bradman Oration later that evening. I was actually coming to regret having signed up for that event which required that I wear a dinner suit, but the prospect of having another cricket chat with these guys lifted my morale. And as the next chapter, which deals with Rahul Dravid's address, will reveal I would never have forgiven myself had I missed it.

Ultimately, the two highlights of the Indians' Canberra interlude occurred off the playing field—the powerful oration by Dravid, and the opportunity to meet some of the Indian media contingent. The cricket itself was essentially devoid of meaning and rather than preparing the Indians for the rigours of the coming summer, it quite possibly lulled them into complacency, leaving them woefully underdone. The Manuka track had yielded a feast of runs the week before in the Sheffield Shield match; it was now dead. If Cricket Australia had wanted to deceive the Indians as to the bounce and seam of Australian wickets, they could not have chosen a better venue.

That Manuka Oval strip had lived in my imagination long before I ever saw it. It was described in the very first cricket book that I had ever read—Johnnie Moyes's, *with the M.C.C. in Australia 1962–3* to which I have already alluded. The description of Manuka Oval that had so fired my boyish imagination had actually been written by *The Sydney Morning Herald* journalist, Tom Goodman. Goodman had stepped in to complete the book when Moyes had died suddenly of a heart attack in January 1963, in the midst of that Ashes series.

Goodman described the venue in 1963 as the, 'tree lined Manuka Oval, Australia's prettiest cricket ground'. As pretty as Manuka may have been in 1963 though, it cannot currently claim to be more picturesque than the Adelaide Oval. Such pedantry aside, it is a pleasant, intimate ground, which is generally filled to provide an agreeable atmosphere each year for the Prime Minister's XI fixture.

In 1963 the Prime Minister's XI played the MCC at Manuka. What made that fixture so fascinating to me was that Sir Donald Bradman had, at 54, come out of retirement to lead the home side at the personal request of the prime minister, Sir Robert Menzies. Sir Robert opened the Bradman Pavilion before play started. According to Goodman, a crowd in excess of 10,000 was present. Most were, reportedly, hoping for a once in a lifetime opportunity to see The Don, who had not played since the close of the 1948–49 season, in the flesh.

Apparently everybody, including the MCC players, were willing Bradman to succeed. Many were hoping for some glimpse of the genius they had heard so much about from family, friends or even total strangers who had seen him in his prime. Unfortunately his innings ended in abrupt disappointment, rather like his final Test match appearance in England when he was bowled for a duck. He clipped a crisp boundary, but then played on to an innocuous ball from English pace-man Brian Statham. The bowler was evidently horrified at his own handiwork, as was the injured Australian player Alan Davidson, who was umpiring at the bowler's end. Goodman reported that Statham threw his hands to his mouth in anguish as The Don departed, along with a large segment of the crowd. Unless I missed something obvious, neither Wes Robinson nor Tom Cooper will be recalled in the same breath as Bradman in coming years. However, they batted with more aplomb and to greater effect at Manuka Oval than did the great man.

As impressive as I had found the Indians in the nets, they faltered badly on the opening day of the tour. Again, with hindsight, there were worrying intimations of the same crippling deficiencies that had plagued their ill-fated tour of England. Robinson and Cooper plundered their attack, albeit on a tame track. I was puzzled as to why Rahul Dravid offered the home side first use of the wicket. The stumps score on the first day of 6/398 seemed to justify my doubts. Robinson cruised to 143 while Cooper looked untroubled on his way to 182, occasionally producing explosive hitting. Of particular concern was the bizarre performance of key Indian pace bowler Ishant Sharma who left the field twice in the course of bowling a mere 5.3 overs. He appeared to be troubled by the same left ankle injury that had forced him out of the England series after Edgbaston. He was a vital component of the Indian attack and in the net session had looked genuinely hostile. During the rancorous 2007–08 series in Australia he had developed a psychological ascendancy over Ricky Ponting, who was much closer to his peak form than he had appeared in recent months, particularly in Hobart.

The Indian management provided the usual pieties to the effect that his fitness was of no concern and that it had always been intended that he only bowl six overs. But his minimal contribution left the attack looking threadbare. Whatever the future holds for Robinson and Cooper, they were considered surplus to requirements for the Big Bash. The Indians should have been disconcerted at the lack of headway Umesh Yadav and Vinay Kumar were able to make against a very modest batting line-up. The worrying lack of bowlers able to routinely hit the deck at 145 km/h should have sounded alarm bells for me. In the absence of Ishant Sharma, the Indian attack looked incapable of taking twenty Test wickets under Australian conditions.

I was however lulled into suspending my own judgement by some of my new-found friends among the Indian media contingent. My decision to take the contrived Chairman's fixtures seriously was vindicated by the opportunity to meet some wonderful Indian journalists, some of whom became good friends over the summer. In particular, I enjoyed the insights into the tourists provided by Harini Rana, Ashish Shukla, Samip Rajguru and Abhinav Punshi. All were wonderful companions with an encyclopaedic knowledge of Indian cricket.

Samip discovered from Tim Gavel that I was an army officer and would elaborately stand to attention and say, 'Good morning, Sir!' whenever I entered the box, much to his and my amusement. He was a reliable source of fun. Harini Rana was a fascinating young woman whom I grew to like and admire over the summer. At only 26 she was already the chief cricket correspondent for India's leading English news channel, *Times Now*, and possessed poise and authority well beyond her years. Her cricket networks were quite extraordinary and I was soon in awe of her work ethic.

She was an unobtrusive and soothing presence in the box and I enjoyed some fascinating chats about Indian cricket with her over the summer. She was one of a family of talented girls who had excelled academically before becoming engineers. For a time she contemplated training as a commercial airline pilot, but was dissuaded from undertaking the time-consuming and expensive training needed on account of the uncertain prospects for employment a few years ago before the airline boom hit India. I am obliged to her for unlocking the mysteries of Twitter for me. She was a prolific contributor to this medium throughout the series and I never looked like matching her output or her following. Some very senior Australian and Indian cricket writers and cricketers monitored her output closely.

Although troubled by Ishant Sharma's injury, the consensus among the Indian media contingent was that Australia was vulnerable at home to an almost unprecedented degree. They were convinced, based on the brittleness exposed by the New Zealand seamers, that Zaheer Khan would wreak havoc against the top order, and that spinner Ravi Ashwin would thrive under Australian conditions.

It was soon also evident that they were vigilant about what they perceived as a win-at-all-costs mentality among Australian fans and media alike. *The Sydney Morning Herald* ran a silly story about an alleged confrontation between David Warner and some of the Indian players that, to my mind, reflected little credit on the paper and was unworthy of a serious broadsheet. The story was essentially without foundation and misused a photograph that actually showed a group of friends engrossed in conversation.

The Indians were convinced that it marked the opening of an Australian dirty tricks campaign designed to psychologically undermine the visiting team. I recorded a television interview with Harini outside Manuka Oval on the evening after the story broke and was creating a furore back in India. Memories of the acrimony of the Sydney Test of 2008 were fresh among Indians and still rankled. Having served abroad with the Australian Army I am sceptical of our self-image as easy-going larrikins whom other races naturally warm to. In my experience, Australians too frequently underestimate two very important characteristics of other cultures—religious belief and natural reserve. The beat-up in the *Herald* reopened fresh wounds among the Indian media. For many Indians, cricket had been a vehicle for the nascent nationalist movement and was used to rebut English sneers about the alleged manliness of local men. Those writing about Indian cricket and cricketers would do well to study the history of the game and its role in that proud emerging nation, and be conscious of their tone in analysing it.

For their part, Team India probably drew false comfort from their performances in Canberra where Tendulkar and Laxman scored easily and appeared to be in nice touch. Each used the inaugural fixture for batting practice before retiring—Tendulkar for 92 and Laxman for a very nicely compiled 57. As the summer unfolded and Tendulkar's quest for an elusive 100th international century grew increasingly forlorn, I wondered whether the hubris of that retirement on 92 had offended the cricketing gods and cursed his later endeavours. Although the fixture did not count towards his milestone, his retirement from that innings spoke eloquently of a lack of intensity in the visitors' preparation. This was further confirmed when the Little Master did not even deign to play in the three-day fixture which started on the following Monday.

This was a shadow play of charmless irrelevance. Severely affected by rain it petered out into a draw, despite contrived declarations by both sides. It was promoted as the final chance for both Phil Hughes and Usman Khawaja to save their positions in the Australian line-up for the Boxing Day Test in Melbourne, though it is doubtful that runs in such a marginal fixture would have stayed the executioner's axe in either case. Both were unconquered at the end of the match and had secured useful starts when it no longer mattered.

Australian selector Rod Marsh was undoubtedly at the ground to run a final appraising eye over Ed Cowan who had been mounting an irresistible claim for Test selection for the entire season. His 109 for the Chairman's XI sealed Hughes's fate, while Virat Kohli's elegant 132 for the tourists was the harbinger of his emergence as one of their more credible batsmen as the season progressed. My Indian friends regarded Rohit Sharma as better prepared for Test cricket than Kohli but he batted very well in Canberra. Later in the Test series and One Day Internationals he seemed to be the one Indian player with the mental toughness to defy the Australians. They certainly developed an intense dislike for him. The only other interesting development in this meandering, pointless, rain-affected farce was the late appearance at the bowling crease of Ishant Sharma on the final afternoon as if to dispel once and for all any doubts that he would play in Melbourne.

For the last hour of play I had the pleasure of sitting with an old friend of mine, Michael Cooney, who was the speech-writer to Prime Minister Julia Gillard. He is an astute and passionate cricket observer and we had met the previous week at the Australian War Memorial when Rahul Dravid had delivered the Bradman Oration. We were chagrined at the premature conclusion to play, though we vowed to catch up in Melbourne at the Boxing Day Test match. There did not appear to be much out of the five abbreviated days of play at Manuka upon which to base a prediction for that encounter, but hindsight has invested it with more significance than appeared at the time. The Indian attack looked shallow and lacking in penetration and real menace. Tendulkar had baulked at scoring a century when well set, while Kohli had looked polished and confident. Ed Cowan was everything in the opening department that Phil Hughes was not. And as for any idea that Manuka Oval could host a Test match in the near future, the last word belongs to Michael Caton's character, Darryl Kerrigan, in the Australian film *The Castle*: 'Tell 'em they're dreamin'!'

'Before we were competitors, Indians and Australians were comrades.'

Rahul Dravid delivered the 2011 Sir Donald Bradman Oration at the Australian War Memorial in Canberra.

5. *Rahul Dravid*
—the poetic heart of cricket

'Not Dravid. He never paraded his toughness—it emerged between the lines of his performances ...'

... the obvious love he felt—firstly, for his, 'vast, varied, often unfathomable and endlessly fascinating country', and secondly for Test cricket.

Perhaps it says something good about us as a nation that at our War Memorial we revere the service of men who tried to save lives rather than to take them.

When he announced his retirement from Test cricket in March 2012, Rahul Dravid inspired a veritable torrent of wonderful tributes. The estimable Gideon Haigh sent Dravid off in fine style and with his usual eloquence in *The Australian*. Yet for me one of the most moving pieces of cricket writing I have ever read was former England player Ed Smith's tribute to Dravid on the ESPNcricinfo website. With elegance and clarity he seemed to go to the essence of the man. He wrote of his first encounter with the Indian champion:

> When Rahul Dravid walked into the dressing room of the St Lawrence ground in Canterbury on a cold spring morning, you could tell he was different from all the others. He did not swagger with cockiness or bristle with macho competitiveness. He went

quietly round the room, shaking the hand of every Kent player—greeting everyone the same, from the captain to the most junior. It was not the mannered behaviour of a seasoned overseas professional; it was the natural courtesy of a real gentleman. We met a special human being first, an international cricketer second.

I envied both Gideon Haigh and Ed Smith their personal knowledge of Rahul Dravid. Like millions of cricket fans I had long admired Dravid from afar and to me the qualities to which they referred shone like a tenfold beacon in the night.

Dravid delivered Cricket Australia's annual Sir Donald Bradman Oration at the Australian War Memorial on the evening of the Indians' first net session in Canberra. As the event approached my enthusiasm waned, notwithstanding that I had paid $500 for tickets for Tritia and myself. The Indian net session had given me ample inspiration and material for my blog and the prospect of donning a dinner suit and bow-tie was becoming less appealing with each passing minute. Moreover, the evening was falling into the pattern that was to be so prevalent in the Indian summer of 2011–12—wet and unseasonably cool. The leaden skies that had compounded my grief at the Gabba had continued and the summer was to be one of the coolest and dampest for some time. It felt like the sort of night that justified television under the rug on the sofa.

Tritia was equally ambivalent about venturing out. She enjoys cricket but the prospect of sitting through a formal dinner did not exactly send her into raptures. However, for her the clincher came in response to her question:

'How much did you say you paid for these tickets?'

'Two hundred and fifty bucks each.'

'Get dressed—we're going!'

We live close to the War Memorial and we walked to the venue through the misting rain and fading light.

My spirits lifted when I encountered Sai Mohan and Karthik standing outside. Though we had only met that afternoon I already felt at ease in their company and their radiant grins warmed and illuminated the gloomy Canberra evening. Inside I immediately stumbled into Daniel Brettig, a very gifted young man who covers cricket for ESPNcricinfo. We had met at the Gabba Test and I took an instant liking him to him. I suspect that he will enjoy an illustrious career as a cricket writer. He loves the game and writes about it prolifically and well. Providing reliable analysis as a Test match unfolds demands extraordinary concentration and I often relied on him to confirm factual matters. He always had a plethora of statistics at his disposal and he shared these generously. It was nothing for him to idly observe out loud something like, 'Do you realise that was the thirty-eighth consecutive dot ball? I wonder how close to the Test record we are?' At the Gabba we had enjoyed a distant cordiality, but that night I sensed that he was enjoying the constriction of his bow-tie nearly as much as I was and we beamed at one another like old schoolmates meeting after the elapse of too many years and too many marriages. Over the summer, as I formed new and unexpected bonds of friendship with fellow cricket writers, such chance meetings were a constant source of delight. There is a real sense of camaraderie among the occupants of the commentary box.

Then, as I walked into the main hall where the dinner was to be held, I nearly tripped over V.V.S. Laxman and Ishant Sharma and had the brief but courteous chat that I described earlier. The decision to eschew Wednesday night television had already been handsomely rewarded. Next, while I was scanning the seating plan to locate my table

I was tapped on the shoulder by an old mate, Michael Cooney, speech-writer to Prime Minister Julia Gillard. Cooney is an interesting character. We share the Catholic faith—though I suspect he is more zealous these days than I—an interest in American politics and a love of truly beautiful prose, especially the work of the great speech-writers. Cooney takes his craft seriously, though for him it is more a vocation. He loves the Labor tradition and is steeped in the lore of the party with which he is familiar through his exhaustive reading. We have maintained our friendship, notwithstanding the repudiation of my youthful Labor beliefs, through a shared friendship with Kim Beazley and his service with Mark Latham for whom I have retained fondness and regard. When he worked for Latham I used to commend the work of the British Labour modernisers Tony Crosland and Richard Crossman to him and he purported to have found them useful. Cooney had sprouted a beard since I had last seen him. Unlike most Canberra men whose facial hair generates my immediate suspicion that they bake their own bread, engage in glass-blowing and hate the Australian Army, Cooney's whiskers actually suited him. Indeed, to me he bore a passing resemblance to Paul Kinsey, the copywriter at the Sterling Cooper advertising agency in the HBO series *Mad Men*, played by Michael Gladis. The War Memorial smoking policy and the black tie requirement had ensured that he had not accessorised with a pipe and desert boots, but they seemingly would have worked just as well. I had not seen much of Cooney since he joined the Prime Minister's staff, but we rekindled our friendship over the remainder of the summer following this chance encounter. He was to be a source of inspiration for important aspects of this story as the Indian summer unfolded. So the evening had already taken several turns for the better and we had not yet reached our table.

As we sat down, Tritia nudged me while nodding and whispering, 'Not bad seats'. And they were, for we were seated adjacent to Rahul Dravid's table. I think she could have just about reached over and touched him on the shoulder; not that she would have of course. Well I don't think she would have, though she subsequently commented to one her friends, 'He was rather easy on the eye'. She was referring to Dravid, not me. But then he may not have been able to match my effortless mastery of a digital camera. Actually, I regretted not having brought a camera because I would have liked a permanent record of what followed.

Quite simply, Rahul Dravid delivered one of the most eloquent and moving speeches that I have been present for. I have written speeches for a number of prominent Australians over the years and I pride myself on understanding some of the techniques that allow a polished practitioner to build an emotional bond with the audience, including the ability to employ alliteration and subtle changes to the cadence to make the spoken word sing. In particular, I have always loved the speeches of the Kennedy brothers, and in a previous life I had been recruited by Bob Ellis to deliver some of Robert F. Kennedy's most memorable words in a stage production that was to be called *Orators*. Ellis had persuaded Bob Carr to perform as Lincoln and recite some of the sixteenth president's most memorable lines. Sadly the concept was vetoed by Carr's staff who thought it may bring his lofty office into disrepute, unlike appointing Ian Macdonald and Joe Tripodi to the ministry. So Bob Carr's thespian talents were confined to feigned indignation during Parliamentary Question Time. And I rasped away in my Brookline accent under the shower.

In any event, I have never heard an Australian politician deliver a speech that came near Rahul Dravid's Bradman Oration for its humble authenticity. To my mind it was because the man and his message were one.

From our vantage point at the adjacent table, Tritia and I were able to observe him at close quarters. He had an aura. He seemed to have a still, immovable centre, combining the tranquility of a mystic with the implacable resolve of a warrior. Yet, as those who know him aver, he does not need to indulge in brash demonstrations of machismo. Again no one said it better than Ed Smith in his tribute when he reflected on Dravid's most conspicuous attributes:

> I learnt that real toughness takes many different forms. Dravid could appear shy and slightly vulnerable off the pitch; in the middle, you sensed a depth of resilience. Many overseas players liked to set themselves apart from the county pros—as though they had to swear more loudly and clap their hands more violently to prove that international cricketers were tougher than the rest. Not Dravid. He never paraded his toughness—it emerged between the lines of his performances. Instead, he always talked about learning, about gathering new experiences—as though his cricketing education wasn't complete, as though there were many more strands of his craft to hone. His journey, you could tell, was driven by self-improvement.

My wife is very intuitive and endowed with an extremely high level of emotional intelligence. *Sotto voce* she observed of the guest, 'He meditates—look at how calm and centred he is'. I stole a furtive glance in his direction and indeed Dravid seemed to be almost in a trance as Channel Nine's Mark Nicholas went through the formality of introducing him. The most prolific number three batsman of all time had earned the nickname 'The Wall' for his perfect technique and impregnable defence. As he sat awaiting the call to the podium he was a study in sedate permanency appropriate to such a structure. But there was also a beguiling gentleness in his demeanour that I had never observed in an elite sportsman before. Later in the summer, when the hostilities had ceased, Dravid addressed a charity dinner for the LBW Trust where he confirmed Tritia's intuition. Here he verified that he had meditated from a young age. I gleaned this through the running commentary of Steve Cannane on Twitter, who was also an admirer of Dravid's and the author of a delightful book on the backyard cricket origins of some of our cricketing legends titled *First Tests: Great Australian Cricketers and the Backyards that Made Them.* But I digress.

Genuine humility in someone of great achievement is rare yet extremely seductive to those of us who unconsciously project our hopes, dreams and aspirations onto them. We choose to be blind to their defects and bask in their reflected greatness. In an era where fame, or at least celebrity, is divorced from serious achievement I tend to no longer have heroes. As I have matured I have come to appreciate humility in the great and powerful far more than intellect, charisma or a host of other talents with which they may be richly endowed. I can admire great talent in a range of fields of endeavour, but few of the great and powerful really inspire me.

But let me tell you about one who did. During that unforgettable summer in Oxford in 2008 I had a profound experience where I brushed up against that genre of greatness leavened by true grandeur of spirit. It was a fleeting encounter, but one that I will treasure to the grave so indelible an impression did it make on me.

On the 6th of May 2008, Tritia and I set out to buy or rent bicycles for the remainder of our stay in Oxford. It had become obvious that this was the most effective and pleasant mode of transport among the 'dreaming spires' and our central location obviated the need for a car. We had found a bike rental business down the Cowley Road over Magdalen Bridge. We were strolling in that general area when we spotted one of those ubiquitous blue enamel plaques that seem to adorn every second building in England, and that assure you that Winston Churchill or some other worthy spent a night there when they were seven years old, or something of the like. You get my drift. There was no doubting the veracity of this particular inscription though. It stated simply that this was the Iffley Road Track where Roger Bannister had become the first human being to break the four-minute mile on the 6th of May 1954.

'Will we have a look?'

'Yeah, we are not in any real hurry. And you know, this is actually the anniversary of the run' I said. 'That surely means we are meant to have a look. Synchronicity.'

So we wandered in and incidentally discovered that the University of Oxford gymnasium and indoor pool were also located inside. Because we were looking for place to train while living in Oxford we elected to join after we inspected the scene of that epic event of 1954. As we completed the membership forms I said to the young bloke behind the counter, 'You know it's the anniversary of the run today?' He shrugged, underwhelmed at this revelation. Smug clever Dicks littering conversations with historical facts are probably not in short supply in Oxford.

On our way home Tritia said, 'You know I met Roger Bannister back in Australia once.' She had been the media director at the Australian Institute of Sport for a number of years and counted Robert de Castella and Dick Telford among her friends from that time. She knows athletics. But if she had ever mentioned her meeting with Bannister to me before, it had seeped out of my increasingly leaky memory vault.

'Really. What was he like?'

'Very distinguished. He was getting old but you could tell he was just a perfect gentleman.' There was that term that had so often been applied to Rahul Dravid.

We thought no more of Roger Bannister as we headed home on our newly acquired bikes. I quickly needed to change and get to the weekly seminar of the Oxford University Strategic Studies Group, which convened in the Old Library at All Souls College each Tuesday evening during term. Attendance at these seminars was one of the greatest joys of my time at Oxford. Not only was the cast of visiting speakers uniformly impressive, but the setting was also enchanting. The soft English twilight would stream into the Old Library with crests adorning its walls. It was a beautiful space that simply oozed history.

On the same day Sir Hilary Synnott was scheduled to discuss his experiences of nation-building in Southern Iraq. I was one of the few people involved in the Changing Character of War Programme without a significant record of publication or a doctorate so I felt that I needed to be conscientious and extract every ounce of learning available from my time there. And to be honest there was an element of insecurity about working among such an accomplished group of scholars, so I felt I had to be exemplary in application and participation. Consequently, I was one of the first to arrive for each seminar, generally beaten up the quaint old spiral stone staircase by only one other person, a young Singaporean student by the name of Kelvin Ng. He was a gifted and highly motivated Masters student with whom I have remained friends.

As Kelvin and I sat waiting for the room to fill, I became vaguely aware of the sound of the gait of an older man on the stairs. The tread, while not laboured, was slower and more deliberate than the bounding progress of the undergraduates who comprised the majority of the audience each week and whose babbling chatter always announced their arrival well in advance. I became aware of a presence right beside me, a little surprised that in a virtually empty room the new arrival had sat down immediately to my right. I looked up and nodded in his direction and was greeted with a courteous reciprocal inclination of the head.

My companion was a tall, elegantly dressed man attired in the uniform of the Oxford don—monogrammed tie, tweed jacket, corduroy trousers. I briefly returned to my book, *Fiasco* by Thomas E. Ricks. It documented with brutal frankness the folly of coalition operations in Iraq after the defeat of Saddam's conventional forces.

'Do you come to many of these?' inquired the new arrival. I somewhat reluctantly diverted my eyes from my book to meet his gaze.

'I try to get here most weeks. How about you?'

'Oh I try to keep my hand in by getting to a few things—but not so much in the strategic studies field. But I am very interested in nation-building in failed and distressed states and postwar reconstruction.'

'So am I.'

'You're Australian. Do you have chair down there?' The thrust of his inquiry was whether I was a professor of some description. Anxious not to incriminate myself as Sir Les Patterson I refrained from quipping to the effect that I had several around the dining table and two recliners on the back deck. Moreover, there was a quiet dignity emanating from this man that warranted immediate closure of the book that I was reading and a considered, respectful answer. His age and courtly bearing militated against flippancy.

'No, I am actually an army officer. I am here as part of the Changing Character of War Programme. I am a practitioner more than an academic.'

'Australian Army. Presumably you have served in East Timor?'

'Indeed, three times in varying capacities. I speak the local language Tetum, and probably know the place reasonably well. Are you interested in it?'

'I am. Have you served in Afghanistan?'

'Not yet.'

For several minutes he asked me probing questions about Timor. He was very well informed and weighed each answer before proceeding. He was sincerely seeking information rather than demonstrating how much he already knew. He had a very kind, understated manner, which I found compelling. So engrossed was I in our chat that I had barely noticed the room filling around us. Out of the corner of my eye I noticed the arrival of my mate Colonel Tim Bevis of the Royal Marines recently returned from Helmand Province in Afghanistan, and made a mental note to introduce him to my companion so that he might share with him his experiences about that theatre of operations.

Thinking it prudent to close this discussion before the lecture began I said, 'Look, back home I am the Director of the Australian Army's research institution. We have published quite a lot of unclassified material on Timor-Leste. Why don't I give you a card and you can read as much of our stuff as you find useful'. With that I handed over my card with the web address of the *Australian Army Journal* of which I was the publisher at that time, proffering my hand in the customary greeting. He glanced down at the card, looked up and extended his own hand, 'Colonel McGregor— Roger Bannister. How do you do?'

My professional poise deserted me and Sir Les burst out of his cage. 'Today's the day ... you know ... this afternoon I was at the Iffley Road Track and you know ... it is the anniversary of the run and ... and ...'

Like the true gentleman my wife had told me he was, he gently moved the conversation along to spare me further embarrassment. 'How is my dear old friend Landy these days?'

'Pretty well I think. You know he was appointed Governor of Victoria? Did you stay in touch with him over the years?'

'Oh yes, and on the fiftieth anniversary of that race we were in they got us together again.'

When I have reflected on this conversation in subsequent years, the most conspicuous aspect of it was how focused on others Bannister was. He did not need to dominate the conversation, nor puff himself up. He was one of those rare famous men who regard listening as integral to communication.

To kids of my generation this man was as big a name as Neil Armstrong. He was probably one of the first truly global celebrities, given that the expansion of electronic communications and newsreels after the Second World War ensured that news of his achievement was widely disseminated. The quest for that elusive sub-four-minute mile was an epic human endeavour. I was stunned at the synchronicity of all of this. Not only was this the anniversary of the event, but Tritia and I had literally been discussing this man less than three hours before. I do not pretend to understand how such slender threads bind together the most enticing coincidences in our lives. Carl Jung of course famously insisted there are no coincidences. Perhaps he was on to something there. When I have reflected on this chance encounter over subsequent years, it was Bannister's aura and demeanour that made the deepest impression on me. He was a true gentleman—humble and genuinely solicitous of the opinions and comfort of others. Even before I knew his name I knew that this was a man who was by nature truly noble.

However, his exit made even more of an impact on me than had meeting a boyhood idol, or our stimulating discussion of Timor-Leste. About halfway through the question and answer session that followed Sir Hilary Synnott's presentation I felt a gentle tap on my elbow. 'Colonel, I need to slip away early. Would you be kind enough to excuse me?'

Thus the immortal Roger Bannister departed, honouring a code of chivalry that demanded such elaborate courtesy to a middle-ranking Australian Army officer whom he would never see again. I can never recount this story in company without developing a lump in my throat. 'If you can talk with crowds and keep your virtue,/Or walk with kings— nor lose the common touch.' Since that encounter I have been even more attentive to the demeanour of the allegedly great and powerful and have come to attribute much more significance to how they behave toward those who are without worldly influence, especially when they think no one is looking.

There is a curious postscript to that story told to me by Barrie Cassidy that I can't resist telling before I go back to Dravid's Bradman Oration. I'll recount it in his words:

> On May 6, 1954, Bob Hawke was 12th man for Oxford. Rain washed out the day's play. The guys considered what to do with the rest of the day. One of them suggested going to an athletics meeting nearby at the Iffley Road Track. Hawke persuaded them to go to the pub. They went as a team, and missed history. True story.

The dimly lit ANZAC Hall of the Australian War Memorial is a long way from the Old Library at All Souls College, but I suspect that the same quality that I saw in Roger Bannister dwells in Rahul Dravid. Humility and gentility permeated his Bradman Oration. It was a technically beautiful speech, just like a Dravid innings, but the man imbued it with his inimitable spirit. That is what set it apart from what passes for political oratory in this nation today. Dravid spoke with deep love about things dear to him—his country and the game of cricket. And he was doing it as an act of service. He gave his audience a gift rather than ostentatiously parading his genius for the inflation of his own ego. He was there for us, not the reverse.

He seduced me from his first utterance when he paid tribute to those whose sacrifice invests the War Memorial with meaning. And in so doing he gave me cause to wince at the recollection of our own Test cricketers posing in slouch hats in the entrenchments at Gallipoli some years ago. They should not have needed to be told what was wrong with that picture. As Dravid observed at the outset of his speech:

> Yet, but before all else, I must say that I find myself humbled by the venue we find ourselves in.
>
> Even though there is neither a pitch in sight, nor stumps or bat and balls, as a cricketer, I feel I stand on very sacred ground tonight.
>
> When I was told that I would be speaking at the national War Memorial, I thought of how often and how meaninglessly, the words 'war', 'battle', 'fight' are used to describe cricket matches.
>
> Yes, we cricketers devote the better part of our adult lives to being prepared to perform for our countries, to persist and compete as intensely as we can—and more.
>
> This building, however, recognises the men and women who lived out the words—war, battle, fight—for real and then gave it all up for their country, their lives left incomplete, futures extinguished.

As a solider with a professional interest in military history I attend plenty of conferences where such matters are canvassed. But what followed deeply impressed me:

> The people of both our countries are often told that cricket is the one thing that brings Indians and Australians together.
>
> That cricket is our single common denominator.
>
> India's first Test series as a free country was played against Australia in November 1947, three months after our independence.
>
> Yet the histories of our countries are linked together far more deeply than we think and further back in time than 1947.

We share something else other than cricket. Before they played the first Test match against each other, Indians and Australians fought wars together, on the same side.

In Gallipoli, where, along with the thousands of Australians, over 1300 Indians also lost their lives.

In World War II, there were Indian and Australian soldiers in El Alamein, North Africa, in the Syria–Lebanon campaign, in Burma, in the battle for Singapore.

Before we were competitors, Indians and Australians were comrades. So it is only appropriate that we are here this evening at the Australian War Memorial, where along with celebrating cricket and cricketers, we remember the unknown soldiers of both nations.

'Before we were competitors we were comrades.' I would have willingly lopped off a finger to have crafted a line with such perfect symmetry and cadence in a speech for any of the Chiefs of the Army to whom I have served as speech-writer. That opening was pure class and sent a powerful emotional message to the audience. I looked around at Michael Cooney and we simultaneously raised our eyebrows in admiration. No doubt Dravid produced similar knowing glances between opposing fieldsmen on countless occasions as that signature high back-lift seemed to expose his stumps, only to then dispatch a ball to the boundary. Roughly translated, such expressions mean, 'This bloke is away and there is no stopping him now'.

Dravid went on to get that metaphorical double-hundred in words rather than runs. Gideon Haigh wrote at the end of the Indian summer that this oration was the only world-class performance by an Indian over the summer. That was both a fair assessment of Dravid's eloquence and his teammates' play in the Test rubber.

He spoke with great insight about the challenges facing the game and offered some very sound suggestions for its future development.

In particular, he offered concrete proposals to ensure that Test cricket retains its prestige in the face of the challenges posed by the Indian Premier League and the Twenty20 game, which Haigh has brilliantly termed the 'vertiginous candy mountain'. In a later chapter dealing with the challenges facing Test cricket I will weigh some of Dravid's proposals on the future of the game.

But the emotional power of this address came from the obvious love he felt—firstly, for his, 'vast, varied, often unfathomable and endlessly fascinating country', and secondly for Test cricket. Moreover, he amplified these themes through a deep appreciation of the history of his own country and of international cricket. His development of the links between Bradman, Indian cricket, and his own fierce pride in his nation was a piece of rhetorical genius of which such master craftsmen of speech as Theodore Sorensen or Don Watson could have been justifiably proud. It is worthy of extraction in full:

> For one generation of fans in my country, those who grew up in the 1930s, when India was still under British rule, Bradman represented a cricketing excellence that belonged to somewhere outside England. To a country taking its first steps in Test cricket, that meant something.

> His success against England at that time was thought of as our personal success. He was striking one for all of us ruled by the common enemy. Or as your country has so poetically called them, the Poms.

> There are two stories that I thought I should bring to your notice. On June 28, 1930, the day Bradman scored 254 at Lord's against England, was also the day Jawaharlal Nehru was arrested by the police. Nehru was, at the time, one of the most prominent leaders of the Indian independence movement and later, independent India's

first Prime Minister. The coincidence of the two events, was noted by a young boy K.N. Prabhu, who was both nationalist, cricket fan and later became independent India's foremost cricket writer. In the 30s, as Nehru went in and out of jail, Bradman went after the England bowling and for K.N. Prabhu, became a kind of avenging angel.

There's another story I've heard about the day in 1933, when the news reached India that Bradman's record for the highest Test score of 334 had been broken by Wally Hammond. As much as we love our records, they say some Indian fans at the time were not exactly happy.

From that moment he had the audience in the palm of his hand. Two other anecdotes made an enormous impression on me though and both whetted my curiosity about India and had me shifting uneasily in my seat as to my relative ignorance about that emerging global power. I monitor emerging strategic trends as part of my professional duties as an army officer, but share the myopia of most of the Australian strategic community in focusing on China or Indonesia, and viewing either as Australia's most important relationship, other than the United States. There are too few experts on India, though the Foreign Editor at *The Australian*, Greg Sheridan, has toiled manfully to shame governments of all persuasions to take the relationship more seriously. His tireless advocacy in favour of raising the embargo on uranium sales to India was vindicated just before the Indian tour of Australia began. The decisive National Conference of the Australian Labor Party at which that decision was taken coincided with the Gabba Test against New Zealand. Prime Minister Gillard deserved great credit for this change in policy and I subsequently had the pleasure of discussing Dravid's speech with her at The Lodge. But that is a story for later in this book.

Beyond the media, Senior Research Fellow at the Lowy Institute for International Policy, Rory Medcalf, has conducted serious research into the strategic implications of the rise of India for Australia. He produced a very persuasive policy brief for the Lowy Institute arguing for an expansion of strategic, especially naval, ties between the two countries. As he argued in 2009:

> India's emergence as a globalising nation is at last unlocking its vast capacity as partner to other countries in trade, defence and coping with transnational challenges. A mature Australia–India relationship could offer many aspects of economic complementarity and strategic congruence. Australian resources, including energy, could play a key, and in time, indispensible role as India modernises and lifts hundreds of millions out of poverty. And the two countries have many security concerns in common.

The removal of the ban on uranium sales to India has opened the way for a significant escalation of strategic collaboration, particularly in the maritime sphere of the vital Indian Ocean. Yet again, the lack of sophistication of our strategic community curtails the scope of this. The current Chief of the Navy made a telling remark in a speech to the Australian Strategic Policy Institute in December 2011 in which he suggested that the words of the National Anthem might more appropriately have been 'girt by beach' rather than 'girt by sea'. We tend to think of ourselves as a continental nation. Strategic studies scholars refer to this phenomenon as 'sea blindness'. When we think of the sea at all it tends to be the Pacific. So as an alleged strategist, to say that I was mortified to have the history of the Australian–Indian relationship and the broader scope of our common interests beyond cricket explained by a cricketer whom my wife found 'easy on the eye', would be a serious understatement. It should have had me scampering for the exit before he finished. But Dravid's gentle humour and palpable empathy for the audience rendered this a truly memorable night, thus assuaging my feelings.

Anyway let's get back to that speech. The two anecdotes that so enthralled me and led me to resolve to overcome my unforgivable ignorance about Dravid's 'vast, unfathomable country', were these. Firstly, he recalled that when he was captain of India he once looked around the dressing room and calculated that among his players fifteen languages were spoken, including Shona and Afrikaans. He was proud of this diversity.

As an aside he told a delightful story about playing an under-19 match in New Zealand where two young men from opposite ends of the country were batting together. Neither spoke English, nor the common link language Hindi. The result of the match hinged on the partnership between these two tail-end batsmen. As Dravid told it, 'Neither man could understand a word of what the other was saying and they were batting together. This could only happen in Indian cricket. Except that these two guys came up with a 100-run partnership. Their common language was cricket and that worked out just fine'. Audible sighs and laughter swept through the venue at this pearl. I stole another glance at Cooney who was shaking his head in undisguised admiration.

But it was the humility and sense of duty with which he described his sense of responsibility to the Indian people that convinced me, like Ed Smith before me, that I was in the presence of a special man, a man for others who played out of love for his country and its people. Nor can you confect these emotions. Ask Kevin Rudd.

What playing for India meant to Rahul Dravid he expressed thus:

Here, ladies and gentlemen, is the heart and soul of Indian cricket. Playing for India completely changes our lives. The game has given us a chance to pay back our debt to all those who gave of their time, energy, resources for us to be better cricketers: we can build new homes for our parents, get our siblings married off in style, give our families very comfortable lives.

The Indian cricket team is in fact, India itself, in microcosm. A sport that was played first by princes, then their subordinates, then the urban elite, is now a sport played by all of India.

Cricket, as my two under-19 teammates proved, is India's most widely spoken language. Even Indian cinema has its regional favourites; a movie star in the south may not be popular in the north. But a cricketer is loved everywhere ...

One of the things that has always lifted me as a player was looking out of the team bus when we travelled somewhere in India. When people see the Indian bus going by, see some of us sitting with our curtains drawn back, it always amazes me how much they light up.

There is an instantaneous smile, directed not just at the player they see—but at the game that we play that, for whatever reason, means something to people's lives. Win or lose, the man on the street will smile and give you a wave.

After India won the World Cup this year, our players were not congratulated as much as they were thanked by people they ran into. 'You have given us everything', they were told, 'all of us have won.' Cricket in India now stands not just for sport, but possibility, hope, opportunities ... For those of us who make it to the Indian team, cricket is not merely our livelihood, it is a gift we have been given. Without the game, we would just be average people leading average lives. As Indian cricketers, our sport has given us the chance do something worthwhile with our lives. How many people could say that?

These were admirable sentiments. More impressive was the fact that they seemed to provide the talisman for the way Rahul Dravid went about his role as an Indian cricketer. On the Saturday after this address I went to another Indian net session. By the time Dravid had completed his practice the media had departed. There was no scrutiny to encourage artifice. Dripping with perspiration he patiently worked his way through a long line of well-wishers and autograph hunters from the local Indian community. Their presence corroborated what he had said about the socio-cultural significance of cricket among Indians of all ages and walks of life. Among the crowd lining up to touch Dravid were women old enough to be his grandmother. He signed every bat and shirt proffered to him with a modest smile and a nod to each person who for a fleeting second felt the undivided attention of their hero. This man's deeds matched his rhetoric. I was already an unabashed admirer by the end of his Bradman Oration, but the image of Dravid standing under a blazing sun honouring his adoring fans made a deep and abiding impact on me.

Finally, as he concluded his speech, Dravid brought a tear to my eye with story that took me back to that very first summer that I picked up a grown-up cricket bat bequeathed by my dead father. Good orators always like to close on a powerful emotional note, but Dravid's conclusion carried special significance for me. He said in that gentle lilting accent of his:

> Before I conclude, I also want to talk briefly about an experience I have often had over the course of my career. It is not to do with individuals or incidents, but one I believe is important to share.
>
> I have sometimes found myself in the middle of a big game, standing at slip or even at the non-strikers end and suddenly realised that everything else has vanished.

At that moment, all that exists is the contest and the very real sense of the joy that comes from playing the game.

It is an almost meditative experience where you reconnect with the game just like you did years ago, when you first began, when you hit your first boundary, took the first catch, scored your first century, or were involved in a big victory.

It lasts for a very fleeting passage of time, but it is a very precious instant and every cricketer should hang on to it.

He had just eerily described a phenomenon that I had experienced often during my own modest playing career. In the years following my father's death I believe cricket and the bat and pads he had given me at our final Christmas became invested with special significance. I could lose myself on the pitch or in the field, which I suspect was an unconscious way of avoiding grief simply too deep for an eight-year-old to bear. Over the years, as my skills improved and my love of the game deepened, cricket used to transport me to a place of bliss like that which Rahul Dravid described. As he stepped down from the podium I leapt to my feet to join the standing ovation with tears streaming down my face. It would have had to have been a cracking episode of *NCIS* to have justified staying home that night. I knew that I had heard a great speech. Moreover, I had basked in the luminous energy of a very substantial man.

I happily concede that I cannot match the eloquence of Ed Smith, so I defer to his estimation of what Dravid meant to world cricket. Suffice it to say that, based on my observations that night and over the ensuing series, he captured the essence of the man perfectly. Ed Smith wrote on Dravid's retirement:

I am an optimist by nature. I do not think that sport is perpetually declining from some mythical golden age. But sometimes I cannot avoid the sense that a certain type of sportsman is an increasingly endangered species. I have that feeling now, as Dravid declares his innings closed. No longer will he take guard with that familiar hint of politeness, even deference. No longer will he raise his bat to the crowd as if he is genuinely thanking them for their applause—the bat tilted outwards in acknowledgement of the supporters, not just waved frantically in an orgy of personal celebration. No longer will he stand at first slip, concise and precise in his movements—a cricketer first, an athlete second. No longer will the high Dravid back-swing and meticulous footwork link this generation with the great technicians of the past.

It would be nice to argue that no cricketer is irreplaceable, that sport is defined by continuity rather than full stops, that there will soon be another Dravid, another champion cricketer of timeless steel and dignity. But I don't think there will be. I think Dravid will be remembered as the last in a great tradition of batsmen whose instincts and temperament were perfectly suited to Test match cricket. It is not an exaggeration to say that a whole strand of the game—a rich vein that runs through the game's poetic heart—departs the scene with India's greatest ever No. 3. Playing Twenty20 cricket won't teach anyone to become the next Rahul Dravid.

In years to come, perhaps too late, we may realise what we have lost: the civility, craft and dignity that Dravid brought to every cricket match in which he played.

Tritia left not long after the formalities concluded. At her exhortation, I remained to discuss the speech with Michael Cooney. 'Mate, am I getting soft in my old age or was that simply superb?'

'No mate, that was a cracker. I'm going to show it to the boss.' (By this he meant the Prime Minister.)

Jokingly I pleaded with him: 'Whatever you do, don't do that mate. Neither of us will ever work again if either of our employers read this thing. Do you reckon it was all his own work?'

'Yeah, and you know why? He never seemed to be at the edge of his emotional register. He was very self-contained, never reaching or groping as though it was unfamiliar emotional terrain. You can just tell.'

I conceded that Cooney was probably correct and later Indian journalist Sai Mohan, who knows Dravid well, confirmed his personal authorship. 'He is an avid reader and he loves history and biography. He is actually an intellectual. He really laboured over that address.' Likewise, V.V.S. Laxman writing in the Indian press on Dravid's retirement referred to his friend's refined reading tastes and his propensity to steal away on his own to visit bookstores when on tour.

Eventually it was time to go home and I walked out into a cold and misty Canberra evening. The national capital excels at thrusting out a cold clammy wintry paw right up until Christmas, which was now a mere ten days hence. The walk down the grand boulevard away from the War Memorial was what a euphemist might call invigorating. I walked out of the War Memorial between two silent, immovable sentinels who maintain a permanent vigil. Weary Dunlop and John Simpson Kirkpatrick are deemed to represent the best of Australians bearing the privations of war. They are the only individuals commemorated by personal statues outside the memorial. Both were humble men—healers rather than killers. I suspect they would have liked Rahul Dravid. Whenever Tritia passes Weary's statue she walks over and touches his hand. Now, whenever I look at that lifelike, benign face I can understand why she does this. Perhaps it says something good about us as a nation that at our War Memorial we revere the service of men who tried to save lives rather than to take them.

As I walked down the centre of the splendid Anzac Parade aglow with the lights that illuminate the other monuments to Australia's wars, not a single car passed to interrupt my reflection.

It was eerily quiet and the mist and rain created a strange ambience for a summer evening. The very elements seemed to encourage introspection, and I was in a deeply reflective mood. The remarkable oration that I had just heard had exercised a profound effect upon me. I had been a soldier for the better part of my life and I loved the Army and my country, although I had grown less fond of its cricket team in recent years. I pondered whether Australian cricket could produce a man like Rahul Dravid. I sadly concluded that it could not. As I strode down our magnificent national boulevard the rain quickened and the chill deepened. I was oblivious to both.

Lillee stormed in as the shadows lengthened—an elemental, irresistible force of nature ...

6. The Boxing Day Test

As it turned out, the Melbourne Test provided the only genuine contest of the summer.

... to me the Test turned on the effect that this decision had on Siddle.

... the machinations in the federal coalition over the successor to Holt constituted political soap opera of the highest order.

In his masterful account of the Ashes series in Australia in the summer of 2010–11, Gideon Haigh adopted a novel and brave methodology. He published unaltered his reports to the two publications for which he covered the series. He was filing daily match reports for the *Business Spectator* and columns for *The Times*, which imposed a demanding schedule requiring judgements within an hour of the close of each day's play. That was the journalistic equivalent of batting without a protector. He was willing to expose his contemporaneous analysis to those with perfect hindsight.

This made a very favourable impression on me. It was a brave approach. As he explained: 'Players don't have the luck of magisterial hindsight, rewriting events to leave out the bad shots they played, the long-hops they served up, the catches they dropped; it's fairest to be read in parallel. And let's face it: if you were right all along, where would be the point in watching?'

Punditry frequently demands predictions, or at the very least editors and readers demand that pundits venture predictions and vent criticisms. Academic journals are the ideal vehicles for equivocation and measured, heavily qualified opinion. Newspapers, magazines and blogs are not.

My background in political reporting and analysis had inured me to the risks of prediction, of pontificating on complex events, notably elections. I was often wrong—never more spectacularly than in 1996 when I was one of three pundits who predicted that Paul Keating would defeat John Howard in the federal election. That public humiliation was a salutary lesson to a rash, opinionated young man. I have since tried to confine my predictions to things I understand better—the past for example—though my training as a military historian has made me wary of venturing dogmatic opinions, even about the past. These days I am much less invested in perceptions of my omniscience; to be human is to be fallible and I am wrong as often as I am right.

Nevertheless, I elected to try to match Gideon's integrity in writing this story. As the summer unfolded I wrote a blog recording my immediate impressions of play in the Test series or my snap judgements on who enjoyed the ascendancy on any given day. Looking back on what I wrote I was reasonably pleased with my analysis, which is not to say that my judgement was impeccable. The blog, as a type of journal of my experiences and thoughts during this time, is more than a reminder of what took place in the Test series against India; it prompts me to be honest about the impressions that I formed even where it reveals my own fallibility. No 'magisterial hindsight' for me either, at least when it comes to the Tests.

For reasons I have already explained, I was sentimentally disposed towards the Indians before the Boxing Day Test began. My journey from rabid cricket patriot towards cricket purist has been long and incremental.

I am a sentimentalist and a traditionalist and some elements of the contemporary game disappoint me. However, like Ed Smith, I do not subscribe to the fantasy that there was a magic cricketing Camelot which has passed into the mists of memory, where batsmen automatically walked when out and fieldsmen chivalrously applauded the scintillating shots of their opponents.

As a kid I used to go into mourning whenever we lost a Test match, especially against England. But somewhere during that unipolar moment when Australia was unbeatable I steadily began to lose respect for our national side. I could admire the sheer unprecedented genius of Shane Warne. On his day Mark Waugh was as aesthetically pleasing as any batsman I have seen, while Glenn McGrath was clearly another all-time great. But as a playing unit—in the authorised jargon *du jour*—I found them a pretty unappealing bunch. There is a difference between being competitive with an indomitable will to win, and being a pack of graceless bullies. It seems to me that our blokes lost sight of that difference somewhere earlier this century, if not before. When Peter Roebuck demanded that Ricky Ponting be sacked as captain of the Test side in the wake of that nasty Test against India in January 2008, he was inundated with supportive mail far outweighing the hate mail. Even polls in the tabloid press seemed to point to a chasm between the national team and the country at large. They were neither widely respected nor much liked. So wanting were the Australian team in maturity and insight that they thought the country was lacking in patriotism.

For my part, I had long before abandoned them. The sledging and spitting struck me as despicable and phony-tough. There was never any real prospect of the batsmen on the receiving end of this stuff retaliating physically, though I recall Viv Richards frightening the living daylights out of Tim Zoehrer when he once had too much to say from behind the stumps. And McGrath squealed when he got some of his own medicine from a batsman. Apparently the wives of Australian players were exclusively off limits for salacious references. Those of lesser races were open slather. And therein lay the rub. One of my old Rugby League coaches from Toowoomba used to describe exponents of one-sided toughness as, 'Barbers' cats mate—they can dish it out but they can't take it'. He also had another quaint aphorism for blokes whose fistic prowess did not match their loquacity, 'He couldn't beat time with a stick brother. He won his last fight by fifty yards'. I suspect a few of our alleged hard men of the last decade occupy this category. I would like to watch them run their spitting–sledging routine past an All Blacks lock rather than a diminutive Sri Lankan batsman.

The Australian team's drubbing at the hands of England in 2010–11 had rekindled my dormant patriotism but, as I previously confessed, a combination of events had seduced me into supporting the Indians and wishing them well. Those same factors had blinded me to what should have been obvious deficiencies in their line-up. All of which is a long-winded way of conceding that I had predicted that if Ishant Sharma was fully fit, then India would win the Melbourne Test. He was, and they did not.

In seeking exculpation for this folly, may I plead that I had ignored my own misgivings. The Indian team's pop gun attack, their supine capitulation in England, and what was already an obvious lassitude in their out cricket, in addition to ceding soft runs to opponents, was indicative of a lack of mental toughness and cohesion in the team.

Yet just two weeks before, Australia had succumbed to a very modest New Zealand line-up in Hobart reawakening in me disturbing images of the flaky batting against England the previous season. Nor had the gripping two-wicket victory in Johannesburg quelled the considerable doubts sown by that pitiful 47 in Cape Town. While much good work and fearless self-examination had taken place off the field in Australian cricket, I thought India should win if they played to their potential. This turned out to be a spectacular triumph of the heart over the head, though I hastily arrived at a more realistic appraisal of the visitors after Melbourne. The most prescient analysis came from Ian Chappell who predicted that Australia would benefit from the pace and bounce of the home pitches, and that the Indians would struggle. I believe Chappell has one of the most incisive cricket brains in world cricket and I had the opportunity to review the summer with him in some depth towards the end of the Adelaide Test. I will explore his lucid views of the series in more detail in that chapter. On the very first day of the summer he perceptively wrote of the forthcoming series against the Indians:

> A few months ago [the four tests against India] would have loomed as a daunting task even under Australian conditions. However, following a disastrous tour of England, India now has as many unanswered questions as their hosts. They have an attack that is heavily reliant on one injury-prone fast bowler Zaheer Khan. India's best batsmen are aging and are way past their best in the field and the younger generation players have a distinct dislike for short-pitched deliveries.
>
> If the young Indian players thought fielding and batting was difficult in England then they're in for a rude shock in Australia; the grounds are bigger and the pitches are bouncier.

As it turned out, the Melbourne Test provided the only genuine contest of the summer. It ebbed and flowed for the first three days. India had their chances, but failed to capitalise at the decisive points of the match.

The unseasonably wet and cool conditions that were to affect the eastern seaboard throughout the summer prevailed on the morning of Boxing Day as I dragged myself out of bed in the dark to get the early flight to Melbourne. Unlike my trip north for the Brisbane Test, I was in high spirits. The Boxing Day Test is one of the great Australian sporting rituals and the opportunity to view it from the vantage point of the media box was one to be savoured. The mood of the passengers heading to Melbourne was buoyant. A couple of the blokes in front of me would already have struggled to pass a random breath test and gave every indication that their next alcohol-free day would not be until the New Year.

I was almost the only person in the terminal not sporting some form of official Australian cricket paraphernalia. If anyone had read my treasonous mind and identified me as an incipient Benedict Arnold because of this, they were too polite remark on it. In fact the only people on the receiving end of some good-natured ribbing were the handful of hardy souls flying Qantas. We in the Virgin line were smug and teased the tiny band of stalwarts boarding Qantas with, 'You'll be sooorrrrrry!' Memories of the abrupt grounding of Qantas by its chief executive officer the previous October were still fresh and rankled with the public. Soon we were on our way like kids bursting out of the school gate for the last time.

Melbourne was equally gloomy and damp and I wondered whether I had really needed to get up so early. As I took the taxi from Tullamarine, I actually wondered whether there would be any play that morning. However, in typical Melbourne fashion, gloom gave way to brilliant sunshine sufficient to permit 89 overs during the day. On the way to the ground I dropped my luggage at the Hotel Windsor, one of my favourites anywhere, before ambling towards the ground amid the throng of enthusiastic fans.

No other venue matches the Melbourne Cricket Ground for the sheer electricity of a big match day. Whether it is the local football code or Test cricket, the cavernous enormity of the ground and the volume of people it contains creates an atmosphere that I have not experienced anywhere else. Lang Park, when full of rampant Queenslanders during a State of Origin match has something of the same intensity. However, the MCG is simply so much larger that the veritable wall of sound that reverberates around it is inimitable, at least in Australia.

In my mind, a young nation like Australia applies the term 'traditional' a little too readily. The traditional Boxing Day Test match is of relatively recent advent. For instance, during the first Indian tour of Australia that made such an impact on me as a child, the Melbourne Test started on the 30th of December 1967 and straddled the New Year. In the days of the long MCC tours of Australia with five Test matches spread over the period of November through to February, Sydney and Melbourne would alternate between hosting two Tests of each series. During the 1962–63 tour, the sole Melbourne Test, which was the second of the series, began on the 29th of December, while in 1965–66 Melbourne hosted the second and fifth Tests with the earlier fixture scheduled for the 30th of December.

Australia was away on tour over the summers of 1966–67 and 1969–70, so no Tests were held at the MCG in those seasons. The Melbourne Test was scheduled to begin on the 31st of December as recently as the 1970-71 MCC tour of Australia, a match that had the distinction of being abandoned on the third day without a ball having been bowled. The abandonment of the third Test during that series meant that the originally scheduled six Test matches became seven with the final being played in Sydney in February 1971. Thus the 'tradition' of Boxing Day test matches at the MCG is not exactly the equivalent of Anzac Day.

However, in the years since Ray Illingworth's team snatched The Ashes, Boxing Day and MCG Tests have become synonymous—and there have been some epic clashes. Two performances that remain vivid in my memory were from the summers of 1981–82 and 1982–83. The first was an explosive spell of fast bowling from Dennis Lillee, who ripped the heart out of a formidable West Indies batting line-up to bowl Australia to victory despite their being scuttled for a paltry total of 198 on the opening day. With a baying MCG crowd at his back, Lillee stormed in as the shadows lengthened—an elemental, irresistible force of nature—to remove Desmond Haynes, Colin Croft, who had been thrown into the breach as night watchman, and finally Vivian Richards with the last ball of the day. The West Indians were reeling like Liston before Ali at 4/10 at the close on Boxing Day 1981. When the stumps of the apparently invincible Richards were shattered, our living room erupted into cheers and hugs reminiscent of VJ Day. Lillee went on with the job the next day claiming 7/83 on the way to ten wickets for the match.

It was a lion-hearted performance that bore all the hallmarks of the vintage Lillee so revered by my generation—controlled aggression, technical mastery, menace and an absolute refusal to concede defeat in any circumstances. Victories over that seemingly invincible West Indies line-up led by Clive Lloyd were exquisitely rare in that era, so it was one to be savoured.

The following summer Australia won the Ashes series 2–1. The fourth Test in Melbourne is deservedly recalled as an epic. Australia was in dire trouble, chasing 292 for victory when their ninth wicket fell at 218 with the dismissal of Rodney Hogg. This brought Jeff Thomson to the crease to partner Allan Border with Australia still requiring 74 to win.

Whatever his many strengths Thommo, who averaged 12.81 over his Test career, would be among the last men with whom I would choose to bat for my life. Yet he nearly steered Australia home on this occasion with a gutsy, if streaky, 21. The catch that ultimately dismissed him nearly went to ground before being clutched lovingly by Geoff Miller off the bowling of Ian Botham. England snatched victory by a mere three runs. During the final wicket partnership of 70 runs in 128 minutes, Border and Thomson declined to run 29 comfortable singles as they sought to give the strike to Border as the more accomplished batsman. It was the most exciting conclusion to a Test match that I have witnessed, including the tie between Australia and India in 1986.

So I arrived at the MCG media box alive with anticipation. Having missed the Hobart Test I was delighted to catch up with the media crew. I was seated directly in front of Gideon Haigh and Peter Lalor of *The Australian*, with Wayne Smith not far off. It was great to see them all again. I mentioned how much I had enjoyed Gideon's piece about newly installed Australian opener Ed Cowan. The day after the announcement of the Test team he had written about his friendship with the Cranbrook Old Boy who had eschewed his home state in the hope of forcing his way into Test cricket from Tasmania. Cowan had a reputation for being cerebral and had recently written a book. Gideon's article intrigued me; perhaps Australia would produce a cricketer with an intellect to match Rahul Dravid's yet. Maybe it already had. Gideon wrote of their relationship and I quote it at length as I think Cowan will make a contribution to Australian cricket well beyond runs. We do not produce many well-rounded men these days and he may be one of the few:

Consider this a disclaimer. Over more than 20 years' writing and reporting cricket, I have had to describe the selections of scores of new Test players, puzzling occasionally over what it must feel like to undergo the experience, but in general treating it with much the same dispassion as I would any news item.

Yesterday that all changed. Australia's latest Test cricketer, Tasmania's Ed Cowan, is a friend of mine. A good friend, too: I've stayed at his home; he's been a guest in mine; I use a bat he gave me when I play for my club in Melbourne; he's the author of a book I helped with the writing of. This is going to be awkward ...

So I'm thrilled, and I'm gratified also, because Ed is not only an accomplished cricketer but a thoroughly good, kind and honourable man, as I became more completely aware when we collaborated on the book that was published a few months ago as In the Firing Line.

Ed was an admirer of a book by another Ed, also a friend of mine, Englishman Ed Smith. On and Off the Field was a pithy and perceptive diary of English Ed's 2003 season for Kent, during which he was also chosen to play for England.

Would a similar diary about a summer of first-class cricket work here, Australian Ed wondered? Only, I said, if the writer was entirely open and honest—to the point, perhaps, of revealing his true struggles and susceptibilities. I expressed a willingness to help if Ed ever wanted to have a crack—just as a mate, no strings attached.

Shortly before last season began, Ed told me he was ready; that being the case, so was I. The reassuring sensation for me was knowing that Ed had a voice, an authentic one. He spoke of cricket with deep knowledge, abiding passion, and sardonic humour. All we needed was for that speaking voice to become the written one.

For a cricket writer as gifted as Haigh to mention Cowan in the same breath as Ed Smith, whose beautiful tribute to Rahul Dravid I plundered mercilessly in the previous chapter, stamps him as a man to watch. He batted with enough assurance and maturity in his debut innings of 68 on the first day of the Test to convince me that he was thoroughly at home at this level. The palpitation-inducing Phil Hughes looked very much consigned to Saint Helena. Nor did I subscribe to the view that Cowan should defer to the injured Shane Watson who should drop down the order to the legitimate all-rounder's slot at six or seven.

Likewise, I was also thrilled to encounter Harini Rana, Asish Shukla, Samip Rajguru and Abhinav Punshi and the Indian media group again. The festive season's mood added spice to the opening of hostilities of what promised to be an absorbing series. My Indian friends were warmly optimistic that this would be their time; the time when they would claim an inaugural series win over Australia at home. After returning the now customary salute from Samip, I gravitated to the back of the box to chat to Harini who exuded her own Dravidian aura of calm. She was enjoying cosmopolitan Melbourne a good deal more than sedate Canberra.

The first day of the Boxing Day Test is incredibly atmospheric and I replicated my strategy from the Gabba of trying to get out of the media box at frequent intervals to experience the roar of the crowd and the vast range of sensory pleasures on offer. The MCG staff was easily the most professional and courteous that I encountered at any ground over the summer. They were manifestly proud of their venue and committed to making the public's experience as enjoyable as possible. No doubt my media accreditation helped, and I was waved through to any area I was curious about.

One public area that had a real buzz was the wicket-keepers' bar. I was puzzled at the omission of Brian Taber's name from the list of Australian glove-men and racked my brain. Was it only the list of those who had kept wickets for Australia at the MCG? Surely Taber had done so?

As I walked back into the box I encountered Jim Maxwell, my human *Wisden* pouring a cup of tea, and asked him about it.

'Can you think of a reason why Brian Taber's name is not on the list above that bar downstairs? Is it meant to be every Aussie keeper?'

'Unless it is only for those who have played a Test here', he suggested. 'Did he?'

'I would have thought he played here against the Windies in '68–69 at the very least. But you should go and ask the librarians; they know absolutely everything. And you'll be famous if you've found a mistake.'

I was unaware of the MCG Library, but at Jim's suggestion found my way there. And I was immensely glad that I did. The staff were a terrific bunch of people who took enormous pride in their work. No inquiry was too trivial. I was semi-apologetic in invoking their assistance, but they waved aside my reservations.

'No we love helping media people. Gideon uses us all the time. We love him.' That hardly came as a surprise, though the hint of some fallibility in Jim Maxwell's memory did. It turned out that Brian Taber had never played a Test match at the MCG, hence his omission from the honour board downstairs.

As it turned out, Barry Jarman kept for Australia against Sir Garfield Sobers' touring team in what was indeed a 'traditional' Boxing Day Test in 1968. But if Jim Maxwell's memory was slightly askew on that matter, my own failed dismally on another.

As I have already recounted, the summer of 1967–68 has a very important place in my memory. The tumultuous political events surrounding the disappearance of prime minister Harold Holt in December 1967 cemented my earlier interest in politics. I had become interested in news and current affairs in the wake of the assassination of president John F. Kennedy in Dallas in November 1963, and from that day forth took to reading the newspapers as soon as my parents had finished with them. The Kennedy assassination riveted me and marked the end of my childish oblivion. After the 22nd of November 1963 I was always aware of a world beyond childish games in the backyard in Toowoomba. My mother bought me a copy of the Theodore H. White classic *The Making of the President, 1960* for my tenth birthday. Although a shy kid in the wake of my father's premature death, I had a precociously advanced reading age and was a source of constant irritation to teachers on account of my constant quest for answers to irrelevant questions about US politics. It did not help my grades in primary school, but formed the basis for a reasonably lucrative career as a pundit for a time last century.

The death of Harold Holt elevated Australia into the big league. Lyndon Johnson, whose only claim to fame to my mind was that he had been in the motorcade in Dallas, flew in for the memorial service. Over the ensuing weeks the machinations in the federal coalition over the successor to Holt constituted political soap opera of the highest order. I spent much of that summer on an idyllic holiday at the Gold Coast. From the perspective of middle age, that summer inevitably seems almost perfect—lying on the beach listening to cricket on an Astor transistor radio, inhaling an intoxicating mixture of sea breeze mingled with suntan lotion. My mother's preferred label was a lotion called Quik Tan, risibly marketed as a sunscreen. A more appropriate sobriquet may have been Quick Burn though, as it was essentially cooking oil perfumed with some kind of fragrance to conjure up the sense of being in the Caribbean or some other exotic locale where the jet set gathered. Remember the jet set from those 1960s ads?

They all smoked Peter Stuyvesant. And if they dodged lung cancer, they now presumably have melanoma from using Quik Tan. The 'nanny state' and the *Trade Practices Act 1974* all lay in the future.

This was also, as previously mentioned, the summer when I was enthralled by the Indian touring team led by the Nawab of Pataudi Jnr. Anyway I listened to large segments of play against the Indians and avidly read every newspaper that I could get my hands on. I have fond memories of Pataudi's courageous batting in the Melbourne Test when Graham McKenzie was rampaging though the Indian batting order. In one of my columns for *The Spectator Australia* I made an error in asserting that the Australians had objected to Pataudi using a runner during his innings. He had torn a hamstring batting against Western Australia in the opening fixture of the tour and was afflicted by this injury throughout the Melbourne Test.

I had a distinct memory that Bill 'The Phantom' Lawry, had objected to Pataudi using a runner, whom I thought may have been Dilip Sardesai. According to my flawed memory Lawry, a dour and uncompromising competitor, objected that the Indians were using too swift a runner and insisted on another being appointed. On the opening day of the Boxing Day Test, I encountered Bill Lawry in the corridor on his way to the lavatory and struck up a conversation about the incident.

'Bill, did you object to Pataudi having a runner in the Test here back in 1967?'

He pondered for a moment. 'No. Doesn't ring a bell. Anyway it would have had to have been Simmo. He was the Captain and it's the captain's call on whether someone gets a runner. It couldn't have been me.'

Deciding that some of the humility that I had so admired in Rahul Dravid was in order, I deferred to the memory of someone who had actually played in that Test over my own childhood memory. After all who knows what hallucinatory qualities Quik Tan possessed in addition to its SPF factor of minus 1.5? Nonetheless, I entertained a niggling doubt and beat the now familiar path back to my chums in the MCG Library.

'Did Bill Lawry object to the Nawab of Pataudi using Dilip Sardesai as his runner here in the 1967–68 series?'

The duty librarian leant on his desk and mulled this one over for a moment. 'I don't think anyone would have objected to Sardesai running. He was one of the slowest blokes between wickets in that side.' If The Phantom had already humbled me, then that degree of precision on the part of the librarian delivered what the shrinks term 'ego deflation at depth'.

'Oh. I see', I said as I beat a hasty retreat back to the box. Later that day the librarian came around to the media box with the score-sheet and reports from that match, and personally handed them to me. I was absolutely stunned at this degree of professionalism. Moreover, having mistakenly impugned Lawry's sportsmanship I felt I needed to hastily make amends to him. This was easier said than done. The Channel Nine commentary position was not readily accessible to mere mortals from the 'Speccy' and my encounters with most of their team had been by chance in the corridor. Nevertheless, I had always found them approachable, especially Michael Slater and Ian Chappell.

Rather than trying to barge into their box clutching the score-sheet and rambling incoherently about the event as I had with Roger Bannister, I decided to pass the incriminating document to Lawry through an intermediary. I scribbled a note to him to the effect that I was sorry to have queried his memory and resolved to get it to him when I next saw Roz Kelly or one of the other members of the Nine Network team whom I knew. However, as I was taking a walk to get some fresh air I bumped into

Richie Benaud. He was heading in the direction of the gents and as politely as I could I explained that I was trying to get a note to Bill Lawry. Would he mind terribly?

'Not at all. It would be my pleasure', he smiled. He interrupted his passage to the lavatory, turned on his heel and went straight back into the Nine commentary box to deliver the paper. As with Roger Bannister, his behaviour was the generous, courtly act of a man now in his eighties. And it made a similar impression on me. No one was looking and he owed me nothing, simply the assured concern for others of a man with nothing left to prove. I admired him for that—and his ability to delay his ablution. In the afternoon of life, I could not delay a trip to the gents for a conversation with Scarlett Johansson. It was a very gracious act.

The story, however, does have sequel. When I was writing this chapter early in the autumn of this year, I consulted Garrie Hutchinson and John Ross's *200 Years of Australian Cricket: 1804–2004* to clarify some of the media reports of that series, notably the account of the Brisbane Test of 1967–68 which the Indians nearly snatched from Australia through the efforts of M. L. Jaisimha who had arrived in Australia only days before the Test match. He scored a fine double of 74 and 101. For that Test match Bob Simpson handed over the captaincy to Bill Lawry as part of his transition out of the Test team. In an explanatory note titled 'Quick Singles' the authors commented under the heading A Tough Cookie, 'In his first Test as Australia's captain Bill Lawry showed an uncompromising attitude. He refused to allow India's Borde to have a runner, but was overruled by the umpires'. Rather than relying on my Quik Tan-addled memory, perhaps I should have relied on my insights into American politics and framed my question toThe Phantom thus, 'What did you know about the refusal of runners to Indian batsmen in 1967–68, and when did you know it?' Anyway let's return to the Boxing Day Test of 2011.

For the first two days the optimism of the Indian media appeared justified. I awarded them the honours narrowly on day one and thought the match was theirs to lose at stumps on the second evening. Their bowlers forced their way into strong positions twice, only to fail to deliver the *coup de grâce* to an obstinate Australian tail in each innings. Moreover, their batting was exposed as skittish against genuine pace. In the end Australia won by 122 runs with all their pace bowlers making valuable contributions. Pattinson emphatically repudiated any reservations that I had entertained about his performance against the New Zealanders, while Hilfenhaus discredited my assessment of his performance at Manuka Oval just three weeks earlier. Indeed, the Australian pace attack operated impressively as a unit. They oozed menace and hostility and established a mental ascendancy over the Indians, including their three venerable champions, that was sustained through the remainder of the summer.

And adding insult to injury, Siddle contributed a valuable 41 runs in the Australian first innings while Pattinson achieved his highest first-class score with a lusty 37 in the second. Indeed, his partnership of 43 for the final wicket with Hilfenhaus in Australia's second innings exercised a psychological impact beyond its value in mere runs. It elevated the total required for an Indian victory to 292, a feat exceeded only once on this ground when South Africa scored 4/297 to defeat Australia in 1953.

Having reached 2/214 in reply to Australia's 333, India looked poised to lead on the first innings. Yet this tide was not taken at the flood. This in large part was due to Siddle who became incensed at having clean-bowled Dravid only to have the dismissal overturned for creeping over the front foot line.

He renewed his assault with unprecedented ferocity and struck a crucial blow by bowling Tendulkar, who appeared comfortably on the way to his 100th international century.

One can sometimes invest such instances with too much significance, but to me the Test turned on the effect that this decision had on Siddle. He exploded onto the bat in a manner reminiscent of Lillee against the West Indies thirty years before. Apart from his decisive removal of Tendulkar in each innings, he softened up the remainder of the Indians for his partners. As in Brisbane I felt he created the conditions for the success of the other pace-men. The Indians unforgivably conceded a handy lead to Australia, which meant that batting last was always going to be a challenge. Even so, they had Australia reeling at 4/27 in the second innings and may yet have prevailed except they were again unable to capitalise on their early breakthroughs. Their decision to veto use of the umpire decision review system also cost them dearly. They should have had Hussey twice on his way to a vital 89, though it must also be conceded his golden duck in the first innings would not have survived video scrutiny.

In my retrospective on the match written at the close of play on the final day, I concluded that India had serious weaknesses to which I had been wilfully blind in Canberra. Whereas I had thought their attack looked thin the real problem lay elsewhere:

> Rather the real problem was that their vaunted batting line-up failed in the most abject fashion, bringing back chilling memories of the recent debacles in England. Apart from an entertaining period on the second afternoon, when Tendulkar and Dravid dominated the bowling, taking the score from 2–97 to 2–214, the Indians exhibited their customary vulnerability to the ball rising sharply off a good length. They seem intimidated by the pace and aggression of the Australians. If this is happening in Melbourne then they need to

be very worried about the decks in Perth and even Sydney, which is evidently greenish this summer.

Gambhir looks out of his depth in Australian conditions. Giving his wicket away early is placing pressure on Dravid whose advancing years warrant offering him some degree of protection. He was bowled through the gate three times in this match albeit by a no ball on one occasion. For a man who bears the sobriquet 'The Wall', that is a parlous and unaccustomed state of affairs. There is no easy answer to the opening issue. Rahane does not seem to be ready for this level. But surely Rohit Sharma must be selected ahead of Virat Kohli in the wake of this defeat. The batting needs spine.

Even more troubling is the listless form of VVS Laxman. He accumulated only three runs in this match and each of his failures came at a tipping point when a genuine champion should have stamped his authority on the match.

...

But as a unit the Indian batting which looked so imposing on paper has fallen at the first hurdle. The bigger worry for them now is that such a bruising encounter with the brash young Australian quicks will undermine their mental equilibrium. The memories of England must be vivid.

For years Australian teams sought to demoralise and unhinge touring teams. That threat has sounded shrill since the retirements of Langer, Hayden, Warne and McGrath. The unraveling of the Indians in Melbourne yesterday make it now seem a serious prospect, unless they can recover quickly. They need the mental toughness of the old guard. But their form may not be sufficient to guarantee their ongoing selection. The younger brigade do not look impressive.

Australia has dispelled a lot of demons from last year, including the loss in Cape Town, with this thoroughly deserved win. India faces some tough questions. And answers are needed soon.

As I conceded earlier, my best predictions often involve an element of hindsight. As the players gathered for the presentations and formalities a mere seventy minutes after tea on the fourth day of the Test, I turned to Gideon Haigh and queried him, 'How did I get them so wrong? I have seriously overestimated their batting'.

He was generous and philosophical, 'It happens to all of us, mate. I wrote New Zealand cricket off in the most comprehensive fashion imaginable in the middle of the Bellerive Test and look what happened there. But I think their top order is just getting a bit old'.

I took some solace from his words. I walked back through the parklands around the MCG in the direction of the Windsor in the company of my Indian friend Ashish Shukla. He was in glass-half-full mode and more confident than ever that India had Australia's measure. He correctly pointed out how much more dangerous Umesh Yadav had been in this match compared to his ineffectual efforts in Canberra, while Zaheer Khan had produced some simply unplayable deliveries.

However, I now vividly recalled watching Stuart Broad dismantling this batting order in my Port Douglas hotel room, and attributed even more weight to the sober prediction of Ian Chappell that the Indians lacked the technique and temperament to prevail under Australian conditions. And so it came to pass. *Après Melbourne, le déluge.*

Yet the 100th Test match at the Sydney Cricket Ground will forever be Michael Clarke's Test. His massive score of 329 elevated him to the ranks of the immortals. (Gregg Porteous © Newspix)

7. *The Sydney Test*
—*the big tease*

'There seems to be a conga line led by a chap in a gorilla mask wending its way through the crowd at the Vauxhall Road end.'

This was the first time in the history of Test cricket that a single innings had yielded two partnerships in excess of 250 runs (ah, the beauty of those statistics).

One by one, like Indian middle-order batsmen on tour, many of the certainties of Australian life fell before the forces of economic and social change ...

Clarke represents the human dimension of commercialisation of the game, and the reduction of the Australian team to a brand and the various forms of the game to franchises.

Cricket is a statistician's dream. Discussions among purists and savants are dominated by the numbers rather than by the aesthetics, perhaps because the numbers seem to speak for themselves. Broadcasters like Henry Blofeld paint wonderful word pictures as did John Arlott whose gravelly commentary during the 1972 Ashes series in England thoroughly enthralled me. When I was a child, Ashes series in England occurred in the depths of the Toowoomba winter and I would lie in the darkness listening to the cricket on an ancient radio that my mother had inherited from her aunts.

Cricket and radio are inextricably linked with my memories of childhood and teen years, but just as summer evokes the aroma of suntan lotion and sea breezes, when I think back to broadcasts from England I can still conjure the whiff of Vicks VapoRub which accompanied the perennial winter colds and flu. And such was my affliction as I lay in the cold dark night listening to Bob Massie dismantle England at Lord's during the winter of 1972.

For me the true beauty of cricket on the radio is in those long passages when seemingly nothing is happening. Any passage of play, that an American would mistake for a rest period, inevitably conjures broadcast genius of the highest order. 'There seems to be a conga line led by a chap in a gorilla mask wending its way through the crowd at the Vauxhall Road end.' Or this marvellous piece from Christopher Martin-Jenkins during one *Test Match Special* broadcast of an England–India Test last year:

'Did you realise that Geoffrey Boycott has never owned nor worn a single pair of jeans?'

'That is quite extraordinary, isn't it?' ventured Jonathan Agnew.

'I would have thought so.'

But invariably, descriptions of cricket—whether in print or on radio or television—are sprinkled with little-known trivia: 'This is now the highest opening stand by Australia against India at the MCG since ...' and, 'Pattinson will be the first Australian to take a hat-trick on debut since Damien Fleming if he removes Ryder with this the last ball of the eighth over of New Zealand's second innings'. That latter comment from the Gabba Test match was made all the more enjoyable because I was sitting directly in front of Fleming, surreptitiously watching his imperturbable demeanour as it went to air. Anecdotes and trivia are grist to the cricket lover's mill, but the raw data from the Sydney Test in January 2012 described an Indian humiliation of gargantuan proportions.

Consider these facts. From the dismissal of Shaun Marsh on the evening of the opening day until Australia declared its first innings closed, India was able to claim just one wicket at a cost of more than 600 runs. India lost the Test match by an innings and 68 runs. But even that statistic flatters them. Australia lost only four wickets for the entire Test against India's 20. Speculation was rife in the media for much of India's second innings that the visitors would fail collectively to match Michael Clarke's massive 329 not out. It was India's sixth consecutive defeat in as many Test matches away from home with only one redeeming, but ultimately irrelevant statistic—they actually reached 400 away from home for the first time since December 2010 when they suffered yet another innings defeat. And when Ravi Ashwin deposited a towering six into the stands to take India past 364 it constituted their best away batting performance in 18 innings.

As Indian journalist Sambit Bal bleakly concluded at the end of the match:

> These numbers are useful only for one purpose: they are evidence of India's rediscovered wretchedness away from the subcontinent. The nucleus of this team still carries a group of remarkable cricketers who contributed massively to erase the painful memories of touring, and how it must hurt them to be part of this horror streak, which now seems interminable.
>
> And for a proud bunch of players, nothing would sting more than this statistic: Not since 1968, not even in the hopeless era of the 1990s, which some in this ground have painful memories of, have India lost six away matches on a trot. Between 1959 and 1968 they had lost 17.

Indeed, the Sydney Test was lost on the first morning when M.S. Dhoni exposed his fragile batting order to a rampant Australian pace attack when conditions most favoured them. The incipient revival of Australian fortunes that some had detected at the Gabba was corroborated by the bowling attack in Sydney. That the Australian pace attack was capable of intimidating much stronger batting line-ups than New Zealand's was now undeniable. My scepticism was no longer sustainable. The Australian pace trio of Siddle, Hilfenhaus and Pattinson was simply superb. The collective effect of their sustained aggression was to unhinge the Indian batting order by denying it respite or easy runs. In particular, Pattinson reminded me of the young Dennis Lillee in the early stages of his career. He generated real pace and hostility and was constantly in the batsman's face—an unnervingly abrasive presence.

To some extent, when I reflect on the Sydney Test match, the events off the pitch take on more significance. The match was so gruesomely one-sided that I frequently wandered away from the spectacle to savour the atmosphere in the Members' Enclosure. Like the Boxing Day Test match in Melbourne, the New Year Test in Sydney is firmly rooted in the calendar and attracts a large and socially diverse crowd. Ever since my cricketing epiphany at Lord's in 2008 I have purchased tickets for the opening morning of the Sydney Test match. My wife and I go as part of an eclectic group comprising an American-born colleague of mine, Albert Palazzo, who abandoned baseball for cricket with the zeal characteristic of all converts, and his uncle through marriage, Max Benyon, one of the founders of 2MBS-FM, the classical musical station in Sydney. This has become an annual event for us, and Tritia has grown particularly fond of Max, who seems to become younger each year as he advances through his 70s. He is fit and agile and a wonderful advertisement for regular tennis, though I harbour a suspicion that yoga or Pilates may also contribute to his superb bearing and supple movement. As a youngster he had seen Bradman play at the SCG in his final season of Test cricket and he has a fine appreciation of the game. He listens intently to the ABC commentary and uses field glasses to observe play closely. I trust him more than the third umpire on the close calls and he is a source of measured thoughtful analysis as the day unfolds.

For his part, Al is an incongruous figure at a cricket Test match, replete with New York Yankees cap, Brooklyn accent and hot dog—he brings the trappings of Yankee Stadium to the SCG. As I argue below though, the SCG may well be on its way to becoming a pallid imitation of Yankee Stadium. But I will get to that shortly. Back to my friend Al who, despite having taken out Australian citizenship, resolutely supports every touring team that comes here. He is comfortable with this treachery and genuinely delighted to have me defect to his cause this year. We were a forlorn pair in the Churchill Stand as the carnage of the first morning unfolded and the increasingly triumphant crowd sensed a rout. To honour this recent family tradition of attending the first morning in Sydney with Tritia, Al and Max, I forfeited my spot in the media box for the day. But the pleasure of watching the opening day with our little group more than compensated, as did the opportunity to immerse myself in one of the iconic tribal celebrations of the Australian summer. The period from the Boxing Day Test through to the Sydney Test match, with the Sydney to Hobart yacht race in the background, have taken on a ritual significance for me over the years. Those events, along with the Australian Open Tennis, define summer to me in the afternoon of life the way cricket and ninja star throwing did as a boy.

Briefly, here is what happened on that first day in Sydney. India limped to 191 and was reeling before the Australian pace battery the whole time.

Winning the toss and electing to bat in Sydney demands a score of at least 400. Tendulkar looked unassailable and seemed to be in, but then he was gone after an enticing cameo of 41 that had promised so much more. I also thought Virender Sehwag and Dravid had weathered the storm before they were abruptly dispatched. Each of their wickets fell immediately after I had assured Al, 'Mate he is finally in now. He'll be right!' Only some lusty Twenty20 style hitting from Dhoni spared India an even more pitiful total.

The Australian innings began and the Australian top order wobbled at 3/37 with the new boys Warner, Cowan and Shaun Marsh all dismissed cheaply, the last for a duck. At no point in the summer did Marsh realise the potential intimated at in his 141 on debut against Sri Lanka. Going into this series, the media debate had been dominated by speculation that Ponting and Hussey had reached the end of their careers and that the batting order required the same infusion of youth that had energised the bowling attack. The Sydney Test emphatically ended that debate. Ponting scored 134, ending a hiatus in his century-generating capacity that had seemed permanent. Hussey compiled an impeccable 150 that assisted his captain in crushing India's dwindling vestiges of hope for an inaugural series win in Australia. Yet Ponting, the only batsman dismissed on the second day of the Test, and Hussey, who played superbly, provided mere footnotes for historians of the game.

The partnership between Ponting and Clarke produced 288 runs, while that between the skipper and Hussey, 334. This was the first time in the history of Test cricket that a single innings had yielded two partnerships in excess of 250 runs (ah, the beauty of those statistics). Yet the 100th Test match at the Sydney Cricket Ground will forever be Michael Clarke's. His massive score of 329 elevated him to the ranks of the immortals. He eclipsed my boyhood hero Bob Cowper as the highest-scoring Australian in a Test at home, giving me a tiny twinge of sadness as he breezed by Cowper's 307. Fleetingly, I recalled February 1966 with a clarity that I cannot summon for 1996.

Ishant Sharma dropped Clarke on 182. Other than that blemish, the innings was of symphonic breadth and perfection. At his best Clarke is one of the most graceful batsmen I have seen and this innings overflowed with his signature fluent driving. He has played more valuable innings in more adverse match situations, notably in Cape Town in 2011 and at Lord's in 2009, but the sustained self-mastery and sheer physical endurance entailed in an innings of this magnitude sets it apart. In addition to eclipsing Bob Cowper's milestone, Clarke erased a number of other names from the record books during his majestic progress. He replaced the long forgotten R.E. Foster as the highest Test scorer on the SCG. But in becoming the first triple centurion in a Test on that ground, he also passed some much more illustrious players— Wally Hammond, Doug Walters and Brian Lara. And as if to illustrate that he had been touched by the divine, he removed Sachin Tendulkar with the ball just as he seemed destined to secure that elusive 100th international century in India's second innings.

By breaking Tendulkar's ominous partnership with V.V.S. Laxman, Clarke cracked the Indian second innings wide open. The partnership seemed to be taking root and promised to force the match into a fifth day. Some among the Indian media contingent thought that they may just escape with a draw should the weather intervene. To them, the series hinged on this Test and that partnership. If they continued to resist until stumps on the fourth day the series could be retrieved. Clarke abruptly ended this speculation.

Moreover, Clarke seemed to end, once and for all, doubts about his fitness to lead the Australian team. His relationship with Australian fans had been uneasy up to this point, partially as he was seen as usurping the popular and somehow more authentically Australian Ricky Ponting's position. To me, Clarke seemed a discomfortingly ambiguous figure to Australians and their ambivalence, if not overt hostility, towards him was a manifestation of something deeper.

Clarke does not conform to the orthodox archetype of Australian masculinity. It was reported he and Simon Katich clashed when Clarke suggested that the traditional team song be sung early in the evening of a victory over South Africa to allow him get away to join his then girlfriend Lara Bingle for a date. That this story leaked out at all suggested an uneasy relationship between Clarke and the rest of the team.

While memory can play tricks, I believe he is the only Australian captain whose entry to an Australian ground has been greeted with booing and derision. That did not happen to Greg Chappell in the wake of the underarm incident or even in the midst of his run of seven ducks, four in a row. It may have happened to Kim Hughes, whose public tears as he relinquished the captaincy of Australia in the wake of crushing defeat by the West Indies in 1984 led to a public debate over Australian masculinity. But if it happened I do not recall it. Indeed there were eerie similarities between the paths of Hughes and Clarke until that watershed innings in the 100th SCG Test. Both possessed a sort of boyish innocence bordering on vulnerability. Likewise, neither seemed to be able to command the unreserved respect of their teams. When Clarke left the team in New Zealand to deal with a crisis in his relationship with Bingle the media commentary was scathing. One insult from a member of the public was representative of the sneering contempt of a large segment of the public—'Man-up you pussy'. Blog comments were routinely of this nature.

Clarke's taste in designer clothes and unashamed enjoyment of shopping expeditions with his girlfriend seemed to affront cricket lovers. He was evidently too soft—dare I say it, almost too effeminate—to constitute an authentic Australian hero. But that epic Sydney innings ended, or at least suspended those doubts. The timing of his declaration was impeccable, leaving the records of both the popular 'Tubby' Taylor and The Don intact. The media unanimously applauded this act of self-sacrifice and his placing of the team ahead of personal gratification.

For my part I was somewhat sceptical. Clarke is managed and packaged cleverly. Retiring at 329 not out smacked of contrivance to me. Frankly, I would have respected him more for running down Lara's world record and batting on. India was never going to escape by that stage and Australia ultimately won with more than day to spare. In his defence it must be conceded that for a time the Tendulkar–Laxman partnership looked likely to make time and weather an issue, and Clarke did not have my benefit of hindsight.

On the other hand, I never harboured the reservations about Clarke that the majority of fans did. On his day he is simply beautiful to watch and I have never doubted his courage despite his lack of overt machismo. My concerns run deeper. To me Clarke represents the human dimension of the commercialisation of the game, the reduction of the Australian team to a brand, and the various forms of the game to franchises. Let me qualify this. I do not have any right to scorn him for taking the money and extracting as much from the game as he can, while he can. But as I have repeated *ad nauseam*, I am a traditionalist. To me, commercialisation, even more than corruption, is the existential threat to the game that I loved as

I grew up. Michael Clarke is but a symptom of this phenomenon, not its cause. Would I choose dinner with Lara Bingle over singing with Simon Katich while Brad Haddin sprayed champagne over me? As my friend Al from New York would conclude, 'You kidding? Get outta here!'

Because the lopsided nature of the Sydney contest reduced some of its appeal, I became fascinated by things other than the almost gluttonous accumulation of runs by the Australians against an opponent who had almost stopped chasing the ball by the end of the second day. The Members' Enclosure provided a wonderful snapshot of Australia at play, and Test cricket makes odd bedfellows in Australia. At one point on the second day of the Sydney Test I strolled through the Members' and Ladies' Pavilions. Seated closer than they ever could have been in the parliamentary chamber were the former prime minister Bob Hawke, a serving Minister of the Gillard government Anthony Albanese, and retired Liberal politician Bruce Baird.

Back in the 1980s I knew them all through my involvement in politics. At that time Anthony Albanese was a young firebrand from the left of the New South Wales ALP. In cricket terms, he was often given the new ball to take up the attack to the right of the party during the set piece battles over contentious issues at various state and national party conferences. Throughout much of the life of the Hawke government, Albo—as he has long been affectionately known—was enraged by what he and the rest of the left saw as the sell-out of traditional Labor values by the Hawke government. For his part, Baird was a key minister in the reformist Greiner government elected in New South Wales in March 1988. As transport minister, Baird had carriage of a significant portion of the microeconomic reform that Greiner championed. This involved significant cuts to jobs and reductions of uneconomic transport routes.

During this period I worked, in turn, as an official of the right-wing head office of the New South Wales ALP and a political adviser to the NSW opposition leader, Bob Carr. I even managed a stint on the staff of the left-wing education minister in the Unsworth government, Rodney Cavalier. This astonished his colleagues on the left and my patrons on the right at the time. He jokingly referred to me as his cricket adviser. It was a reasonably accurate description of my skill set in public policy at the time. There will be more of Rodney Cavalier later in the story, for I was to stumble across him for the first time in years outside the SCG Trust box with actor Rhys Muldoon for a very agreeable chat on the final day of the Test. As Chairman of the SCG Trust, Cavalier has had to wrestle with many of the trends in the evolution of cricket of which I started to become more conscious during the Sydney Test.

To return briefly to my unusual career as a political staffer in the 1980s—I was a strong supporter of the Hawke government's economic reform agenda, which simultaneously made me an enemy of Albanese and Baird. Even at the time, the incongruity of opposing the microeconomic reform of the Greiner government as rampant neo-liberalism while defending Hawke and Keating against the left, required cognitive dissonance—or chutzpah, depending on your point of view. The key adviser to Baird in those days was a young bearded fellow by the name of Barry O'Farrell who was elected premier of New South Wales in March 2011. He was a collegial character with friendships across the aisle, as they say, and I have always enjoyed his company. In a coincidence of Bannister-like proportions, BOF—as he is referred to in shorthand—and I both share the same birthday the 24th of May, though he is younger than I. In 2011 he offered me the job as his speech-writer and I was sorely tempted to take it. Ultimately however, I was persuaded to stay on and write for the current

Chief of the Army, Lieutenant General David Morrison. Why? Well he and I were born on exactly the same day—the 24th of May 1956. He is senior, but I am older by a few hours.

However, back to Sydney on the 4th of January 2012 where I had no sooner seen that political trio than I stumbled into Barry O'Farrell strolling behind the stands. We had a long chat. I told him that I had just seen his old boss Bruce Baird, Hawkie and Albo and we reminisced about that turbulent time and how much of the Greiner agenda was subsequently left undisturbed. Indeed, these days I am struck by the convergence between the two major parties over economic management despite the rancorous tone of our public debates. There is a fair degree of unanimity about the desirable macroeconomic settings required for a prosperous nation. Even governments of the centre-left support the maintenance of budget surpluses and lower taxes these days. This in part explains why the culture wars are conducted with such ferocity. Political parties need significant points of difference to mobilise their base vote and in an era of economic change people look for rootedness and meaning in symbols. I cannot get too indignant about this, nor join with those who claim that contests over culture and symbols are dangerous. If politics is not about debates over meaning and identity, then what is it about? I digress and am perilously close to a soapbox that my current profession rightly denies me.

On this occasion Premier O'Farrell was accompanied by his former colleague Andrew Tink, another veteran of that era who left politics a few years back and subsequently published a couple of very well received biographies on William Charles Wentworth and Lord Sydney. It was terrific to see him in such good fettle at the Test match as he had been in seriously ill health the preceding year.

My ideological fervour of those years has cooled with the passage of time. Yet it was a heady period to be a young man close to the nerve centre of national politics. Paul Kelly provided the definitive account of this era in *The End of Certainty* and expanded on it in the even better sequel, *The March of the Patriots.*

As previously mentioned, since the float of the Australian dollar by the Hawke government in 1983, the Australia of my youth has been radically transformed. According to Paul Kelly, Hawke and Keating presided over the dismantling of the 'Australian Settlement' distinguished by its three pillars of wage arbitration, the White Australia policy and heavy tariff protection for industry. While the White Australia policy was long gone by then, the float of the Australian dollar in 1983 generated tremors that eventually shifted the foundations of the Australian economy and ultimately our way of life. Our lives have been improved, but also made less predictable by competition. In particular, the character and tempo of work has changed dramatically.

The cozy myth that Australians are laid-back, along with the concept of lifelong employment with a single employer, was demolished. Since that time we have worked harder with less security than ever before and it shows in the way we relate to one another and the things that we regard as valuable. Great Australian enterprises in public ownership were either privatised or corporatised. Who remembers the PMG? TAA? Remember house calls by the family doctor? Remember pubs that closed on Sundays? Or pubs that closed at all? The list of institutions, customs and rituals that were swept away by the wave of economic reform was long and part of a civilisation now extinct. For a long time I was critical of this from both the left and the right, but over time I came to believe that the ends justified the means and that there was no credible, viable alternative.

One by one, like Indian middle-order batsmen on tour, many of the certainties of Australian life fell before the forces of economic and social change that were unleashed by the exposure of the Australian economy to the discipline of the global market. It struck me that, for a time, cricket—especially Test cricket—remained immune from much of this change. I suspect that this explains its special place in the Australian way of life. Amid so much change—an end to certainty—there was a reassuring familiarity about the rituals of the summer game. Test cricket, especially the radio commentary on the ABC, provided the soundtrack of our summer.

While it is difficult to generalise about such matters, cricket brought Australians together as a national audience. Unlike our football codes, which have always derived support along regional lines, the Test cricket team truly represented the nation. It seemed to enjoy enormous prestige and to palpably affect the national mood, especially when it was winning at home. I clearly remember the recriminations surrounding the capitulation of the Australian team to the West Indies, which culminated in the weepy resignation of Kim Hughes as captain in 1984. Of course I recognise that plenty of people would dispute this, but I suspect that the proposition is broadly valid, or at least was until recently.

I reflected on this during that week early in 2012 when those two Labor warhorses—Hawke and Keating—renewed hostilities over which of them was entitled to the greater credit for his role in the great transformative project of the 1980s. Obviously, I do not propose to express an opinion on that controversy. Together they constituted a formidable team, as did John Howard and his treasurer Peter Costello. In each case the whole seemed to be greater than the sum of the parts and both pairings achieved substantial structural reforms that directly contributed to the prosperity of the nation. I am inclined to agree with commentators such as Gerard Henderson who argue that the Howard government built upon the legacy of economic reform bequeathed by their Labor predecessors and that there was considerable common ground between them.

Of course Bob Hawke was also a handy cricketer whose passion for the game was well known, so it was no surprise to see him at the Sydney Test. But his physical presence was not the only thing that inspired these reflections on the nexus between globalisation and the changing character of Test cricket.

For a time Test cricket was one of the most resilient elements of our civil society. It had been both a unifying force in the face of the fissiparous forces created by globalisation, and a palliative in times of anxiety and uncertainty. Historians have long pointed to the significance of the Depression in shaping popular attitudes to Bradman, so this phenomenon is not novel. But there are ominous signs that the game may be changing irrevocably in response to market forces.

In a thought-provoking piece in *The Spectator Australia* to which I referred earlier, Nick Bryant bemoaned the impact of modernisation on the charms of Australia's traditional cricket grounds. The Adelaide Oval has undergone significant redevelopment, and during the 100th Sydney Test there was much discussion of the imminent demolition of the M.A. Noble, Bradman, and Messenger Stands, which will all be replaced by modern facilities in time for the 2015 World Cup.

This has aroused the ire of conservatives, but Adam Smith's 'invisible hand' wrote the script. The commercial demands of football and Twenty20 cricket are driving this push for 'functional multi-user entertainment facilities'. Even my use of such abominable language—

of which Don Watson has been the most pungent critic—reveals how irreversible and pervasive the ideology driving the transformation of sport into a commodity has become.

Here is where my old boss Rodney Cavalier re-enters the story. After lunch on the opening day of the Sydney Test Jim Maxwell interviewed him about the changes to the Sydney Cricket Ground, which will entail demolition of some of the historic grandstands and the renaming of the Noble Stand. To hear a traditionalist such as Rodney Cavalier describing the commercial imperatives behind the modernisation of the SCG on ABC radio during the 100th Sydney Test was incredibly revelatory. Cavalier possesses deep cricket sensibilities and genuinely cares about its traditions. However, in that interview with Maxwell he sounded like he was conducting a seminar at the Harvard Business School. The SCG will be a cricket ground in name and memory only. The aim is to make it a venue for use both day and night and for a wide range of purposes.

As Maxwell pursued him over the details of the modernisation of the ground, Cavalier was frank about the fact that the SCG could not derive its character purely from being a cricket ground. Nor would all the expense and disruption significantly increase the capacity. Asked about this, Cavalier conceded:

> Not a great deal more. Maybe 2000 or so more, but the future of spectator sport is not in capacity—in fact quite the opposite. The smart money in places which think intelligently before it builds stadia, in North America and Europe, isn't about capacity, unless there are guaranteed hirings like English soccer where you get attendances of 60–70,000 every week. In North America they're building stadia with 30–40,000 anticipating attendances of baseball, American football.
>
> ...

It's about creature comforts for the spectators—whether they're members or the public, it's about improving the dining rooms and the bar and giving it a really fine experience. What you have to do in the modern grounds business is not just be available four, or five, or eight days a year—you come here most days and nights, you've been here. You've seen how many events we've put on. And it's the location of choice for charities and fundraisers.

One cannot argue with any of this. However, the pressure to extract every ounce of commercial value from the SCG and to realise that the Sydney Swans Australian Football League team is its most frequent user must inevitably confer upon it a character that Doug Walters would just not recognise. Neither would the legendary Yabba—the famous barracker from the Bodyline era.

As an aside, it seems that there may be a direct link between the derivation of that term 'barracker' and the original users of the SCG. The original plot of land upon which the SCG was established was purchased using military funds by the commanding officer of the North Devonshire Regiment, then on colonial duty at Victoria Barracks during the 1840s. He hoped to host matches against the finest cricket teams in the Empire. This new cricket ground was located adjacent to the Barracks and it seems that officers and soldiers from Victoria Barracks became known for their raucous cheering. This disturbed nearby residents and other spectators, and the appellation 'barracker' came to be applied to the visitors from the barracks. The British Army had changed little in that era from what the Duke of Wellington caustically remarked comprised, 'The scum of the earth enlisted for drink', so there may be something to this story. Yet Victoria Barracks in Melbourne lays claim to the same term and I am unable to arbitrate with any certainty on that particular Sydney–Melbourne rivalry. Still, my publisher who served as the senior general at Army Training Command when it was located at Sydney's Victoria Barracks insisted that the story was an entrenched part of cricketing folklore there.

Yabba, while vociferous, was without political clout. And the case for the changes to the SCG seems irrefutable. Certainly, Barry O'Farrell made it sound persuasive enough to me when we spoke again on the Thursday afternoon of the Sydney Test. He had time for an extended chat because Tendulkar had been dismissed by Clarke just as he arrived. BOF had come to the ground when the Little Master had entered the 70s confident that he would arrive to see that milestone ton. I was waiting outside the Trust box with Harini Rana as the Premier arrived and I asked him more about the planned changes to the ground.

He was insistent that the Trust had got it right. He argued that there had been a real risk that the SCG may not have been deemed fit to host Test matches in the future without the modifications to facilities that his government, the Commonwealth and the SCG Trust eventually funded. For what it is worth, I believe the case for change made by the Premier and Cavalier was compelling, even if it was brutally unsentimental. Nonetheless, the changes to the capital city grounds are emblematic of other changes that may have more adverse consequences.

I had just finished chatting to the Premier when I turned around to see the former Indian great Ravi Shastri being interviewed on the viability of Test cricket by an English documentary crew. Sam Collins and his mate Jarrod Kimber were making a film about this Australian summer under the working title *Death of a Gentleman*. They were part of an interesting and talented group of guys with whom I found myself in the Brewongle Stand media centre on the second day of the Test match.

They, like Jim Maxwell when the idea of my own story of this summer of cricket was taking root, considered there to be no guarantee of the survival of Test cricket in any recognisable form and were making a documentary canvassing the attitudes of current and past cricket luminaries to this issue.

Meeting Sam and Jarrod turned out to be a wonderful stroke of luck. I had spent the first day in the Churchill Stand enjoying our 'traditional' day at the Sydney Test match. When I arrived at the main media box before play on the second day, I found to my chagrin that I had been allocated a spot in the Brewongle Stand—euphemistically termed the 'overflow area' by Cricket Australia. Dragging my bruised ego there I was becoming a rapid convert to the Cavalier plan to tear down the Bradman Stand and to rebuild it from scratch to expand the media facilities.

In the elevator ascending to the seventh floor of the Brewongle, I became aware of a tall urban-chic male and a camera crew crammed in beside me. We were all making light of being bumped out of the Bradman Stand, though I was privately interpreting this as a significant demotion. I wondered whether, as the summer unfolded, I would find myself moving incrementally to the car park with a set of binoculars provided by a smiling, reassuring Cricket Australia media officer.

As the doors opened and we emerged on the seventh floor my co-passenger extended his hand. 'Sam Collins. How do you do?' He was the personification of Cool Britannia with groovy Clarke Kent glasses, fashionable stubble and nonchalance that would have not been out of place in one of those glossy fashion supplements in *The Sydney Morning Herald's* magazine. This, allied with the understated, impeccable manners and bearing, left me unsurprised later when I learnt that he was an Old Etonian.

'Malcolm McGregor. English mate? Are the BBC interested in the 100th Test?'

'No, we're independent film-makers', he said as he groped for his business card. 'How about you?'

'I'm accredited as the cricket correspondent for *The Spectator*, but I'm trying to pull together a book on my own as well.'

'The English *Spectator*?'

'Yeah, sort of. There's an Aussie supplement. I'm paid by London, but my stuff only appears down here.'

'What's the book about?'

As we ambled down the corridor I gave him the short version of what I was trying to say about Test cricket. As I veered into the print media room he said, 'That sounds interesting. We might need to talk to you if you are amenable. Why don't you have a look at our website. It sounds to me as though we might be examining some of the themes in which you are interested. Are you going to Perth?'

'Yeah, I'll be at all the Tests.'

'Then let's catch up there, or Adelaide.'

'Love to.'

On entering the overflow print area I was thrilled to see Harini Rana and Samip already set up and pensively shifting their gaze between screen and pitch. Buoyant at my corridor chat with Sam and the prospects for collaboration in the lonely task of producing this story, I overlooked Samip's failure to deliver the usual military courtesies. Harini smiled wanly, conveying immediately what she thought of India's prospects as Clarke and Ponting resumed at 3/116.

It was then that she introduced me to Boria Majumdar, yet another fortuitous benefit that flowed from being moved to the Brewongle. As I mentioned earlier, I have enormous regard for Boria's scholarly work on Indian cricket and his observations on the impact of globalisation on sport influenced me deeply in the conclusions that I formed during the writing of this work. And it was wonderful to reminisce about the beauty of Oxford and twilight cricket on the South Parks wickets.

Had I been in the Bradman Stand I may have missed meeting him, Sam and Jarrod and my summer would have much the poorer for that. I found myself among a group of people who were all trying to come to grips with some of the bigger issues confronting traditional cricket in the face of globalisation and I could not have planned any of it. This was a wonderful windfall. Yet again, the inexplicable slender threads of synchronicity had connected me to the very people I needed to meet.

As Clarke and Ponting remorselessly extinguished India's hopes, I had the opportunity for extended discussions with Sam and Jarrod who employ the name 'The Two Chucks'. It was soon clear that they had very serious knowledge of, and love for, cricket. Our initial instincts that we might be tilling the same ground turned out to be correct. They had sent an emissary around to fetch me to their viewing area where it became apparent how sophisticated their approach to film-making was. I was instinctively drawn to them, as I am to most creative people. I envy those with gifts for creating beautiful music, prose or film. You can sense the presence of authentic talent in these areas, much as you can tell a Laxman is different in the nets.

It turned out we shared a love of the game. They were also immensely good fun. Sam was more reserved and measured, but over time I came to realise he had a terrific sense of humour. Jarrod had one of those faces that are probably placed on 'Wanted' posters in teachers' colleges across the world with mandatory warnings, 'If you get one of these, isolate them from the class immediately'. He had a distinct hint of mischief in his face and a mouth that readily spread into an engaging, infectious grin. Like all my colleagues in the media boxes over the summer, his mastery of cricket history and statistics was depressingly impressive. If you ever need to know the five English counties Marcus North played for, and your search engine is down, ask Jarrod. And he is without doubt the most hilarious tweeter on cricket on the globe. Over the ensuing months I was occasionally reduced to tears as he tweeted his pithy observations about the England–Pakistan series and England in Sri Lanka.

Like Langer and Hayden, Sam and Jarrod appeared to be an odd couple in that they were so physically dissimilar. Sam was male-model tall and lean while Jarrod was shorter and chunkier. His only attempt to match Sam's unconscious sartorial style was a ubiquitous United States Marine Corps utility cap in urban camouflage, which remained on his head in even the finest of restaurants over the summer. Yet like so many apparently unlikely pairings, they were a perfectly balanced team. Perhaps that was because, to paraphrase Rahul Dravid, they both spoke cricket so fluently.

As the title of their documentary *Death of a Gentleman* suggests, they shared my pessimism as to whether Test cricket can survive over the long haul. It struck me as an interesting paradox that so historic an occasion as the 100th Test on the Sydney Cricket Ground should graphically illustrate the apotheosis of the trends likely to marginalise Test cricket. My reminiscences about the economic debates of the Hawke era with Barry O'Farrell, and later chance encounters with senior Labor senator John Faulkner and Rodney Cavalier, deepened my conviction that there was something in Jim Maxwell's preseason speculation as to whether this would be the last of the summer wine.

There are no easy answers to this dilemma. Although I am a traditionalist, I can see the merits of the market arguments. This matches my own journey from conservative country boy, through Whitlamite romanticism and back, over five decades. In some ways, the recurring tensions between neo-liberals and paleo-conservatives within the broader conservative movement find perfect expression in the arguments between those who long for the bygone era of chivalrous amateurism and those who support the untrammelled operation of the market. Ever since Bob Hawke floated the Australian dollar, every showdown between the market and sentimentality has been resolved unsentimentally. Maybe the right will soon emulate the left and spend the next decade in ideological schism over 'The Cricket Question'.

My instinct as an historian is to be cautious about 'presentism' in the form of breathless claims that we find ourselves in unprecedented times. For much of the past decade I have watched authors who have purported to discern 'revolutions in military affairs' and 'new' ways in war achieve instant success, only to have their places on those endless shows that everyone watches in airport lounges with the sound turned down taken by even newer gurus.

Having said that, there is a sense that cricket is in uncharted waters. The Packer revolution under the rubric of World Series Cricket does not provide a true precedent. Kerry Packer embodied the old Australian Settlement, with his monopoly businesses flourishing behind licensing schemes. Keating was repulsed by him and vastly preferred dealing with Rupert Murdoch whom he considered to be truly attuned to the *Zeitgeist* of post-Cold War globalisation. His falling out with Packer at the fag end of the Hawke–Keating era made his argument with Bob Hawke over their legacy look like a lovers' tiff.

Certainly, Bob Hawke would have recognised the World Series Cricket rift with the Australian Cricket Board as a classic industrial dispute from the era of collective bargaining during which he rose to national prominence. Essentially, the Australian cricket team unionised itself and entered into a cosy award arrangement with Packer.

They participated in a wage breakout that would have made the metal workers blush. As such, World Series Cricket was not so much the harbinger of the current era of fast-food cricket as the apotheosis of the centrally regulated wage fixing system that became unsustainable in the wake of deregulated capital markets. Whatever Bob Hawke thought of Packer's raid on the cricket establishment, he showed what he really thought of such an approach to wage fixing during the pilots' strike in 1989. Since that time, elite cricketers have thrived as celebrities on lucrative individual contracts. However, the money is only available at the very highest levels. Grade and state cricket are in a parlous state.

Of course, World Series Cricket pioneered the coloured kit and the changes to rules and customs that are recognisable in the even shorter form of the game that emerged. But despite the routine pieties from senior players and past greats to the effect that playing for one's country remains the ultimate test of character and ability, Test cricket is under threat. Crowds are dwindling and neither television audiences nor the players can achieve an emotional connection with a game when it is played in front of empty stadiums. This depressing observation was made most eloquently by Rahul Dravid in his Bradman Oration.

The curtain came down on the Sydney Test inside four days. Despite the history-making significance of Clarke's triple century and the explosive bowling of Siddle and Pattinson backed by the subtle variation of Hilfenhaus, Sydney was most memorable to me for the off-field action and the stimulating discussions about the larger trends in the game.

I was very sad for the Three Tenors of the Indian batting order—Tendulkar, Dravid and Laxman. The comprehensive defeat by an innings and 68 runs ensured that, regardless of their achievements in the game, they would retire never having conquered Australia at home. Sidarth Monga summed it up thus:

> It's all over, as Bill Lawry would say. Sachin Tendulkar: 22 years of international cricket, five Test tours to Australia. Rahul Dravid: close to 16 years of international cricket, four tours to Australia. VVS Laxman: same as Dravid. They will never win a Test series in Australia. How broken the three must feel. Australia, the land that loved them and also broke their hearts, had to be part of the reason they kept going at their age.
>
> Australia, the big tease. Australia, where they came within three wickets or an enforced follow-on of winning a series in 2003-04. Australia, where they played the most bitter Test in recent memory but couldn't bat out two sessions and a bit. Australia, where Tendulkar is closing in on 2000 runs at an average of 58, where both Laxman and Dravid have more than 1000 at averages of over 45. Australia, where they shall never win a Test series.
>
> The dream didn't even reach Perth.

Perth was on my mind as I walked out the gate amid a gloating army of drunken Australians in sombreros. The Duke of Wellington may have issued them with red coats. I was deep in thought about the next Test and whether India could salvage any respectability, and also what I should write next about the disintegration of an Indian side that I had rated so highly and the re-emergence of the Australian side, especially its ageing champions whom I had written off. As I walked towards my appointed rendezvous with Tritia for the drive back to Canberra I saw a tall figure in the gathering gloom as distinctively British as Nelson's Column. Sam Collins and his camera crew were interviewing the Australian fans as they poured out of the ground.

He towered over a couple of drunks whose match analysis seemed to be, 'Tendulkar go home!'

He nodded and winked. I nodded back.

'How goes it mate?'

'Your lot thinks they will win The Ashes back on the evidence of this. They're pretty cocky.'

'I warned you about the ugly Australian!'

He nodded silently, an almost imperceptible smile parting his lips.

'See you in Perth.'

'See you in Perth.'

As [Grant] famously wrote in a dispatch to Lincoln and the Cabinet after a bloody battle in the Wilderness next to the Rapidan River, 'I propose to fight it out along this line if it takes all summer'.

8.   If it Takes All Summer

... there are nevertheless some interesting analogies on how soldiers and sportspeople respond to crises.

... India, like Ulysses S. Grant in the brutal Overland Campaign of May and June 1864, needed to show more resilience.

... it is tempting to see the applicability of Grant's quote to the plight of the Indian touring team which found itself heading to Perth amid widespread predictions of a whitewash in the wake of its poor preparations in Canberra.

I have previously mentioned that idyllic summer of 1967–68 when my boyhood love of Test cricket intersected with a fascination for Australian politics. This summer lives on with vivid, sensuous immediacy for me and I can still summon up the aromas and sounds of that long holiday in which it always seemed afternoon. That year our family spent an extended period on holidays at the Gold Coast and I still recall it is as the most perfect summer of my life. Already an inveterate cricket listener I lay basking in the warm sun, drowsing to the gentle buzz of the cricket on the radio. So enthralled was I by the exotic Nawab of Pataudi Jnr. and his Indian team with their unpronounceable names, that I was seldom without the transistor glued to my ear. On one family outing during the Brisbane Test I wandered through a lush national park in the Gold Coast hinterland listening to India's desperate run chase at the Gabba. The crackling transistor dropped in and out at the most inopportune moments, but I was able to hear my hero Bob Cowper strike the decisive blow for Australia when he dismissed the Indian centurion M.L. Jaisimha just as it was looking like the Indians may run down Australia's total.

Events of greater significance than that one-sided Test series left the summer of 1967–68 seared into my consciousness though. On the 17th of December 1967, Australia's seventeenth prime minister disappeared while swimming at Cheviot Beach near Portsea. While the assassination of John F. Kennedy had jolted me out of infancy and sparked an interest in current events, I was now old enough to take a more serious interest in the unfolding drama surrounding the death of Harold Holt. I was absolutely riveted by the drama of the futile search for his remains off Cheviot Beach and transfixed by the arrival of the President of the United States, accompanied by some of the very secret service agents who had been in that fateful motorcade in Dallas, to attend the memorial service for Holt in Melbourne.

This temporarily moved cricket from centre stage that summer. Holt's death was surrounded by mystery and spawned nearly as many lunatic theories as had Kennedy's. But it was the politics of the succession that thoroughly intrigued me and weaned me on to a diet of Australian political news thereafter. I was ultimately to spend a substantial part of my working life either participating in or writing about the type of machinations that so fascinated me over the summer of 1967–68.

The definitive account of the intrigue, number crunching and sheer bastardry within the Liberal–Country Party coalition that ultimately yielded John Grey Gorton as leader of the Liberal Party—and hence the replacement for the interim prime minister, 'Black Jack' McEwan—were chronicled by one of the granite figures of Canberra political journalism, Alan Reid. His account of the manoeuvering within the coalition, *The Power Struggle,* was a masterpiece of the genre. I elected to receive this book as the prize for topping my Year 11 English class and I still have it, bearing the sticker recording my success, on my shelves among my vast book collection.

Given the many thousands of words I have written about politics over the years, it may surprise some readers to learn that by far the largest collection of works in my library is on the American Civil War, a passion that almost predates my love of cricket and which I have pursued without interruption since the age of about seven. Readers of earlier parts of this story might understand how little I am capable of exercising moderation in my passions and so might imagine how many volumes of the Civil War populate my shelves.

My interest in things American, especially the Civil War, frustrated my father, whose contempt for Douglas MacArthur and the United States Army knew no reasonable bounds. His was an attitude widely shared among veterans of the Allies' New Guinea campaign. My mother's lamentations about my interest in the Samurai aside, I rather suspect that my father would have been almost as gravely offended by my obsession with American military history as by my adulation of the other enemy from New Guinea.

I am often drawn to my knowledge of military history when I look for analogies or metaphors to describe situations. As I argued earlier, Clausewitz offers lessons of general applicability about the complex interplay of morale, chance and friction in adversarial contests. While not breaching Rahul Dravid's prohibition on employing warlike metaphors to describe sporting contests, there are nevertheless some interesting analogies on how soldiers and sportspeople respond to crises. To me, it seemed that the most disturbing aspect of India's defeat in Sydney was the lack of resolve that they displayed when the going got tough. This was most graphically exemplified by the lack of vigour and enthusiasm they displayed in the field. At times their cricket bordered on slapstick in its incompetence. It was not of a standard befitting a proud nation that had quite recently enjoyed the number one Test ranking. This had also been a feature of their defeats in England and they appeared at risk of actually unravelling in pitiable fashion over the final two Test matches in Australia unless something dramatic was done.

What analogy from my reading on war sprang to mind? India, like Ulysses S. Grant in the brutal Overland Campaign of May and June 1864, needed to show more resilience. They needed to absorb the hit they had taken and knuckle down to the daunting struggle that lay before them. In the words of Grant, they needed to resolve to fight it out without quarter. As he famously wrote in a dispatch to Lincoln and the Cabinet after a bloody battle in the Wilderness next to the Rapidan River, 'I propose to fight it out along this line if it takes all summer'. Grant was essentially distinguishing himself from other Union generals who immediately suspended their plans in the face of a single reverse.

Since my childhood I have read voraciously on the American Civil War. It had thoroughly beguiled me even before I entered the Royal Military College, Duntroon to start officer training some thirty-eight years ago on the 14th of January 1974. Both the causes of the war and its conduct were the subject of exhaustive study at Duntroon. Even cadets enrolled in the engineering stream were obliged to study Jackson's Valley Campaign in intricate detail along with the campaigns of Napoleon. And the promotion examinations to captain emphasised campaign studies from the American Civil War well into the 1980s.

We were taught by an array of impressive men, notably the redoubtable Professor L.C.F. (Len) Turner—a global authority on both the Napoleonic Wars and the American Civil War—and also by a kindly, urbane man by the name of Alec Hill, whose reputation as a veteran of El Alamein added lustre to his prodigious teaching skills. Both men inspired awe in us, especially Alec Hill who had met the legendary Montgomery in the Middle East. They were world-class scholars who had been to war as young men. We had just missed the end of the Vietnam conflict and had joined an army deeply wounded by its experience there. This was compounded by drastic cuts to its strength after the end of National Service. Few of us ever expected to see active service. Those of us who have served into this century lived to learn the folly of that expectation. Thus men like Turner and Hill held us enthralled with their academic knowledge embellished by experience of war.

Turner and Hill were both generous mentors to me and encouraged my scholarly interest in the American Civil War. I remain deeply indebted to them as they imbued in me a love of this era of history that abides to this day. One of my fondest memories from my time at RMC was the evenings devoted to informal discussions of military history at Turner's residence in the grounds of Duntroon. These were attended by a group of men who went on to be the high priests of Australian military history. The most eminent of them was Robert O'Neill, a Vietnam veteran and Rhodes Scholar; he ultimately held the Chichele Chair of the History of War at Oxford. And there was David Horner, another young man with regimental service in Vietnam who has made a seminal contribution to the writing of Australia's military history from the Second World War to the present. Many years later I was fortunate to study under O'Neill's successor as Chichele Professor, Hew Strachan. I spent a couple of terms at Oxford reading into the first-hand accounts of the British Army observers who spent time with the Union and Confederate armies. The highlight of my research was the discovery of personal correspondence from Robert E. Lee in the private papers of Viscount Garnet Wolseley who wrote extensively on the Civil War. Among the Wolseley papers were personal letters from Lee to his wife and family and correspondence between Wolseley and Lee's nephew Fitzhugh Lee who later became the Governor of Virginia. However, I digress.

As much as Len Turner loved the Civil War, he was prone to chuckle on occasions that the curriculum at Duntroon was guilty of producing a generation of Australian officers who, in the words of the British historian Basil Liddell Hart, were able to 'enumerate the blades of grass in the Shenandoah Valley'. Len suspected that, while all military history was useful to aspiring officers, we may have been better advised to allocate as much time to the assiduous study of Bob O'Neill's biography of the North Vietnamese Commander Giap as we were then devoting to G.F.R. Henderson's biography of 'Stonewall' Jackson.

Nonetheless, he enthusiastically supported me when I proposed that my honours dissertation deal with the historiography of the generalship of Robert E. Lee who fought Grant to a bloody stalemate during the celebrated Overland Campaign of the summer of 1864. The fate of the great American republic turned on that campaign more so than on the battle at Gettysburg the year before. Both Grant and Lee knew that the resolve of the Union for the war was weakening and Lincoln's re-election depended on the successful prosecution of the war in Virginia in 1864. Lee, for his part, hoped to bleed the Union armies white in order to undermine Lincoln's campaign against the former Union general George McClellan who was arguing for a negotiated peace.

As a young army officer in the making, I was mesmerised by Lee's masterful use of interior lines to constantly cut off Grant's hosts as they remorselessly advanced into the Confederate heartland. My views reflected the intellectual consensus of the British school of Civil War historians who, apart from Liddell Hart and J.F.C. Fuller, overwhelmingly subscribed to the 'Lost Cause' school of historiography. Under this, Lee was the brilliant chivalric figure whose military genius was brutally subdued only by Grant's unimaginative employment of his immense advantage in numbers and materiel. Grant, we assumed, was oblivious to casualties and was somehow dishonourable, or at least unskillful, in not being able to vanquish Lee through envelopment. While Lee was the architect of the Napoleonic master strokes of Second Manassas and Chancellorsville, Grant's signature battles were the bloody frontal assaults at Spotsylvania Court House and Cold Harbor.

However, in the wake of the two global wars of the twentieth century, Grant's reputation as the butcher of Cold Harbor underwent dramatic rehabilitation. Modern historians concluded that Grant had maintained relentless pressure on Lee, confident that he would defeat him through attrition. His boast that he intended to 'fight it out along this line if it takes all summer' had been routinely cited to demonstrate his lack of strategic imagination. On the contrary, it revealed that he alone among the senior leadership of the Union armies shared president Lincoln's insight that Robert E. Lee's army had to be destroyed to end the war. Mere capture of territory, especially the capital of the Confederacy, would not subdue the insurrection while Lee and his army were capable of armed resistance.

Fuller in particular situated Grant in the context of the carnage of the Western Front of 1916 and concluded that he had indeed been a prophetic figure who, along with his protégé William Sherman, had grasped the essentials of industrial age warfare before many European officers. While there is a grain of truth in this contention, it exaggerates the extent to which the Civil War really was a 'total' or 'modern' war. Fuller pioneered this theory, which was taken up with enthusiasm by New Left Marxists, Progressive historians and proponents of American exceptionalism, with equal conviction. All exhibited an insular disregard for the Civil War as a classic example of nineteenth century warfare, recognisable more as the last Napoleonic war than as the first of the purported 'modern' or 'total' wars.

Over the better part of a lifetime I have followed the trends in Civil War historiography. It is impossible to really understand the United States of America without some understanding of the legacy of this war. Moreover, debates over the war provide piercing insights into contemporary American anxieties and aspirations. As a military professional it is possible to discern what the US Army thinks about modern warfare by examining what it is teaching cadets at West Point about the Civil War.

My admiration for Lee has waned both on account of my own changes in attitude to the cause he served, and my intensely personal rediscovery of Ulysses S. Grant. In the unadorned prose for which he was famous, Grant observed of one of his fellow Union generals of the American Civil War, 'He got started wrong and just never got right'. Over the years Grant has subtly won me over as an admirer. He was an exceptional general although he was a mediocre president. But his memoirs, only completed on his deathbed, are a masterpiece of clarity and homespun common sense.

Lee was an exceptional commander, but I no longer accept the 'Lost Cause' interpretation of him as a knightly figure without blemish who reluctantly chose loyalty to his state over his duty to the nation. His loyalty to Virginia ran deep and such state loyalty was not uncommon among his generation. But the war was about slavery and any arguments to the contrary are sophistry, as the leading historian of the Civil War, James McPherson, has demonstrated beyond any reasonable doubt. Since the publication of his epic work, *Battle Cry of Freedom,* McPherson has published prolifically on the decisive influence of slavery on Southern secessionists. The state rights theories of war causation have been comprehensively discredited, as have the crude economic deterministic theories of the Progressives. Still, on any view of it, Lee was a formidable general with extraordinary charisma who inspired his outnumbered armies to feats of arms that should have been beyond them. However, my youthful adoration of him has dimmed considerably.

Leaving aside my long-standing professional interest in these matters, I was forced to reappraise Grant from a purely personal perspective when I reached a pivotal crisis in my life—alcoholism. Grant was clearly similarly afflicted and at critical junctures in his career his drinking nearly brought him undone. While I am unconvinced that he was drunk at Shiloh, there is sufficient evidence that he occasionally 'fell off the wagon' at inopportune times. And he clearly suffered from the neurosis that afflicts problem drinkers who seek to abstain from drinking through the exercise of sheer unaided willpower. His triumph over this serious condition filled me with admiration for him and led me to reappraise him in my later years.

One of the most poignant images of him for me is that of him sitting alone whittling while waiting anxiously for news of his army locked in a deadly wrestle with the Army of Northern Virginia in the Wilderness around the Rapidan River in May 1864. To alleviate his nerves he chain-smoked cigars, a habit that eventually caused the throat cancer that killed him. Having grappled with my own share of these demons I came to feel that I had a personal sense of who Grant was, despite the chasm of years that divided us. And his unkempt appearance, with his battered campaign hat and absent the sash and sword worn so ostentatiously by his fellow generals, make him an accessible figure even today. The face that stares at us from the cover of his biographies is contemporary, whereas Lee seems a patrician relic of a vanished plantation society. Over time, such changing perceptions led me to repudiate the evaluations of the relative merits of the two men that characterised my undergraduate work.

Although I should resume the cricket story, it is tempting to see the applicability of Grant's quote to the plight of the Indian touring team which found itself heading to Perth amid widespread predictions of a whitewash in the wake of its poor preparations in Canberra. How had it come to this? In Melbourne there were a couple of tipping points when it appeared that India could put their stamp on the match. Slumping from 2/214 to trail Australia's 333 by 51 was unforgivable. Even then, the efforts of the Indian bowlers to reduce Australia to 4/27 in their second innings seemed to revive the prospect of victory. Yet at key moments there was a worrying hint of the same lack of grit that had characterised this team in England just five months earlier. The abject collapse on the first morning in Sydney seemed to set the tone for the remainder of the series. While 191 was never going to be enough, it was the indolent, unprofessional cricket of the second and third days that provided a disturbing insight into the psyche of the touring team. The bowling looked perfunctory, and the chasing and throwing from the field smacked of surrender. It appeared that they were disintegrating and drifting to a 4–0 whitewash as they had in England. This suggested that there was something wrong in the ethos and morale of the team. What was urgently needed was for one of the old guard to adopt Ulysses S. Grant's sanguine approach and propose that his teammates fight it out along this line, 'if it takes all summer'. My sense was that this had to be Rahul Dravid—the moral centre of gravity of this team—even though he was not the current captain.

On my blog I predicted this:

> It is unlikely that the jittery middle order will get much respite from the pressure being exerted by the Australian fast bowlers, though conventional wisdom is that this Perth track is not as bouncy and fast as that of earlier eras. India did indeed win here on their last tour, albeit with a more balanced and aggressive attack than they are fielding here. Much will hinge on the performance of Ishant Sharma. He has bowled with courage and fire and his figures do not reflect his consistent menace. Although Zaheer Khan has made headway against the Australian top order he lacks the express pace that tends to achieve the best results in Perth. India is simply unable to maintain the level of intimidation and menace that the Australian attack has been producing, and it is beginning to define the series.
>
> With hindsight it looks as though this tour got started wrong with a soft preparation in Canberra against modest opposition on a dead track. At the very least an 'Australia A' fixture on the WACA or another fast surface would have been more valuable. Having got started wrong they must get it right. Another loss here will seriously erode the credibility of Indian cricket.

Remarkably, my passions—cricket, Australian politics, and the American Civil War—all coalesced in the most synchronistic fashion during the Indian summer of 2011–12. In an enticing coincidence, a touring Indian team was again emphatically defeated 4–0 over an

Australian summer in which our domestic political scene was punctuated by Machiavellian scheming over the leadership of the governing political party. Here is how it happened.

Encountering my old mate Michael Cooney at the Bradman Oration at the Australian War Memorial in Canberra eventually proved to be a turning point in the way that this story unfolded. It was great to see Michael, but my status as a Labor renegade and long-standing friendship with Tony Abbott does not make contact with me a career-enhancing move for ambitious Labor staffers. Cooney has always been more magnanimous than this and has an eclectic range of friends vastly more conservative than I.

But despite our constant assurances that we must stay in touch, our social contact in the previous year had been confined to attendance at one representative rugby match in Canberra in which my beloved Queensland Reds had been hammered by the ACT's Brumbies. At that time Cooney had been working for the education minister in the local ACT government, Andrew Barr. However he was recruited by Julia Gillard as her speech-writer when she became Prime Minister, thereby returning from the wilderness to which he had been consigned by Kevin Rudd on account of his connection to Mark Latham's Iraq policy. Working in the Prime Ministerial Office is demanding enough and he and his wife Cathy have a young family. So I had not seen a lot of him until the night of Dravid's stunning speech at the Australian War Memorial.

However, as this summer unfolded we saw a lot more of one another, beginning with our shared time at the lacklustre fixtures in Canberra staged as part of the Indians' preparation for the Test series. We began to exchange text messages and arranged to meet at the MCG during the Test match. Cooney has an excellent rugby and cricket brain and he provided some thought-provoking ideas about the way cricket coverage has changed in response to the pressure of the 24-hour media cycle. I will acknowledge his valuable insights in that regard later in this narrative.

He liked my account of the Bradman Oration and the fact that I had given credit to his boss for having had the courage to push the sale of uranium to India through the ALP's National Conference. Favourable opinions about Julia Gillard were not in wide circulation in December 2011. Indeed, the latest round of speculation about a challenge to her leadership was inspired by Gillard's perceived humiliation of her predecessor Kevin Rudd in her speech at that same conference. She had omitted Rudd from her lengthy encomium to the achievements of former Labor prime ministers. Amid the tributes to Gough Whitlam, Bob Hawke and Paul Keating, Gillard overlooked Rudd's *tour de force* performance in roofing insulation installation. Nor had her coup on uranium sales to India endeared her to the foreign minister who neither approved of the plan nor had been consulted about it. As I was busy at the Gabba Test I had paid only cursory attention to all of this.

When Cooney told me that he had passed on a copy of Dravid's speech to the Prime Minister I asked him, 'Do you think I could have a yarn to her about the book? I'd like to make the link between the Bradman Oration and the broader India relationship. Given that she put some skin in the game to get the uranium sales through, she would have something worthwhile to say about India and why it matters. She doesn't need to go through the usual crap about her earliest memories of cricket. I am actually interested in her substantive views on India as a rising power.'

'She might do it. By the way, did you know Tim [Tim Mathieson, the Prime Minister's partner] is a cricket fan? He might talk to you about cricket.'

'Actually I knew that, mate. He was at the Shield game at Manuka Oval. He and I, and his personal security detail, were the crowd. I'd be happy to have a talk to him. I'd be grateful for any access you can help me with to either of them.'

With that we parted at the gate of Manuka Oval after that miserable, inconclusive Chairman's XI fixture promising to meet for dinner in Melbourne. As it turned out dinner in Melbourne was hard to organise as I attended a tribute evening for Peter Roebuck and then was obliged to do some live Melbourne radio interviews on the evenings of the third and fourth days' play.

Nonetheless, Cooney and I exchanged text messages throughout the Test match. His tone was exultant as Australia's march to victory became inexorable. I had confided my treachery to him and he crowed at my discomfort, especially when my new hero Dravid was bowled in the second innings. 'I though they called your man The Wall?' he sniggered as Pattinson shattered his stumps for the third time in the match, including once off that Siddle no ball I described earlier.

As the match drew to a close Cooney rang me, 'Mate do you need a lift home to Canberra. I am going to stop overnight in Oxley near Wangaratta with a mate of mine, Matt Corboy, whom I think you'd like. He's a mad National Party member who loves the Latin Mass and a few beers. I like him despite the fact that he's a Nat and a Richmond supporter. He's a really down-to-earth bloke. The thing that unites us is that we are both teaching our kids to hate the Greens! You'd fit in well'.

I declined with regret as I had already arranged to link up with Tritia in Albury, which is her hometown. She was relishing returning to her roots and spending some quiet time away from my cricket obsession. But I would equally have enjoyed Cooney's company and chance to debrief on the Test. Invariably the end of each Test match left me feeling empty. The atmosphere and camaraderie of the media box is very engaging and the prospect of dining alone and then writing a lengthy blog entry in my hotel room before getting the next morning's train from Spencer Street to Albury was unappealing.

In parting I asked Cooney, 'Mate, any progress with your boss in terms of having a chat about India?'

'Not yet. But I'll ask, don't worry. She is definitely in Sydney for the Test for the first day and also the Jane McGrath events. I reckon we should be able to hook you up with her there. She'll be doing the ABC commentary at some point and we can probably pick you up on the way to the box.' At this point I did not know that I was to overflow away from the electronic media boxes in Sydney.

'Will you be with her?'

'For sure. I am trying to get to as many days of cricket as I can. But Sally Tindall will probably cover the media piece for the Test.' With that we parted and undertook to meet at the SCG.

I thought no more about Prime Minister Gillard until I arrived in Canberra late on the Friday night after the Melbourne Test. When I logged on I was surprised to find an email from Sally Tindall of the Prime Minister's Office inviting me to Kirribilli House the following Sunday for the reception for the Australian and Indian teams. In closing, Sally indicated that she had scheduled a private meeting for a few minutes with the Prime Minister in the garden at her Sydney residence to answer my questions about the relationship with India.

I was stunned and simultaneously grateful to Cooney who had clearly intervened to deliver this generous access. The only problem was that it had all come far too soon and unexpectedly, and it was simply impossible to be in Sydney at the appointed time due to family commitments over the New Year. I hastily composed a profusely apologetic email to Sally Tindall explaining my inability to accept her offer at this stage and requesting that she consider facilitating a meeting with the Prime Minister during her time at the SCG during the Test.

As in Melbourne, Cooney and I played telephone tag throughout the Sydney Test, so he gave me Sally Tindall's mobile number. Sadly this was all to no avail. The Prime Minister proved elusive in Sydney. She was heavily committed and my position in the Brewongle meant that I was not on hand when she visited the ABC and Channel Nine studios for her customary slot as a guest commentator. Cooney reassured me that he would arrange a meeting with her even if it entailed waiting until we were both at the Prime Minister's XI fixture against Sri Lanka in Canberra in February. In any event, he and I caught up during the warm-up in the nets. Over a cup of coffee we had an amusing conversation while watching Ricky Ponting working on his technique. I asked Cooney what he made of the plans for the demolition of the M.A. Noble Stand and the rest of Rodney Cavalier's and the Trust's plans for the ground.

'Well we have stumped a fair bit of dough for it, so obviously the federal government gets the need for this. But I would like to discuss his ideas for reform of the Labor Party with Rodney Cavalier. I thought he might like to pilot his idea for primaries where anyone who broadly identifies with the ALP can vote for pre-selection candidates within the SCG Trust first. Who does he answer to? Maybe we should just let everyone who buys a ticket to the AFL or the cricket have a vote on who the chairman of the SCG Trust should be. Maybe then Rodney might not be as enthusiastic about the merits of grass-roots democracy if we suggested that this applies to him. I reckon he might find Ray Hadley takes his job on that basis.'

Clearly Cavalier's critique of the contemporary ALP rankled with Cooney who must have been feeling besieged as the speculation about his boss's tenure mounted in early 2012. Like 1968, the normal hiatus in political reporting had not occurred and leadership speculation was bubbling away with an unusual intensity over the summer recess.

But my attempts to meet the Prime Minister took an unexpected twist, and ultimately we did catch up. Strangely, it occurred through the unlikely link of my passion for the American Civil War and my speculation about the malaise in the Indian team revealed by the massive defeat in Sydney. The chapter on the Sydney Test emphatically described the magnitude of the defeat which led Ian Chappell to predict that India was well on the way to conceding a 4–0 whitewash just as they had against England a few months earlier. As one of the few analysts not to have installed India as favourites at the outset of the series, his views demanded serious consideration. My sense that the Indian team had started wrong and never got right might also have been deemed to apply to Julia Gillard. And in the most remarkable manner she decided the same thing. How that came to pass I shall explain shortly.

My sense that the Civil War analogy was apposite was reinforced in Perth. India had showed even less application there. While I was watching that Test I wrote a blog along the lines I have written here, with my thoughts on Grant, Lee and the American Civil War titled, 'He got started wrong and just never got right'. It had unexpected repercussions beyond cricket and facilitated my oft-postponed meeting with the Prime Minister.

Whether or not I had drawn too long a bow when I likened the situation facing the Indians with the Union Army in 1864, both Cooney and former leader of the ALP and deputy prime minister Kim Beazley wrote to tell me how much they had enjoyed it. Kim was based in cold, wintry

Washington DC as Australia's Ambassador to the United States of America and was homesick for the WACA. He normally attended the Perth Test without fail each summer. He sent me a gracious email saying, 'The Civil War historiography was terrific and I enjoyed it more than a Tendulkar ton!'

I certainly didn't expect it to come to the attention of the current leader of the Australian Labor Party, yet I clearly underestimated the efforts of her speech-writer Michael Cooney. Thus did the line from Grant find its way into Julia Gillard's first major address on the economy that formally opened political hostilities for the year in February 2012. As Gillard said to the Australia–Israel Chamber of Commerce in Melbourne on the 1st of February:

> I was recently reminded, while reading about the cricket of all things, of the famous oath of the American Civil War General Ulysses S Grant, who said he would, 'fight it out along this line if it takes all summer'.
>
> There's something of that determination and clarity in my Government's approach in 2012.

I had not been aware of the speech but had received a text message from Cooney on the 31st of January saying, 'Got the Grant quote up!' This puzzled me, but I thought no more of it until my mobile phone rang the next morning and an exasperated Cooney raged, 'Did you see what Tony Walker said in the *Fin Review*?' I confessed that I never read the *Financial Review* these days, nor do I adhere to my old routine of reading the papers quite so early in the morning. Occasionally, in my days as a political staffer, I had waited at Taylor Square for the first copies of *The Sydney Morning Herald* to be prepared to brief Bob Carr for his radio offensive which would begin at 5.30 in the mornings.

Fuelled by drink, I was generally more effective at midnight than at 5.30 am. But that is another story.

Of course that routine preceded the advent of the ceaseless 24-hour news cycle, the internet and various forms of social media. These days I enjoy the lazy ritual of reading the papers over a coffee at the Artoven Bakery in Manuka on the way to work. It is a comforting ritual that I discovered when suffering badly from jet lag in the winter of 2010. Dom and Rose and their eclectic cast of characters are open by about 3 am and I got into the habit of going there and watching the soccer World Cup with a coffee. The habit has stuck, though I pore over the papers at a more civilised hour these days. I am philosophical about the fact that much of the news has already been rendered irrelevant by the contemporaneous reporting of the electronic media. However, I enjoy the columnists Paul Kelly, Greg Sheridan and Janet Albrechtsen. Which is a long way of explaining that I reluctantly admitted to Cooney that I did not have the foggiest idea what he was upset about, nor did I regret that I was no longer on a political staff and tied to the news cycle.

As it turned out Tony Walker had lampooned Gillard for citing the quote from Grant that had appeared on my blog. He blustered that her analogy was fatuous and that, in any event, it was probably dishonest to claim she had found a reference to the Virginia Campaign of the summer of 1864 in a cricket article. I felt sorry for Gillard. The conventional wisdom that she was economical with the truth struck me as being unduly harsh and essentially exacerbated by sexism. Walker's interpretation of the significance of Spotsylvania was naïve and revealed a lamentable lack of any serious grasp of the historiography of the Civil War. Indeed, if he had actually read the blog piece that he had accused Gillard of not having read he would not have made this error.

But being a media guru means never having to say you are sorry. Despite the Prime Minister's staff providing evidence of the blog material and the extensive development of the argument, Walker moved on to his next topic. The folly of Walker's argument was best exposed by James McPherson—arguably the best contemporary historian of the war—who wrote in *Battle Cry of Freedom:*

> Grant's purpose was not a war of attrition—though numerous historians have mislabeled it thus. From the outset he had tried to maneuver Lee into open-field combat, where the Union superiority in numbers and firepower could cripple the enemy. It was Lee who turned it into a war of attrition by skillfully matching Grant's moves and confronting him with entrenched defense at every turn.

When it comes to interpretation of the significance of the assault at Bloody Angle in the context of Grant's overall strategy in the Eastern Theatre I am inclined to prefer McPherson's view to Walker's, who seems not to have published anything else on the Civil War since February. No doubt his long-awaited work on the Civil War is being timed for the Christmas market.

As luck would have it I had the chance to commiserate with the Prime Minister about this issue. My mate Barrie Cassidy is an old mate of her partner Tim Mathieson and had arranged for Tim to host me to the Lord's Taverners Dinner the night before the Prime Minister's XI against Sri Lanka. I was interested in talking to Tim as I had seen him at every day of cricket at Manuka over the summer and it was clear he was a serious watcher. Through Barrie's intercession I was invited to drinks at The Lodge to welcome the Sri Lankans and the plan was that I would then stroll down to dinner at Manuka with Tim to discuss the cricket.

However, the invitation specified that military members were to wear service dress and this gave me pause to think about going on to dinner.

While it looks sharp, service dress with full embellishments is not especially comfortable, particularly when it involves sitting through a long formal dinner. So I resolved to give the dinner a miss.

I soon regretted this decision. As I was shuffling along in the receiving line to be welcomed by the Prime Minister I stumbled across Gideon Haigh heading in the opposite direction. He was the guest speaker at the dinner. Had I known this I would not have missed it for quids.

We simultaneously burst out laughing at one another's attire while pointing at one another like delinquent schoolboys. 'Check you out!' we each blurted. I suspect that my long hair and casual dress over summer had inspired some doubts as to whether I was really in the Army, while for his part Gideon takes enormous pride in never wearing a collar and tie. This has been the source of contention on the ABC television show *Offsiders* where his insistence on wearing a T-shirt makes fitting him up with a microphone a challenge. Barrie Cassidy subsequently offered me a handsome reward for an incriminating photo of Gideon in his suit. But acting on the aphorism that what happens on tour stays on tour, I preserved his privacy. Indeed we both lit up at seeing one another. Neither of us had been to the one-day games and I think we each drew nostalgic comfort from memories of the Test series in the media box at various grounds.

However, for me the highlight of the evening was the chance encounter with the Prime Minister. I was deep in conversation with Michael Cooney towards the end of the evening when she strolled over. Her opening gambit revealed two things: she is a consummate politician, and she is easy and informal company. I was instinctively drawn to her and found the intensity of the animosity directed at her by the public and media inexplicable upon actually meeting her.

She said, 'That blog photo doesn't do you justice'. This was her way of subtly rebutting Tony Walker's claim that she had not actually read the civil war material for herself and a guaranteed way to make a man in the afternoon of life pretty much assume the consistency of putty.

'You're better in person yourself.' I immediately felt gauche and quickly apologised saying the Chief of the Army would not be thrilled to learn I had flirted with the Prime Minister. It must be said however, that she is a striking looking woman that television does not show to advantage. She has the most remarkably translucent skin. It makes her quite arresting in person. She laughed this off before asking, 'How do you and Cooney know one another?'

'I think Christopher Pearson introduced us.'

At the mention of her fierce critic and close friend of Tony Abbott she mirthfully rolled her eyes. 'Don't tell me any more!' Her laughter and sense of mirth is infectious and never seemed to be far from the surface.

I put my request direct to her that I would like a chat at some point about broader Australia–India issues before I put this story to bed. She was very gracious, turning to Cooney saying, 'We should be able to work that out?'

Then she looked at me with a wry smile and said, 'We have a bit on our plate at the moment. I hope you are not in a hurry.'

'I read the papers. I know it is tough. May I stay in touch with the staff and work it out?'

'Sure. Aren't you going to dinner with Tim?'

'No, not dressed like this. But it was nice to be invited. I'll probably regret it. I nearly didn't go to the Bradman Oration and would have kicked myself if I had missed that speech by Dravid.'

'That was very good speech.' I gave her another mental tick. 'Good luck.' I meant it.

With that I took my leave. Finally I had managed to track down the elusive Prime Minister and put my request about an interview directly to her. It had been worth the wait. This indeed was a summer of strange coincidences. Sadly, events transpired and this interview never took place. Yet again I left a summer cricket function and walked into a gloomy, drizzly Canberra evening, this time puzzled at the chasm between the public image of the Prime Minister and her charm in person. The scheduled Prime Minister's XI fixture against Sri Lanka was cancelled without a ball being bowled. It was not however, an omen. She won a leadership ballot handsomely later in the month, though at the time of sending this work to print her hold on the leadership of her party still seems tenuous.

Dougie brought up his century and exactly 100th personal run in the session by depositing Bob Willis on the other side of the rope off the very last ball of the day. (News Ltd © Newspix)

9. Perth and a Real Fremantle Doctor

Adam Gilchrist simply shredded an English attack here in December 2006.

Tours of Australia had the potential to degenerate into something akin to the death spiral of a stricken aircraft.

She [Carmen Lawrence] is serious about the nexus between scholarship and public policy.

It was the Australian captain Steve Waugh who popularised the term 'mental disintegration' to describe the steady erosion of the cohesion of Australia's cricketing opponents, especially when they were touring in this country. During the Waugh era Australia were ruthless opponents and the country itself provided an austere and demanding environment, which added to the pressure on touring teams. Australia provided the most severe inquisition of international cricket with a potent combination of human, climatic and natural factors all conspiring against visitors.

The cumulative effect of the relentless stress produced by high quality opponents—even among the state teams—and the hot, hard grounds was enough to sap the will of any visiting team that did not possess abundant mental toughness. Tours of Australia had the potential to degenerate into something akin to the death spiral of a stricken aircraft.

Minor flaws were exposed and then exploited, leading to catastrophic failure and ultimately a nosedive to oblivion. Clausewitz would have referred to this as undermining the centre of gravity of the enemy. Such was the fate of England in 2006–07.

This type of inglorious capitulation had become the defining characteristic of most English touring teams to Australia after 1986. Of course, England had extracted vengeance at home in 2009 and utterly humiliated Australia on its own soil in 2010–11. However, as India headed to Perth in January 2012, there seemed to be a very real risk that they were on the verge of unravelling on the way to a 4–0 whitewash—an exact demoralising repeat of their disastrous tour of England in 2011.

Perth is obviously a long way from other Australian capital cities and is isolated by the largest Australian desert. Travelling, whether by land or air, requires thought and preparation and the WACA ground epitomises this. With its sun-baked playing strip it is physically challenging for Australia's Test opponents and has earned the reputation for being especially fast and producing threatening bounce. But it is not just the distance that has to be travelled, or the physical challenges of its environment that is the key to the WACA Test. This Test fixture has, over time, developed a mystique of its own. It has come to embody not just the physical, but also the mental disintegration of Australia's cricket opponents, destabilising if not completely disintegrating their centre of gravity.

This mystique stirs the imagination, no more so than for the visiting media who often reduce this Test's uniqueness to hackneyed Hollywood 'Wild West' clichés. The 'Western' in front of Australia invariably ensures that reports of matches at the rustic little ground are sprinkled with metaphors of gunfights and shootouts at the O.K. Corral. A Test at the WACA customarily constitutes a 'High Noon' for whichever team is under pressure at that point of a series, with batteries of rival fast bowlers riding into town to stare one another down like the Earps and the Clantons.

And then there is the perennial insult to genuine locals delivered by visiting commentators who jostle to be the first to describe the afternoon sea breeze as the 'Fremantle Doctor'. More than one Western Australian I spoke to expressed their irritation each time it is uttered by a blow-in seeking to sound authentic. As it turned out I had a very stimulating encounter with a real Fremantle Doctor during this Test, but more of her later.

Back to the gunslinging metaphors. As with all clichés, there is at least a grain of truth in them. Genuinely fast bowlers can generally extract more bounce from the Perth strip than from most Australian pitches. Yet, despite its reputation as a fast-bowling nirvana, it has also produced some very swift scoring. Adam Gilchrist simply shredded an English attack here in December 2006, scoring the second fastest century in Test cricket off a mere 59 balls, while West Indians Roy Fredericks in 1975 and Chris Gayle in 2009 blasted their way into triple figures off 71 and 70 balls respectively. The pair each launched violent assaults on very capable attacks. Fredericks thrashed the vaunted Lillee–Thomson duo to pave the way for the only West Indies win of the 1975–76 series, while Gayle cleared the boundary rope six times in an innings of cyclonic ferocity which only narrowly failed to steer his side to victory.

Doug Walters' feat in scoring exactly 100 runs in the final session of the second day of the Perth Test against England in December 1974 is etched in Australian cricket mythology. Dougie brought up his century and exactly 100th personal run in the session by depositing Bob Willis on the other side of the rope off the very last ball of the day. I saw Dougie's heave over the rope at the WACA live on television. That was the summer that colour television was being rolled out to Australia. While I watched the majority of the Perth Test on our antique family Motorola, I actually saw the moment when Australia reclaimed The Ashes in vivid colour through the window of an electrical goods store in an arcade in Surfers Paradise in January 1975.

Televised coverage of Test cricket only really arrived in the summer of 1970–71 when Ray Illingworth's team seized The Ashes from Australia. For the first time the ABC telecast the whole of each day's play from every venue rather than just the final session, with even that often denied to the host city. Those early black-and-white broadcasts would probably arouse mirth or pity among today's cricket audience. They seem incredibly antiquarian when viewed now.

To his great credit Kerry Packer later revolutionised the coverage of cricket, but in 1970 there was only a single camera so every second over was viewed from behind the batsman's back. The replays were rudimentary and shed little light on what had happened especially in the event of a sharp catch in the gully, which was invariably outside the scope of the lens. After much excited shouting from Norman 'Nugget' May, we would be treated to a replay, which generally showed the batsman flashing at a ball followed by some shaky camera-work which revealed a group of grinning fieldsmen ruffling the hair of the catcher. They could usually capture a clean bowled, but compared to today's coverage it was laughably basic.

While Norman May and Frank Tyson provided agreeable and incisive commentary, even then I preferred to turn down the sound and listen to the radio description of play. The game was really not the same without McGilvray. These days, when I am cursing the third replay of a routine leave outside off stump and the interminable reminiscences of Tony Greig, I remind myself what watching cricket was like that year when John Snow turned the Test series into a coconut shy and the favoured shot of the Australian top order was a hasty squat with bat perpendicular to avoid a bouncer. Not surprisingly, such uninterrupted television coverage fuelled the family addiction to cricket. We took our sustenance during the scheduled breaks in play and I barely missed a ball of that series. Well, there was one significant ball we did miss. In the very first Test ever played on the WACA ground, a tall elegant right-hander by the name of Greg Chappell made his debut for Australia against England. With Australia reeling before a new-ball attack, as they so often were in the series, he joined a brave, underrated Victorian named Ian Redpath. The Australians staggered from 3/17 to 5/107 before Chappell and Redpath stabilised the innings. Redpath scored an impeccable 171, but Chappell, one of the most perfect stylists ever to play Test cricket, scored a century on debut. He took a long time to get off the mark and grafted through an ordeal by fire at the hands of Snow, Shuttleworth and Lever on the way to his maiden Test century. He took an excruciating 48 minutes to register his first run but hit his last 60 runs in only 13 overs.

With the largest television audience in Australian history on the edge of its seats urging Chappell on, the ABC, in a display of bureaucratic buffoonery that would have made an East Berlin border guard appear flexible, returned to normal programming in the eastern states. In Lincoln Tyner's wonderful documentary, *Cricket in the '70s: The Chappell Era*, Ian Chappell recalled that the viewers in the east, who were three hours ahead of Perth local time, were obliged to sit through the evening news. I can remember the collective groan going through our living room as the cricket coverage was abandoned with Greg Chappell in the 90s. As a family we were loyal supporters of the ABC, especially their authoritative evening news bulletin, but this was a programming judgement of the kind that in later years prompted Kerry Packer to call Channel Nine and profanely terminate the services of whichever idiot had made a decision that had caused his ire. On this occasion I would have gratefully found a spot for Packer as chairman of the ABC. As it turned out we got to see the replay of Chappell clipping Ken Shuttleworth for 2 through mid-on thirty minutes after it had happened. I recently watched it again and recognised the boyishly chirpy voice of Drew Morphett describing the shot from the commentary position. He sounds no different today. Neither Chappell's nor Redpath's tons were in the rapid-fire category of those mentioned earlier, as vital as they were to Australia's survival on that occasion.

Of those lightning centuries on the WACA, the feats of Gayle and Fredericks demand the most respect as they were achieved by opening batsmen who stared down the fabled WACA bounce at its most fierce. In the Perth 2012 Test, David Warner synthesised all of the most remarkable elements of these innings, reaching his century as an opener off just 69 balls and bringing it up with a brutal six off Vinay Kumar in the manner of Doug Walters.

It was an extraordinary innings and one that quelled any doubts about his capacity to thrive in the long form of the game. Setting the Australian cricketing scene alight he blasted 89 off only 43 balls against South Africa in a Twenty20 match at the MCG in January 2009. Australia had slumped to its first home Test series defeat in sixteen years against South Africa the previous month and the media and public alike were thirsty for the next messiah. Warner's innings dripped with disdain for the South Africans and seemed to promise much more. I might add in passing that it is the only

Twenty20 innings that I have watched live that I can actually recall with any precision. I watch both the shorter forms of the game the way I enjoy music in the elevator riding to the top of a very tall building—it makes quite a pleasant background noise, but please remind me which version of something of true merit it was.

As for Warner, he has exorbitant natural gifts of hand and eye, and his batting is complemented by his freakish catching and throwing. He generates quite explosive power through his forearms and has an ability to jolt the ball with a short-armed punch that, more often than not, sees it race along the ground. Interestingly, for a player who excels in the Twenty20 format, he lofts surprisingly few shots. But until that brutal 180 in Perth against the hapless Indians there were still unresolved questions as to whether he really was a Test opener. Granted, he had carried his bat in Hobart amid a woeful Australian capitulation, but I was unconvinced by him until Perth. Nor was he in terrific form going into that match. Gideon Haigh told me that he had watched Warner in the nets the day before the Test. Here were his impressions:

> A batsman like Warner need only be slightly astray in his timing to look entirely wretched—and Warner did. He barely hit a ball in the middle; he was bowled several times. It wasn't just me that noticed it either. Onlookers around me were shaking their heads and rolling their eyes. His record in Perth before the Test was poor, and I suspect that bore on his mind. Perth gets in your head; a year earlier, Phil Hughes had been completely psyched out by the shade and hardness of the pitch.
>
> What made Warner's innings notable was that after scratching around for his first dozen balls, he just threw the kitchen sink at it. It wasn't completely indiscriminate: he went straight, in view of these being the WACA's shortest boundaries. He also played

vertical or horizontal bat shots—it's the in-between ones that get you into trouble at the WACA because of the extra bounce. The most telling moment, I thought, was in the last over, bowled by Zaheer, when he decided to play for stumps. He played defensively and missed all six deliveries. He became again, briefly, the anxious novice that I'd seen in the nets. Next morning he came out and teed off again. Fascinating approach to batsmanship. May not work against spin—and it didn't in Adelaide.

I thought the interesting thing about Warner was that he began the game in such terrible form, and decided on a shit-or-bust response. It was counter-intuitive, and quite West Australian in its way, like Bondy borrowing against an already overstretched balance sheet.

I take the conservative view that quick runs are not as important as the timeless virtues of taking the shine off the ball and shielding the number three from the most potent exertions of the opening bowling. In that regard I believe Ed Cowan is an ideal Test opener with sound technique and an implacable temperament who can secure his end while others flourish. Perhaps I am simply old-fashioned, but those are the qualities I look for in an opener. Through gritted teeth I will occasionally concede that, in my lifetime, the two men who possessed them in greatest abundance have been Geoffrey Boycott and Bill Lawry. But nothing can detract from that innings of Warner's. It was a violent rampage that was both symptom and cause of the mental disintegration of the Indian team on its tour of Australia in 2011–12. The chatter on the field divulged the extent to which the Indians had surrendered. Evidently Virat Kholi and Ishant Sharma were reduced to issuing dire warnings of the fate that awaited the Australians when next they toured India where the pitches would be less conducive to their battery of pacemen. That is the rough equivalent of lying bleeding on the footpath and warning the bloke standing over you that your big brother can fight.

Both teams arrived in Perth having won their last Test matches at the WACA. India won the third Test of their last Australian tour here in January 2008. Perth was also the scene of the only Australian victory against Andrew Strauss's men in the Ashes series of 2010–11. In one of those infrequent spells that label him as an enigma rather than an impostor, Mitchell Johnson ripped the heart out of the English batting order to bowl Australia back into the match after another insipid batting performance. Johnson bowled very fast and seemed to have the ball on a string. Briefly, that customary process of expediting the mental disintegration of the tourists seemed to have been resumed after an inexplicable hiatus over the final two days in Brisbane and the entire Adelaide Test. Australia arrived in Perth having taken six English wickets for 1137 runs over England's last two innings. Mitchell Johnson scythed through them, apparently restoring the status quo. But it turned out to be an aberration. By the end of the series it was the Australians whose psychologists and pharmacists were groping for palliatives. The Argus Review into the parlous state of Australian cricket was the response to this calamity.

Likewise, India nursed happy memories of their last appearance against Australia at the WACA in 2008. They had defied the predictions of mental disintegration after losing the spiteful SCG Test in January and bounced back to vanquish Australia in Perth. In that Test Irfan Pathan and Ishant Sharma gave the Australians a dose of their own medicine. They had teetered on the brink of the fabled mental disintegration after collapsing precipitately in Sydney. In that rancorous encounter a draw had seemed quite likely before India lost wickets in a flurry to a seemingly innocuous Michael Clarke. But in Perth they refused to be intimidated and India prevailed. But these memories of Indian resilience in 2008 were quashed before lunch on the first day of this year's clash.

The foreboding that their top order had been shell-shocked by the Australian pace attack in Melbourne and Sydney expressed on my blog was vindicated when, having been inserted on the opening morning by Michael Clarke, the visitors were scuttled for a paltry 161, losing their last six wickets for just 30 runs.

Steve Waugh would have recognised the symptoms. The Test match was effectively over by stumps on the first day, by which time Australia had reached 149 without loss. Moreover, Cowan and Warner went on with the task the next day compiling an opening stand of 214 to ensure that India's best prognosis was for a draw, and that this slimmest of hopes could only be achieved by occupying the crease for more than two full days in their second innings. At no stage of the summer—apart from the stands between Dravid and Tendulkar in Melbourne and Tendulkar and Laxman in Sydney—did the Indian batting order inspire confidence that they could defy the Australian attack for such a sustained period. That Cowan–Warner opening stand was easily Australia's best against India at the WACA and fell just three short of Australia's best ever against India—the 217 by David Boon and Geoff Marsh in Sydney in 1986.

In Perth the younger Marsh failed yet again, falling for 11 to Yadav who had displayed considerable courage by hurling himself at the rampant Australian openers for little return for nearly two sessions. Indeed, the subsequent Australian batting was unimpressive and tapered away from 0/214 to all out for 369, of which the cumulative contribution of Marsh and the Sydney plunderers—Clarke, Ponting and Hussey—was a mere 50 runs. Yet it was enough and with hindsight it was always going to be enough. India was yielding to mental disintegration. You could sense it in the lack of zeal in India's out cricket and their listless body language—they had succumbed to the processes of mental disintegration. After Sydney, the dream of a win over Australia in Australia was dead. By the end of their first day in Perth, their grip on the Border–Gavaskar Trophy had slipped to that of a technicality, and by the end of the second day they were well on the way to losing their self-respect. At stumps on the second evening India was 4/88 and poised to lose by an innings inside three days. By now the mental disintegration was gathering pace and my sense was that the series was effectively over. Moreover, their failure to reach 200 in either innings in Perth was rendered all the more indefensible as the Australian attack was, by the standards of the Sydney Test, depleted.

The wrecker, Pattinson, was out with an injury, his place having been taken by Mitchell Starc with Ryan Harris providing the mandatory fourth prong of the WACA pace attack. Yet again, the Australians hunted as a pack with all the fast bowlers taking wickets at vital stages. I thought Hilfenhaus was the pick of them though they all bowled well. In particular, Starc had improved on his somewhat pedestrian debut at the Gabba. He suddenly looked like everything that Australia had hoped Mitchell Johnson might be—a left-arm quick capable of late movement off a good length. He snared Tendulkar in the second Indian innings to confirm that he belonged at this level. Over the summer I thought some of his spells in the limited over matches were genuinely hostile and augured well for his development. If Shakespeare was correct in Henry V that 'All things are ready, if our minds be so' then Starc does not seem to be burdened by the strange mental affliction that has plagued Johnson's career and made him the subject of more amateur psychological analysis by the media than any other Australian cricketer in my memory. Starc's mind seemed ready for the fray in Perth and he bowled well.

Ryan Harris's body rather than his mind has perennially been his problem. He is a wonderful competitor with all the elements that comprise a formidable Test fast bowler. He generates real heat and he is relentlessly at the batsman off a good length. He has a broad, beaming face that conceals a classic fast bowler's aggressive temperament and the body of a rugby back-rower, but his superficial robustness cannot conceal a defect in his knees that has rendered him injury prone. His bulk masks a surprising fragility. Too often he has enticingly produced an explosive spell in a Test before going on indefinite sick leave. Sadly it appears he will play fewer Tests than his ability warrants. In Perth he was at his hostile best dismissing Tendulkar cheaply, which his captain badly needed after offering first use of the wicket to an opponent.

If one characteristic defined the Australian bowling effort against India all summer it was their consistent adherence to a fuller length around the line of the fifth stump. Those close to the team ascribed most of the credit for this improvement to fast bowling coach Craig McDermott. It worked, whatever the explanation. Tendulkar, Gambhir and Sehwag were consistently left groping outside off stump at quick deliveries leaving them. The statistics were brutally revealing. In eight completed innings last summer, India failed to reach 200 on four occasions and their opening partnerships were uniformly paltry, never reaching 30.

As in Sydney, the anticlimactic nature of the cricket was compensated for by some very enjoyable social encounters and the camaraderie of the media contingent among whom I was now feeling quite at home. And the WACA is a lovely ground, smaller and more intimate than the MCG and SCG. Moreover, for the first time in the series I felt as though I was in the midst of a classic Australian summer with its scorching heat and aromas of barbecued beef, insect repellent and sunscreen. The heat in Perth was searing.

On the first day I made my way to the media box, which was an interesting improvised structure made of canvas supported by metal scaffolding. Military life has inured me to working under canvas in considerably more adverse conditions than this, but the press position was completely open to the elements with no windows and hence the breeze constantly eddied though. While this provided natural air conditioning, it made writing difficult if you were seated in the very front row. After an hour I would have readily swapped this for the luxury of my previous overflow area in the Brewongle Stand in Sydney. My seat was exposed to the breeze, which lifted the butcher's paper under my computer into my face at the most inopportune moments and blew my rough handwritten notes away several times.

Some compensation was provided by the immediate presence of Sam and Jarrod—The Two Chucks—to my immediate right, and Gideon Haigh, Smithy and Peter Lalor just behind me. The banter lifted morale and offset the physical inconvenience. Likewise, Harini, Samip, Boria and a young man called Mathew T. George, with whom I had enjoyed some stimulating discussions about the Indian team in Sydney, were all seated nearby. Pretty soon we were engrossed in play under the cloudless, idyllic Perth sky. I soon realised how sensuous an experience watching cricket at the WACA can be. Being exposed to the elements one hears the steady buzz of the crowd and the contact of bat on ball is energising and creates an electric atmosphere.

While earlier I scorned the practice of journalists to so readily apply Western and gunslinger metaphors to WACA Tests, I must concede that Perth has a frontier town aspect. It is a long way from the eastern states, and while I wasn't expecting tumbleweeds to blow down the streets or the pubs to have hinged saloon-like wooden doors, there was an atmosphere of rambunctious optimism and fast money that puts the whole Western Australian crony capitalism scandals of the 1980s in context. The Members' bar must be the least formal of any Australian ground with shorts and yachting shoes the norm. Snobs would sniff at the fast money ambience of all this, but after the cool wet summer I had left in the eastern states I revelled in the heat of an authentic Australian summer and the palpable energy of a boom town. Having been an official of the Australian Labor Party I have never been uncomfortable in the presence of fast money or spivs.

After lunch on day one in Perth I strayed into the area provided for the broadcast media in the Lillee–Marsh Stand while I was wandering around to get the feel of the WACA. It turned out that the marquee was purely for the print media. Jarrod turned around and winked at me. He had dropped onto the fact that our passes entitled us to locate ourselves in a small room adjacent to the ABC box just along the corridor from the Channel Nine position. It quickly became apparent this was an overflow area for those with enough initiative to seize it and it had the prized cricket-watching advantage of being right behind the bowler's arm.

'Mate, is it okay to be in here?' I inquired.

'No one has thrown me out yet', he beamed.

'Connectivity good?'

'Perfect.'

'I'll be right back!' I said as I quickly went to retrieve my laptop from the Antiguan-style marquee. I even made a mental note that the lavish remains of the Channel Nine lunch were for once not under the vigilant eye of a private security guard. I was starting to like Perth more by the minute.

On my return Sam and Jarrod were chatting to Harsha Bhogle, just about my favourite cricket broadcaster and invariably the Indian commentator seconded to the ABC radio team for every Indian tour in recent memory. His love of the game and indefatigable optimism, no matter how dire the plight of his countrymen, also makes him beloved among Australian listeners. The question I was most asked by cricket lovers with whom I discussed my travels as part of the media road show was, 'What was Harsha like?' Sadly I can only say that I would have liked to be able to answer more authoritatively based on a longer exposure to him. However, in our fleeting encounter after being introduced by Jarrod, he seemed to be the same in person as he is on air—a genial, self-effacing gentleman. His cheeriness was infectious.

No sooner had I left Jarrod and Harsha to their chat than Jim Maxwell sidled in from his latest on-air segment. I had chatted to him before we boarded our flight to Perth in Sydney the day before the Test and we had exchanged pleasantries in the Qantas club. He was always encouraging about the story I was writing and he asked about its progress. On this occasion Jim had come to the break-out area for one chat in particular. Seated behind a computer screen to our rear was the legendary Australian cricket captain and Channel Nine commentator, Ian Chappell. I had seen Chappelli, as he is fondly known at all the Test grounds, over the summer and he appeared to have an admirable work ethic. Between his on-air commitments he would work the phones like any journalist and devoted considerable time to research on various cricket sites.

Chappell's success as Australian skipper had even influenced the categorisation of the era in which he had played. That golden age of triumph is still recalled fondly by those of us lived through it as 'The Chappell Era'. While he was blessed with some outstanding players and perhaps the deadliest fast-bowling pairing Australia has ever fielded, Chappell was indisputably a superb captain. His instinct for the game

was flawless and he had the charisma of a born leader. He moulded
a great team and by sheer force of personality led them to the top of
world cricket. These qualities are still manifest in his demeanour and
conversation. I will recount his views of this particular Indian summer
in more detail later, but the account that follows provided one of my
favourite memories of the Perth test.

After Jim Maxwell wandered in holding a cup of tea and a snack
he graciously introduced me to Chappell with, 'Do you know Malcolm
McGregor?'

'No.' After the obligatory handshakes, Chappelli asked, 'Who are
you working for?' I explained the connection to *The Spectator* and that I
was working on a book. I decided not to look this gift horse in the mouth.
'Is there any way I could have a yarn to you about cricket in general and
this tour for the book?'

'Yeah sure. This isn't going to go much longer. Are you going to
Adelaide?'

'Indeed.'

'Well you know where to find me. Just come and look me up and we'll
have a yarn.' I was extremely pleased to have made this connection. I had
been reading Chappell's columns in the News Limited papers all summer
and had been impressed with his analysis throughout. He had been almost
alone in predicting that the vaunted Indian batting order would struggle
during the series. And he had also been one of my boyhood heroes. So the
opportunity of an extended discussion with him exercised dual appeal.

These pleasantries dispensed with, Maxwell inquired of Chappell:

'Did you really describe Vinay Kumar as the worst Test cricket
bowler that you had ever seen yesterday?' Kumar had taken some terrible
stick, especially from Warner, and had the dubious distinction of having

delivered the ball that had been clouted 98 yards over the boundary to give the young left-hander his century.

'Yeah, bloody oath I did.'

Chappell has a very democratic demeanour and I had noticed that he seemed to enjoy chatting with media colleagues. I had been watching him since Brisbane and he did not give off the unapproachable vibe of some of the network stars. So I decided to buy into this discussion. I was perhaps a little too eager to ventilate my cricket knowledge after a summer of listening to some incredible trivia geniuses in full flight.

'Come on mate, you were Johnny Watkins's captain!'

Jim Maxwell guffawed and sighed, 'Poor old Johnny—I wonder what ever became of him.'

Chappelli quickly qualified his assessment of Vinay Kumar: 'Well I meant the worst medium pacer'.

He then went on to tell the story of how poor Johnny Watkins made his Forrest Gump debut for Australia against Pakistan in Sydney in January 1973. Chappelli is one of the most naturally gifted communicators I have met. He speaks in vivid pictures in a way that I have only heard one other Australian do with the same power—Paul Keating. Ian Chappell is a wonderful raconteur. He is also absolutely authentic, which explains his charm and charisma as a captain. He is direct and he speaks plainly and with conviction. His rendition of the story of how an almost completely unknown leg-spin bowler was plucked from the Newcastle club competition to play for Australia had Jim Maxwell and myself in descending into gales of laughter and warrants retelling at some length. Chappell went on:

> Poor old Watto. You know Harv [Neil Harvey the then chairman of the Australian selection panel] rang me and said, 'Now I know you

are probably a bit surprised about this but we think this bloke has potential.'

I said, 'Harv, what the hell makes you think that? This bloke's not even a bloody Shield cricketer!'

'Well he's taken wickets in Shield cricket. He got you and Greg in a match in Newcastle didn't he?'

'Yeah and did you see how? We were chasing quick runs and were trying to hit him out of the park!'

Chappell shook his head thirty-nine years later with the memory of the exasperation he had felt at being given J.R. Watkins as his front-line spinner in a Test. Whatever ability Watkins may have possessed deserted him when he arrived in the Test team. His short spell at the bowling crease was cringe-inducing. He was pulled out of the attack after a mere six overs, having delivered a spate of wides and long hops that bewildered even the Pakistani batsmen. As Martin Williamson recalled of that disastrous debut:

> He struggled with the ball, but a career-best 36 helped the Aussies set up an unlikely victory. Watkins went on the West Indian tour that followed, but wasn't risked in the Tests, and hardly played at all. Keith Stackpole dubbed him 'possibly the luckiest player ever to represent Australia', and recalled how in one of the tour games 'he almost hit the square-leg umpire with the widest full-toss I've seen.' His always-fragile confidence fractured, Watkins never played first-class cricket again.

I can recall watching that gutsy 36 from John Watkins. He and Bob Massie combined to add 83 for Australia's ninth wicket. Those runs actually won the match because the pair came together with Australia leading by only 85 in its second innings. They gave Lillee, Massie and Walker just enough to bowl at, with Tangles taking 6/15 in a wonderful display of swing bowling, ably supported by Lillee who bowled uninterrupted from one end throughout the Pakistani innings to claim 3/68 off 23 overs. The great D.K. Lillee was never quite the same man or bowler again. His serious back injuries that subsequently forced him out of the 1973 tour of the West Indies dated from this epic performance. He staged a remarkable comeback through a demanding physical regime, but he was a more subtle and less explosive bowler after the 11th of January 1973. One wonders whether James Pattinson, Shane Watson, Ryan Harris and Pat Cummins might not profit from a few tips from Lillee as to how to enhance their endurance.

With that, Jim Maxwell left us and returned to the ABC box and Chappelli resumed his seat behind the computer. It had been an amusing and utterly unexpected encounter. And as he so often was on cricket matters, Chappell was correct about the match ending prematurely. India was only able to take the match into the first over after lunch on the third day. Mental disintegration indeed.

Having already written my blog commending the approach of Ulysses S. Grant to the Indians, I had a free evening in Perth. I had not visited the city for some time though at one point in the late 1990s had been close to Kim Beazley, Carmen Lawrence and Geoff Gallop. On this scorching, cloudless Perth day, Kim Beazley was snowbound far away in Washington DC. For a time, when I wrote the odd speech for him, we used to discuss Australian and British politics, especially his friendship with Tony Blair from their days at Oxford. I used to visit Kim at his lovely bungalow in South Perth. In those days we were both partial to Churchill cigars and would while away hours on his verandah discussing Civil War historiography.

Geoff Gallop had since moved east and taken up a position at the University of Sydney. Of my old comrades, only Carmen Lawrence remained and I had not spoken to her since she left the Parliament ahead of the 2007 election. We had not fallen out, but our lives had taken vastly divergent paths. When I was the token leftist on the *Financial Review*'s opinion page we had grown quite close and I often discussed issues of public policy with her. Before it became conventional wisdom, we had both formed the view that the trade union bloc vote was exercising a pernicious effect on internal democracy within the ALP and that too many hacks were being pushed into Parliament. She once shared with me her view that the famed engine room of the Australian Labor Party was in terminal decline: 'You can only inbreed for so long before the damage becomes permanent. We are seeing that in New South Wales now where the cronyism and inbreeding has fatally damaged the institution and undermined the calibre of the people they are sending to Canberra'. For the record, she expressed that opinion in 1999, a long time before the malaise in the New South Wales branch of the ALP provided such low-hanging fruit for self-styled public intellectuals and political columnists. Of course such views coming from a so-called Labor 'rat' on my part were easily dismissed. When I ridiculed the bid by New South Wales Right journeyman John Della Bosca—surely the most overrated politician of my generation—to run for the federal presidency of the ALP, my views were readily dismissed. When he subsequently imploded over an on-the-record lunch with Maxine McKew of *The Bulletin* he thoroughly vindicated my low opinion.

Sadly, I placed a serious strain on my relationship with Kim Beazley when I lampooned the ALP National Conference in my column in *The Australian* saying that it, 'presides over a social democrat party that was never socialist, and is now not even democratic'. Over time I concluded that reconciliation with the ALP was simply never going to happen. When he sought to have Jack Lang readmitted to the party, Paul Keating urged it not to allow itself to become a party of 'of great and unyielding spite'. From my perspective it is and probably always will be that. While I regretted my falling out with it, which occurred at a time when I was not in the best of mental health, I ultimately felt more comfortable supporting the conservatives. Necessity and conviction came into alignment over time. As the years elapsed I became more conservative on some issues. Such a passage from the left is not uncommon among conservatives who have written in the Australian media. Padraic McGuinness, Keith Windschuttle and Christopher Pearson spring readily to mind. Similarly, the born-again neo-conservatism of the late Christopher Hitchens horrified his former comrades on the far left. Happily, my friendship with Beazley resumed when he left the Parliament and he generously agreed to serve on the board of the *Australian Army Journal* of which I was editor. He was always too nice a bloke to bear grudges and I still deeply value his friendship.

Carmen Lawrence has not become more conservative with the passage of the years. Rather, I suspect she is more left wing now than she was as a member of the Keating government. Sadly, I progressively saw less of Carmen as my relationship with the ALP ceased. Indeed, she must have been stunned at my decision to return to military service in late 1999. Yet, as with Beazley and Gallop, she was a big enough person to accommodate our differences. Our contact, though less frequent, has always been amicable and within minutes of my impulsively picking up the phone to see whether she was available for a last minute dinner, I remembered why I had always so enjoyed her company.

She is luminously intelligent and has a wicked sense of humour, which she only unmasks among those she trusts. And after the bruising experience she had in politics, especially in 1995, she is slow to take people into her confidence. But she is terrific company.

Moreover, she is easily the most intellectually gifted person that I met in my time in politics. There are plenty who have been able to convince a credulous, poorly read media profession that they are scholars or public intellectuals who just happen to be tied down in the legislature because the public interest demands it. This applies especially to the veritable army of alleged Civil War 'historians' produced by the New South Wales Labor Party over the years.

Carmen Lawrence however is the real deal. She is a genuine intellectual with a record of serious scholarship. So too, it must be noted, is Geoff Gallop. Carmen reads voraciously and diversely and has maintained a deep interest in social, political and economic trends both here and overseas. She is a serious about the nexus between scholarship and public policy and any conversation with her demands measured argument and evidence rather than slogans and clichés. What makes exchanges with her even more agreeable is that she is a good listener. She can accept another viewpoint and give you time to outline a case. She would be a stunning tutor in the Oxford system.

Likewise, she never ceases to surprise me with her eclectic tastes in reading and friends. Some years back Kim Beazley urged me to read a book called *Stalingrad* by the British writer Antony Beevor. It was a powerful, superbly written book—military history at its very best.

'Mate, how did you get on to that bloke?' I enquired of the big genial Western Australian one night over curry at the Shalimar restaurant, our favourite Canberra haunt. 'Carmen Lawrence put me on to it.'

Right. The most anti-war politician in the ALP—if not the Parliament—had read Beevor's gruesome account of the siege of Stalingrad before either of us who rather prided ourselves on being steeped in such literature.

So as my taxi took me from the Rydges in the heart of Perth to Carmen's charming town house in Fremantle, I reminisced about those days when I was very actively engaged in politics. A full moon hung low over the rim of the Indian Ocean making me homesick, so I was looking forward to the company of an old mate. I had outlined my ideas about the story I was writing to her over the phone and sent her a link to my blog as we arranged dinner. Nor was I averse to eating a home-cooked meal after the cold box lunches provided by the WACA. While it was a lovely ground at which to watch cricket, the hospitality was the worst of all the Test venues. And Carmen is also a better-than-decent cook. So as the taxi clung to the coast my warm sense of anticipation of resuming contact with the real Fremantle Doctor mounted.

The evening was enjoyable for many reasons. There was the quiet joy of spending time with an old mate, indeed restoring a friendship that had possibly lapsed into mutual incomprehension as we found ourselves on opposite sides of arguments over the necessity of United States military operations in Iraq and Afghanistan. The evening also provided valuable inspiration for this book. I obtained my customary intellectual fix from the good doctor. As we sat sipping a pre-dinner drink in her tiny walled garden covered in fragrant vegetation that evoked memories of Umbria but for the familiar Australian aroma of mosquito coil, she challenged my central proposition thus: 'I am not sure that I accept your fatalism about the inexorable march of globalisation or its acceleration. Have you looked at any of the work by people like Jeff Rubin on the return to the local and the particular?'

Jeff Rubin is an American scholar whose core thesis is contained in his book *Why Your World is About to Get a Whole Lot Smaller.* He argues that continuous economic growth underwritten by inexhaustible supplies of cheap oil is simply unsustainable and that the current tempo of globalisation will slow. 'It is possible that there will be a return to the local and the particular and that people will produce and market more of what they need closer to home', Carmel ventured.

This of course was inconvenient for my hypothesis about the impact of globalisation on cricket. I had considered similar research under the rubric of the 'peak oil' phenomenon in relation to the potential patterns of future regional wars, but I resolved to take up Carmen's suggestion about Rubin's work, which sounded a little similar to that of John Ralston Saul. We had both found his writing to be a refreshing counterpoint to the almost universal recitations of neo-liberal economic theories in the 1990s. Useful people these polymaths—they can steer you to an Antony Beevor or a Jeff Rubin. If Rubin is ultimately right, cricket may recover some of what Ed Smith has referred to as its poetic heart. I made a note to read into him before forming my conclusions on the viability of Test cricket. Certainly the game of cricket that had enthralled me as a boy relied on national identity and tribalism rather than the ethos of the global market with its ancillary culture of franchises and celebrity.

On economic matters I still share some of Carmen's views. While she comes to her conclusions from the left, I am now more a paleo-conservative of the variety that produces *The New Criterion*. But it was nice to find common ground again. Indeed we were also in violent agreement about the parlous state of the ALP. Inevitably we discussed the prospects for a leadership challenge in the New Year. Carmen regarded the leadership speculation as a mere distraction from much deeper issues that the party had ignored or suppressed and which demanded urgent action. She was dispassionate in her assessments of both Rudd and Gillard, the latter proving to be a particular disappointment to her over refugee policy.

Their falling-out was fairly acrimonious as Lawrence felt that Gillard had forfeited any claim to be taken seriously as a member of the left through the policy solution she devised to help Labor leave the Tampa debacle behind after the 2001 election. Indeed, in the twilight years of her career and liberated from the constraints of cabinet solidarity, Carmen invested the asylum-seeker issue with considerable significance. To her it was the defining moral issue in the Australia of the first decade of the twenty-first century. She still feels very strongly about it, but has also embraced green causes both in her local area and at the global level.

As the evening unfolded I was amused to learn that we were both now also former ALP members. Carmen had not renewed her membership. With her engaging, slightly shy grin she said, 'I didn't make any grand gesture. But the points I made about the decay of the branch structure turned out to be correct. My ticket lapsed and no one ever got in touch with me about it!' If I had to place a bet on it I suspect that she would be more comfortable in the Greens these days, though she had personally groomed her successor Melissa Parke in Fremantle, the seat once held by John Curtin. And from what I know of the code of personal loyalty that animates Carmen Lawrence, I cannot imagine her undermining her successor.

The evening drew to a close. It had been stimulating and enjoyable. We embraced and promised not to allow four years to elapse until our next dinner. As the cab drove me back to Perth along a moon-drenched coastal road, the driver eyed me appraisingly: 'She very famous that lady back there?'

'Yeah mate, she was once.'

'First lady prime minister right?'

'No mate, she was premier of Western Australia. The current woman, Julia Gillard, is the first woman to be prime minister.'

'You sure?'

'Pretty sure, mate.'

'Well she nice lady that one back there. She speak up for me. Good lady.'

'Yeah, how was that?'

'I am Hazara. I must leave Afghanistan. They want to kill me. She stick up for us.'

'Yeah, she is a good lady. Very brave.'

'How about you—you famous?'

'No mate, I am not famous—just rich.' We both laughed out loud at this corny jest.

'What you talking to her about if you are not famous?'

'Lots of things, but mainly cricket funnily enough.'

'Ah cricket. Australia win easy. Very good.'

'Yeah mate, Australia will win easy.' We slowed to a halt in central Perth. I elected to back my cabbie's prediction and booked the first plane home the following morning.

Ian Chappell ... speaks in clear, vivid imagery,
listening intently to each question ...

10. *Adelaide*

—*brutal, inexorable arithmetic*

'Not this heavy, unremitting silence, marking what must be the lowest point in Indian cricket.'

... the side with the most elephants always loses.

The safe clichés used to describe Lehmann as a likeable larrikin were all too familiar to me from my study of Australian military history.

... Søren Kierkegaard who, I believe, wisely noted that we live life forwards, but understand it backwards.

And so it came to pass that India spiralled to their second consecutive 4–0 drubbing away from home. Sadly, a series that had promised so much petered out with a whimper rather than a bang. As in Sydney, the main damage was done by the veterans of the Australian batting order, Michael Clarke and Ricky Ponting, each of whom scored double centuries. They came together with Australia at 3/84, having been failed yet again by youth, and proceeded to build a massive 386 partnership for the fourth wicket to ensure that the Indian mental disintegration that began in Sydney accelerated towards the end of the series.

As in Sydney, the arithmetic constituted its own brutal, uninterrupted narrative of Indian humiliation. For the loss of just seven first innings wickets, Australia amassed 604 runs, which actually would have been enough to deliver the third consecutive innings defeat to the tourists since their brief flirtation with respectability at the MCG. However, Australian teams have seemed to harbour an almost neurotic reluctance to enforce the follow-on against even the most modest and vulnerable opposition since India drastically turned the tables on them in one of the most extraordinary Test matches ever played in Calcutta in March 2001. It is worth briefly recapitulating the salient facts of that match in which Australia scored a healthy 445 before bundling India out for 171. Steve Waugh enforced the follow-on and Australia seemed to be making satisfactory inroads into the Indian second innings, including the prized scalp of Tendulkar for just 10, the same modest contribution that he had made in the first innings here. Then V.V.S. Laxman and Rahul Dravid came together to construct a partnership of 376 for the fifth wicket as India stormed back into contention with a total of 7/657. The majestic Indian pair first blunted, and then repulsed the Australian attack before methodically dismantling some of the biggest egos in world cricket and disrupting Australia's apparently inexorable progress to its first series win in India since 1969–70 under Bill Lawry.

Michael Clarke had not played in that 2001 series, though it seemed that the 'never make India follow-on' rule had taken on the same sort of canonical status among Australian cricket captains as some of the military truisms that I had learned as a young cadet at Duntroon such as, never invade Russia in the winter, never fight a land war in Asia, and the side with the most elephants always loses. Whatever Clarke's motive, whether it was the presence of those two Indian master craftsmen in their line-up—albeit as mere shadows of their 2001 selves—or whether he simply decided to rest his bowlers from the enervating Adelaide heat, Australia embarked on an ultimately unnecessary second innings to set India 500 to win.

Needless to relate, India fell well short barely making 200, which on this tour had become a significant measure of success. Again the signs of Indian lassitude and acquiescence were all too manifest by stumps on the first day, by which time Australia was strongly positioned at 3/335, with Clarke and Ponting untroubled and looking impregnable. It was clear that Australia could keep India in the field at its discretion under a brutal sun and then, at leisure, wait for the wicket to break up permitting Lyon to wreak havoc in the final innings. That is essentially what ensued, though Siddle strove manfully to extract assistance from a slow, dry track to claim five wickets in India's first innings. And all the fast men again showed resilience and discipline in bowling an impeccable line and length to debunk the popular myth that there is nothing in the Adelaide wicket for pace bowlers, especially after the first session. It was a crushing, embarrassing defeat for India and watching them shuffle with apparent relief to the gallows over the final three days was almost excruciating. They seemed devoid of fight, almost grateful to be put out of their misery. No one summed it up more succinctly than the Indian writer Sharda Ugra who brutally summarised her country's recent performances thus:

> At the end of the Adelaide Test, the India dressing room might have resembled a funeral parlour. All that would have been heard was the snap of 'coffin' lids shutting, the clatter of equipment being packed away and the low murmur of voices—the sounds of the end of the greatest era in Indian Test cricket.
>
> An end of an era is meant to be, at the very least, monumentally resonant, or to carry a few final traces of splendour at least. Not this heavy, unremitting silence, marking what must be the lowest point in Indian cricket.
>
> Between June 1959 and January 1968, India lost 17 consecutive away Tests. It is the worst stretch by any team in history.

Yet Adelaide 2012 marked Indian cricket's rock bottom, because a decade of progress was signed off with a staggering paucity of performance. In an age of abundance—of experience, talent and resources—Indian cricket ended up rattling empty.

With unsparing honesty she delivered an even more ruthless estimate of the degree to which India had been living on the mythology of an ageing batting order long past its use-by date. This caused me to reflect again on how I had ignored certain disquieting signs in the Indians' recent form and the inadequacy of their preparations in Canberra. I was as guilty as any, invoking my trusty predictive device from my days of political writing, of hedging my bets behind the safe cliché, 'too close to call', while waiting for the benefit of hindsight from which to pontificate on the blatantly obvious. Let me be clear: before the series began I thought India would probably win. More of why I arrived at that conclusion below, but Sharda Ugra could have been writing about me personally when she wrote:

> Whether 0–8 was because of injuries and scrambled batting orders in England, or the meticulous evisceration by Australia, India's constant over the previous six months has been the heavy margin of every defeat.
>
> Revitalised by an Ashes success, England were on top of their game, their batting at its peak. At the start of this series, though, Australia had an inexperienced bowling attack, an inconsistent top three, and two middle-order veterans fraying at the edges. They had just lost their first Test at home to New Zealand in 26 years. India brought what selectors, experts and players themselves called their best possible team.
>
> Like uncertain election forecasters, even the most astute analysts believed Australia against India was, 'too close to call'. Too close to call has ended with one team in a rubble.

Of course Sharda Ugra was writing with hindsight from a sombre Indian dressing room in Adelaide. Yet the one pundit who had seen this comprehensive whitewash coming with prophetic clarity was Ian Chappell. Even when Australia looked to be facing another humiliating summer at home after losing to New Zealand in Hobart, he calmly predicted that India would be unable to handle the Australian pace attack under Australian conditions. When I read this prediction before a single ball had been bowled I was inclined to categorise it as 'courageous' in the manner that Sir Humphrey Appleby of *Yes Minister* fame employed the term. While India had been execrable against England during the northern hemisphere summer, Australia had capitulated ignominiously to the same side on its home soil. This definitively ended the era of the *Pax Australiana* in world cricket. We had been trifled with in our own backyard. To me it appeared that Australian cricket had entered a period of relative, if not absolute and terminal, decline and that the earnest recommendations of the Argus Review notwithstanding, the playing depth simply was not there. Too many players—notably Warne and McGrath—had departed in too short a time frame. Add to their departures those of Adam Gilchrist, Damien Martyn, Matthew Hayden and Justin Langer since the last successful Ashes series, and the enormity of the rebuilding project became readily apparent.

Quite simply, against England in 2010–11 we had looked second-rate, deficient both in skills and mental toughness. Our surrender had smacked of incompetence. Even worse, it had at times been supine. During the dark ages after World Series Cricket, Australian teams had been frequently outclassed, but they were never so obviously cowed by their opponents as against Strauss's men. Nor did any of the newly discovered talent seem to be so precociously brilliant as to warrant installing Australia as favourites before the series started. That troubling collapse in Cape Town seemed to me to be a depressingly accurate measure of where we stood against a first-rate cricketing power. While not dismissing the subsequent win in Johannesburg as purely an aberration, I was pessimistic about Australian cricket in November 2011 and felt that the task of rebuilding would be both long and frustrating.

Ian Chappell had a clear-eyed view of Australia's weaknesses, and I was to have the opportunity to discuss them with him at some length. I came away from my chat with the legendary Chapelli deeply impressed with his cricket intellect and his vivid communication skills. Again, given the lack of any real contest in the middle, my most pleasurable memories of the Adelaide Test were comprised of the human interactions off the field and my interview with Ian Chappell was the highlight of these. It came to pass like this.

I arrived in Adelaide from Melbourne early on the first morning of the Test. The Soviet bloc customer service of Qantas had necessitated an overnight stay in Melbourne. There are surprisingly few direct Canberra–Adelaide flights and none that could have got me to the picturesque Adelaide Oval in time for the start of play on Tuesday the 24th of January. My plan to impose a permanent boycott on flying with Qantas that I smugly and loudly proclaimed on my blog in the wake of the Gabba Test had, as they say in the military, not survived contact with the enemy. By the Perth Test, only the Qantas schedule could accommodate my elaborate plans to get to Perth and then return in time for a beach holiday at Bawley Point on the South Coast of New South Wales around the dates that Tritia and I had arranged. And even then I was grateful that the Indians had not forced the issue into the fourth day. So, after an enjoyable chat with Jim Maxwell in the Qantas club on the way to the Perth Test, I slunk on to the plane wearing my Ray-Bans, chin pressed down firmly on my chest, anxious to avoid detection and hoping that my attempt to board did not culminate in my being diverted to an interrogation room where my disparaging remarks about the airline would be laid out on a table before me by Alan Joyce personally. 'Well Mr. McGregor what do you have to say about this?' Of course such egocentric fear was delusional and overestimated the penetration of my blog, whose followers would have been outnumbered by collectors specialising in stamps from the Virgin Islands or Guam, or the crowd at Cricket ACT's Festival of Cricket in Canberra back in December.

Unsurprisingly, I boarded without incident. Emboldened by this I chanced my arm in booking to go to Adelaide with Qantas, who were apparently indifferent to or unaware of my sledging, on a late night flight from Canberra to Melbourne. And I was glad that I had. On the cab rank in Adelaide I encountered Wayne Smith bursting with his customary ebullience and sheer joy at being paid to cover yet another sporting event, and Robert Smith of Agence France-Presse.

Robert was a pleasant and engaging fellow. We had met on the first morning at the Gabba and I had warmed to him immediately. He emanated a quiet, understated calm and his face spread easily into a knowing worldly-wise grin. As men of a certain age, we were past being driven and obsessive about work and hopefully were able to maintain some degree of perspective about the task in hand. This is one of the few benefits of entering the afternoon of life when the initials PSA no longer denote the Prices Surveillance Authority. Robert now lives in the Blue Mountains from where he sallies forth to cover a variety of sporting events. It seemed to me an enviable lifestyle. As we waited for cabs to take us to the Adelaide Oval he told me that he had been covering the Australian Open the previous week and I gave a glowing account of my beach holiday. It was great to see Wayne and Robert and I could feel my enthusiasm returning.

Rising in the dark in Melbourne to get to what promised to be another lopsided Test, I was already feeling pangs of homesickness and wishing we had stayed at Bawley Point to watch the rest of the Australian Open with the lulling sound of the surf outside our window. But I was part of the great cricket roadshow again and as I approached the Adelaide Oval felt the familiar adrenaline rush.

The attendants at the gate gave my media pass perfunctory scrutiny and waved me towards the media centre. No sooner had I entered the elevator to go to the commentary position than I realised that the only other occupants were Ian Chappell and the stunningly attractive Channel Nine sport reporter Roz Kelly. We exchanged nods. To be honest, I was unsure whether he would remember our encounter in Perth. I cleared my throat nervously and ventured, 'Ian—Malcolm McGregor—you said I could have a chat sometime during this Test. Is that still a goer?'

'Yeah mate, I said I'd do it.' There was a hint of impatience in his delivery as though it was self-evident that once he had committed to something it would happen.

'Terrific. When would suit you?'

'Look, today will be pretty busy, but come to the Nine area after about an hour on day two.' To my astonishment he pulled my card out of his pocket and said, 'So it's about the book right?'

'Yeah. A general summary of what had gone wrong for India and what it might mean for Australia's chances in England next year.'

With that the elevator arrived at the media area. If that conversation suggests that we had journeyed to the equivalent of the top of the Empire State Building allow me to disabuse you. The elevators at the Adelaide Oval were incredibly slow and took ages to arrive at the ground floor for a laborious trip of a mere three or four floors. Castro could have delivered one of his medium-length speeches during the ascent. Chappell and Kelly headed into the 'holy of holies' in the Nine box and I turned left toward the print box. By now I was easily able to finish the sentence for the pleasant young woman standing sentry outside the print media room as she explained to me that as a nobody from a weekly magazine ... I need to go to the overflow area. 'Where is that precisely, Miss?' She positively beamed at my passive acquiescence and gave me directions.

I wandered around savouring the sights and sounds of the opening day of an Adelaide Test. It is a very well-appointed ground and the grassed enclosure behind the Members' area reminded me just a little of the Nursery Oval at Lord's. There were food stalls, marquees and live music. Many of the young women were dressed as though they were attending the Spring Racing Carnival in Melbourne. It was an intoxicating atmosphere, enhanced by cloudless azure skies and blast furnace heat. This is what Test cricket at the height of the Australian summer is meant to feel like. Like Perth, Adelaide produced genuine summer heat. After the persistent wet and unseasonable cool of the eastern states in that Indian summer, it was invigorating and lifted my mood.

The mood in the overflow media area was effervescent. By now most of us had become friends of varying degrees of intimacy and at the least I considered every one of this group a likeable colleague. We had developed an easy *esprit de corps* as the 'overflow gang' over recent Tests. I suspect I was not alone in exchanging the salutations with just a little more warmth and energy than usual, as we were all aware that our shared adventure was drawing to a close. Based on the recent performances of the Indians we may just as easily be exchanging farewells within three days and I was already feeling wan at saying goodbye to Harini, Ashish, Samip, Mathew and Abhinav. I had really enjoyed their companionship over the concentrated period since our first furtive exchanges in Canberra just over a month earlier. But we had shared much in a short time, and I knew I was going to be sad at their departure.

Sam and Jarrod and their crew were also set up and I lit up when I realised that we were sitting in close proximity to one another again. The premature conclusion to the Perth Test had stymied our planned dinner there, but Sam had sent me a text message seeking a firm date for Adelaide while I was at Bawley Point. We had already settled on dinner at Cucina on O'Connell Street at the conclusion of the second day. I later learnt that this was their second home and I basked in their reflected glory each time I visited there since with the *maître d'* always making a fuss over me.

'Dinner is set—but we would like to talk to you on camera for the film. Are you OK to do that?'

'I'd love to.' Frankly I was flattered to be even considered. The Two Chucks had interrogated the veritable who's who of international cricket for their documentary on the future of Test cricket. I could not wait to see what they were going to do with the vast amount of material that they had in the can. Being considered worthy to be any part of it was quite a thrill.

'We also managed to get to Dravid. We'll see what we can do about putting you in touch with him.' With that he surreptitiously slipped me a slip of paper like one of those espionage drops popularised on *Spooks* with the Indian legend's email address on it. 'Be discreet with it. Good luck. He really is terrific.'

Sam and I had discussed Rahul Dravid in some depth over the summer and regarded him as having serious and important things to say about the future of the game. We had agreed that whichever of us managed to first get access to him would attempt to facilitate a follow-on for the other. As it turned out they managed to breach 'The Wall' first and he participated in a delightful teaser for their film's website which they shot just outside the WACA. Their experience of the man was the same as all who crossed his path. Like their good friend Ed Smith, they found him to be a man of grace and dignity. Jarrod told the story of their meeting with the elusive Indian number three whom they had been pursuing over the summer on their website:

> The first handshake was one of a man who'd rather be reading John Keats on his balcony while drinking a shandy. It was gentle, and you could barely distinguish the hands whose silky soft touch guide the ball behind point. Either he was just a man who shook as softly as he catches in the slips, or he was put off by our shabby demeanor and questionable aroma. If it was the latter, thankfully it didn't put him off his game. Once the camera was on he was exactly as you'd expect Dravid to be; thoughtful, decisive, intelligent and passionate.

> Sometimes he replied with a late verbal defensive shot, and other times he answered with an elegantly punched oral drive. But when we spoke, he didn't treat us like the disgusting group of men we so clearly were. He has this way about him that makes you feel like he's on your side. You should be shitting yourself sitting down in front of him, but instead he makes it feel like you're just at a friend's place talking rubbish.

> The second handshake came after the interview.

> It was completely different from the first—this was the handshake of a man who clearly liked the questions he'd answered and was happy we were making the film. It was firm, more like he slapped our hands and then held on. And he didn't just do it to me, or Sam, he went through our whole crew with the same sort of enthusiastic handshake that makes you feel better about yourself and life in general. I'm not sure any handshake has ever made me feel better.

In our own shambolic way, we appeared to have won over one of the keepers of Test Cricket's flame. With one longer-than-he-agreed-to interview and boisterous handshake Dravid had reinforced to us that we knew what [we're] doing and that we could in fact make a film about something as monstrous as Test Cricket's future and present.

My own pursuit of Dravid took on something akin to a quest in search of Moby Dick or The Holy Grail. He replied graciously to my email to his private account on the final day of the Test and through the generous, unstinting lobbying of Harini Rana I continued to seek him out for a serious interview as to where he believed Test cricket was headed but the differences in time zones made it difficult to expand on this initial contact.

As I toiled over this manuscript with the perspective provided by hindsight amid the chill and gloom of a wet Canberra winter, Adelaide took on even more of the aspect of an idyllic, shimmering oasis, which somehow diminished the memory of every experience of the other venues of the summer. The quality of my discussions with Ian Chappell, Ravi Shastri and Wasim Akram accounted in large part for this. I also suspect that I had slowly developed my own craft after a long lay-off from writing so that I was more on top of my game. But my memories of Adelaide sparkle to this day and I shall offer glimpses of each of them in turn.

But the company of The Two Chucks added real spice to my experience of Adelaide. The belated dinner with Sam and Jarrod at the end of the second day's play in Adelaide was simply wonderful. I arrived at Cucina in a gentle twilight, which if it didn't evoke England for them, certainly did so for me. The light dies gently and slowly in South Australia at the height of summer and there was even a hint of light on the horizon when I left them after a long and convivial meal. We enjoyed splendid food and the untrammelled joy of three cricket fanatics speaking passionately about the game they love. They had been thinking deeply about the game and I found their insights fascinating. Their central hypothesis was one with which I intuitively agreed and had been trying to convey on my blog. Yet it was only through this uninterrupted chat that I fully came to appreciate the sheer magnitude and complexity of the task they had set themselves. In passing, this is where I learnt which five English counties Marcus North had played for, as well as learning much more about the intricacies of English cricket upon which I vowed to draw if I eventually managed to persuade someone to take my copy during the Ashes campaign in 2013.

Sam refrained from gloating about the Australian humiliation of the previous summer and I later reflected on some of his shrewd observations about structural weaknesses in the English set-up as they crashed to an ignominious 3–0 loss to the inconsistent Pakistanis. In particular, Sam was sceptical of the extent to which the Australian public had really warmed to Michael Clarke despite the triple and double centuries that he amassed in Sydney and Adelaide. I ventured my theory that Clarke did not personify the typical Australian archetype of masculinity and that many Australian fans, especially blokes, were vaguely uncomfortable with him. I had expounded this theory to them in Sydney, but had become even more convinced of its veracity after attending an event hosted by the South Australian Cricket Association that morning before play in the Test to unveil the statue of South Australian favourite son, Darren Lehmann.

It had been a gala event conducted in the cool of the morning well before play on the lush lawns in the Members' Enclosure. Jim Maxwell of the ABC had acted as master of ceremonies and, to paraphrase Rahul Dravid, the common language of cricket had brought together a diverse cast of political foes from the last century. My old boss Rodney Cavalier was there and had good-naturedly upbraided me for suggesting on my blog that he was an economic rationalist. Readers can judge whether I did him a disservice through reference to the extracts of his interview with Jim Maxwell published in the earlier chapter, 'Sydney, the Big Tease'. I gently ribbed him in return, noting that I had reported his comments more accurately than Labor gadfly Bob Ellis, who cited Cavalier as the source of scurrilous and untrue remarks he allegedly made about Peter Costello's wife, sparking one of the most celebrated and acrimonious defamation trials in Australian history. The remarks attributed to Cavalier were the verbal equivalent of Gavrilo Princip's pistol shot in sparking the ensuing litigious conflagration. The only problem was that they were held by the court to have been the product of Ellis's fertile imagination—like most of his so-called political commentary that invariably places him at the centre of great events as an omniscient observer. Cavalier conceded with a quiet smile that, whatever the merits of my interpretation, I had not fabricated the remarks that I had attributed to him on my blog. Rodney was but one of the political titans present. He introduced me to John Bannon, the former South Australian premier whose reputation took a hammering during the banking collapses that occurred in the wake of the 1987 stock market crash. I had always liked him and admired his approach to politics. He is a serious man who had been in public life for the right reasons. His quiet, thoughtful demeanour was underscored by a slightly vulnerable boyish exterior, which the advancing years had barely tarnished.

Even less wearied by age, nor condemned by the years was Ian McLachlan who had carried the drinks for Australia as 12th man during the Adelaide Test against Ted Dexter's touring team in January 1963. The fate of being 'always the bridesmaid, never the bride' befell him in his later political career when, for a time, he was touted as a potential leader of the Liberal Party and alternative prime minister during the

Hawke ascendancy. At seventy-five he still exhibited the parade-ground bearing and resonant voice that commanded respect when he was, in turn, leader of the National Farmers Federation and later a federal Cabinet minister. It was enticing to see parallels in his failure to achieve his highest potential in both spheres and Darren Lehmann's cricket career. His highest attainment had been to serve as the minister for defence in the first Howard government where his tenure had been characterised by safe hands rather than brilliance. Yet even at seventy-five it was easy to see how McLachlan commanded respect and attention. There was always an other-worldly quality to him as a politician that the cynics attributed to a lack of hunger for the top job or a lack of intellectual weight. My experience of him was that he was very much a product of that old Australia, the passing of which I have mourned on occasions throughout this story. In many ways McLachlan reminded me of the men who served in the Second Australian Imperial Force—the men of my father's generation. They were undemonstrative and suspicious of affectation or surplus loquacity, which they tended to dismiss as evidence of untrustworthiness. In my limited dealings with him I had found McLachlan impressive; a man of few words which were his bond, and an unnervingly direct and appraising gaze. On this cool morning he looked like a brigadier addressing his troops before sending them over the top. The years had been kind to him.

Likewise, the tributes to Darren Lehmann were something of an elegy to talent not fully exploited, of potential unrealised. Of course Lehmann had enjoyed a very successful career playing 27 Tests and achieving a healthy batting average of 44.95. including five centuries. And he was a more than useful slow bowler who could tie down an end, if not inflict significant damage as his best match analysis of 6/92 demonstrated.

Yet somehow there was a sense that so much more had been possible for Lehmann. Some hint of his limitations emerged from Jim Maxwell's generous and humorous tribute to 'Boof', as he has continued to be affectionately known even after his retirement.

A portrait emerged of the type of ocker hero with whom Australians seem comfortable. The similarities to the loveable, rogue image of Doug Walters were striking. Boof, we were assured, loved a drink and smoke and presumably a game of cards in the shed as well. This cozy stereotype of the idealised Australian male left me vaguely uneasy. Australian captain Michael Clarke's ambiguous relationship with the Australian public had, until his epic innings in Sydney, derived largely from his failure to conform to this same stereotypical image of Australian masculinity. Clarke was not out overnight. His partner going into the second day was his vice captain, Ricky Ponting, and I was again struck, as I had been in Sydney during their long stand, by the contrasts in their personifications of maleness. Ponting exudes stoicism and macho competitiveness. Notwithstanding that he is now domiciled in Sydney, he still bears the hallmark of a working-class background from an unfashionable small town in Tasmania. The contrast with Clarke is stark. To paraphrase Paul Keating describing veteran Australian diplomat Richard Woolcott, Clarke could do with having his smooth edges knocked off.

The safe clichés used to describe Lehmann as a likeable larrikin were all too familiar to me from my study of Australian military history. Lehmann's fondness for a drink and smoke may make him a loveable rogue to fans and some commentators, but how representative is he really of the current generation of Australian cricketers, with their army of support staff, dieticians, psychologists, strengthening coaches and spin doctors? Indeed, is Lehmann himself even more nuanced and complex than this beer swilling caricature? His career and personality were celebrated almost the way we used to revere the gifted amateurs such as Keith Miller and Wally Grout, whose off-field antics were the stuff of popular myth. But the contemporary game is now thoroughly professional—the province of mirthless apparatchiks who speak in the language of merger and acquisitions lawyers. For those who wonder why Boof played so few Tests and failed to amass really impressive statistics, maybe this reality needs to be recognised. As it was, there was a vague sense of grievance that somehow fate had dealt cruelly with him, that maybe it was all because he was a South Australian.

The same comforting myths sustain our military self-image. In the popular imagination, our Army since Gallipoli has been comprised of 'natural soldiers'. Just like our idealised cricketers, they are likeable rogues with no patience for formality. They perform best when hung-over, are innately anti-authoritarian and ruggedly individualistic. Much of the writing on our military history and cricket employs this simplistic, comforting mythology as its stock-in-trade. There is too little serious work on the place of cricket in the broader society and culture. Similarly, much of our military history writing is comprised of the reminiscences of family members celebrating the exploits of grandfathers and uncles, or the aggrieved rhetoric of the 'other peoples' wars' school, which insists that our troops were invincible lions led by donkeys from larger nations. There is precious little written about Grand Strategy or war as an instrument of Australian statecraft, or how the Army and society have interacted since Federation. We cling to images of the original Anzacs when describing contemporary young Australians formed by a completely different society, culture and era. Yet you would never know this when reading what passes for analysis of military affairs in this country. Our strategic debate is the poorer for it.

For this insight I am indebted to *The Sydney Morning Herald* columnist and strategic studies scholar Cynthia Banham, who studied the eulogies of soldiers killed on active service in Afghanistan and was struck at the prevalence of the term 'larrikin' in the tributes paid to them by their mates. Surely they were not all larrikins? I have served with a lot of Australian soldiers, including having led them on operations in Timor-Leste. They were a fairly representative cross section of society. Some were introverts, and some were even women. Goodness, some may even have been homosexual. Although we still do not recruit enough young people of Asian or Middle Eastern background, we are light years ahead of Australian cricket in that endeavour. But without labouring the point, they don't all play cards, drink, smoke and carry on like Mel Gibson in the film *Gallipoli.* This perspective influenced the way I viewed the Australian cricket team over the summer and I deal with it in my final chapter in more depth. The excellent young Australian military historian Craig Stockings made this point in a powerful polemic in *The Australian* on Anzac Day this year. Stockings wrote:

> Much of the power of Anzac stems from its idealised representation of the values most of us aspire to, or even imagine we possess, simply by being Australian.
>
> The model of Anzac manhood is physically commanding, mentally stoic, yet mercurial in spirit. In war he fights hard but plays by the rules. He is ready to volunteer in a good cause but has no desire to kill. Yet he will do his terrible duty by his nation and his mates. He may be a little uncultured around the edges but he has an innate sense of fair play and deep democratic urges. He is no conscript, for compulsion is too close to reluctance.

Where he has erred, his mistakes are not his. They belong, by and large, to his incompetent (British) military and political leaders. He may be uneducated, but he is nonetheless clever and endlessly resourceful. Perhaps he had to be coming from the bush. He is every inch the man—'he' cannot comfortably be a 'she'—despite the degree to which the legend is often stretched to make such an accommodation. He is always, always white.

When I discussed this with The Two Chucks over dinner, my thinking had not really crystallised on what it meant for the long-term health of Australian cricket, nor what it may mean for the Army I had joined when Ian Chappell was still Australia's Test cricket captain.

As dire as the challenge of commercialisation is to the long-term future of Test cricket, I do not believe that Australian cricket can indefinitely continue to venerate the myth of the fair-dinkum, invariably white, Aussie bloke as the apotheosis of the Test cricketer. How will we continue to ensure that Australian cricket reflects the society that it represents if such dated, boorish parodies of maleness are presented as the ideal? Where will we find our Ravi Bopara or Monty Panesar if this is how we idealise the iconic Australian cricketer? And why would intelligent women continue to watch or attend it? Nor is it sufficient to cite Usman Khawaja as a rebuttal to this argument. His selection was noteworthy precisely because of its rarity.

Sam was intrigued by this analysis and we agreed to shoot an interview outside the Adelaide Oval on the Friday of the Test match. It had been a wonderful, stimulating encounter with two very insightful cricket commentators. As I strolled into O'Connell Street to flag a cab in the balmy evening, I continued to reflect on the similarities between the popular images of our cricketers and our soldiers. I was aware that on the morrow,

Australia Day, I would have the chance to refine my thinking on these topics even further as I had finally managed to lock in a formal time to chat to Ian Chappell about his impressions of this series and the future of cricket. Moreover, I knew that my name was to be announced in the Commonwealth of Australia Gazette for the award of the Order of Australia in the Military Division for 'exceptional service to the Australian Army'. I was emotional, humbled and ruminative about this as the cab wended its way to my hotel in the Adelaide CBD. The first day of the Perth Test had marked the thirty-eighth anniversary of my arrival as a fresh-faced boy at the gates of Duntroon. This inevitably inspired reminiscences about the Australia of 1974, the changes in the Army and society and how these related to the current format of cricket. And I was excited to be meeting Chappelli who in so many ways embodied these trends. Australia Day 2012 beckoned.

The next morning dawned clear, bright and beautiful with the promise of the continuation of the Adelaide heatwave. Before heading to the ground I enjoyed a leisurely breakfast with the former South Australian senator and Howard minister, Nick Minchin. We had in turn been friends and enemies over politics, but had reconciled some years before. Readers may find my political friendships contradictory if not downright bizarre. In Perth I shared dinner with one of the most left wing members of the ALP since Eddie Ward or Jim Cairns, while in Adelaide I took breakfast with one of the most right wing members of the Howard government. This warrants some explanation, which I will attempt without impinging on good taste.

It was Søren Kierkegaard who, I believe, wisely noted that we live life forwards, but understand it backwards. That certainly applied to me. My behaviour in the 1980s and '90s had been erratic due to the influence of alcoholism which had nearly killed me. I was one of the lucky ones who managed to recover from this malady and have not taken a drink or non-prescribed drug since June 1990. However, the psychological impairment of my addictions continued to afflict me for some time after I stopped ingesting these things. While I know this now, I was oblivious to it when I was taking a wrecking ball to my life in the early 1990s. As Jung declared: 'What is not brought to consciousness, comes to us as fate.'

Frankly I was far too quick to take offence and far too thin-skinned in the immediate aftermath of my drinking career, something I have since learned is not uncommon among those who have drunk to excess, but is a significant weakness in someone who wants to make a living in political combat. I was a talented political strategist with a natural flair for spin and issues management. But my ego was out of control and in short order I fell out with both major political parties. To the best of my knowledge, I am the only person who has worked at the most senior levels of both of the major parties. The ALP classifies apostates as 'rats'. They are welcome to their tawdry little definitions. But when I look at where most of the socialists of the 1970s and 1980s have ended up on the ideological spectrum, their slights carry neither any emotional charge nor credibility with me these days.

My falling out with the Liberals was more morally culpable in that I genuinely breached the trust of some honourable men who had trusted and promoted me, none more so than federal director, Andrew Robb and the then newly elected senator, Nick Minchin. One of the things that contributed to my later-life conservatism, apart from its apparent inevitability as a function of ageing, was the much greater magnanimity of the Liberals in letting bygones be bygones. Their political culture actually does tolerate individual deviance better than the plastic gangster culture of

Labor with its life ban on so-called rats. They seem oblivious to the actual resemblance of the language on which they so pride themselves to the mafia's lexicon, and the incongruity of this in an organisation that preaches that it has the monopoly on compassion. Anyway, Nick Minchin was deeply offended at my betrayal of his party and by the strident criticisms I made of them when I was hired as columnist by the *Financial Review*. We exchanged insults in the media, and for a time a friendship that I had enjoyed fell under strain. However, we patched up our differences some years later and these days I enjoy his company immensely. Despite his fearsome reputation among progressives, including some within the South Australian Liberal Party, I have always found Nick to be a true gentleman. He is easy company and has a self-deprecating sense of humour. He does not take himself too seriously, though he is passionate about conservative causes. Like Carmen Lawrence, he is the real deal—a serious, committed warrior for the causes in which he believes. He would fit easily into the hard right of the United States Republican Party.

On this morning of Australia Day, ideology came a distant second to talk of physical fitness and dieting, issues which I take more seriously than politics these days. He and his wife Kerry are serious snorkellers and I sought his advice on venues where I might try to develop my nascent interest in this form of recreation. We scrupulously avoided talk about Australian politics and concentrated on the Republican primaries. Nick thought the field was unimpressive, but that Romney probably was the only credible threat to Obama. In no time at all it seemed my cab was honking outside the hotel and we shook hands and parted. Like Ian McLachlan, and John Bannon, Nick was a striking advertisement for the benefits of leaving political life. He exuded vibrant good health and his parting advice was that I try to snorkel in the Perhentian Islands off Malaysia at the next available opportunity.

With that I was on the way to the ground and my scheduled interviews with Ian Chappell and Ravi Shastri. It was clear that India, resuming at 2/61, had little chance of escaping with even an honourable draw. We were at the fag end of the Indian summer and I was becoming acutely aware of the demands of the writing of this story. I was now less interested in events on the field and anxious to canvass the views of the numerous former Test greats hovering around the coffee urn in the breakout area in the commentary position.

Ravi Shastri was scathing about India's performance, demanding that the Big Three of the Indian batting order—Tendulkar, Dravid and Laxman—all be phased out to make way for new blood. 'I would retire all three of them in a phased way over the next few months. It should be done gradually, but Laxman must be the first to go. If it was my decision I would have selected Rohit Sharma ahead of him for this Test. And besides their batting, you just cannot hide three guys of that age in the field on Australian grounds.'

He was also highly critical of the openers. 'I believe the failure of the openers has been culpable. Look at the opening partnerships. India has not passed 26 for the loss of the first wicket. That has left the older players exposed to the Australian fast bowling too early in the innings. What must Abhinav Mukund be thinking now? He was discarded far too early after a few poor efforts in England but they have persisted with others who failed there.'

'What about the bowlers?'

'Praveen Kumar is the key to the future. There was a spot on the pitch in Melbourne exactly where he likes to pitch the ball. It was a real shame that he was not available there. But he will be a major part of India's future.'

I enjoyed my discussion with Ravi Shastri, about whom I had been warned by Sam and Jarrod. They had offended him with some of their questions in Sydney and forewarned me that he could be abrasive if provoked. Maybe I was a soft touch because I found him to be very generous with his time and insights. He was finally summoned by the ESPN producer to conduct his next on-air shift to the subcontinent and we parted with a handshake and a generous offer on his part to speak again during the writing phase of this story.

No sooner had Ravi disappeared than Ian Chappell emerged from the Channel Nine box and waved cordially. We had been missing one another over the past two days. On one occasion he was engrossed in a conversation with his old fast-bowling trump card, Jeff Thomson. He held up his fingers to indicate that he would be off the phone in five minutes. But that was optimistic. The chat went for quite a while and I finally slipped away. Running a distant second to Thommo was no disgrace. I was happy to drop further down the queue. At least he did not offer me an overflow interview.

'G'day Malcolm, do you want to have a yarn now?'

'Love to if you are free.'

'Grab a seat.' We sat down on a couple of plastic chairs looking straight down the Adelaide Oval drenched in the harsh light of the midday Australian summer sun. What followed was one of the most stimulating discussions I have ever had about cricket. As I had already learned in Perth, Ian Chappell is a superb natural communicator. He speaks in clear, vivid imagery, listening intently to each question and thinking about it in a deliberate way before responding. I was acutely aware of how busy he was and wanted to focus on two key elements of my analysis with him. Firstly, I asked, 'Mate, you called an Australian win well before this series even started when no one else dared to, and you went for the whitewash well before any one else. How did you see it coming?'

'Well I just watched them closely in England and you know the signs were there all along. Those grounds are smaller than here and I thought that if they struggled on those English grounds they were always going to do it tough here. You can't hide the number of older slower fieldsmen they have. But the bigger issue was the fact that I knew our pitches pretty well. They were always going to play pretty quick and there was going to be plenty of bounce. Indian teams are never as good away from home as they are over there, and again I thought the conditions would really suit our blokes. That top order has been great, but apart from Dravid none of them got any runs in England and I thought if we bowled decently we would expose them on bouncy tracks.'

He sat silently for a few moments then he resumed. 'And you know they showed a real lack of resilience over there as well. They showed they couldn't take a punch. When they went down, they stayed down. If they were under pressure, they folded. That convinced me that they lacked cohesion and fighting spirit. And again you get found out in Australia if that is your weakness.'

'What is the problem?'

'Well, look at Sydney. Clarke, Ponting and Hussey are just scoring at will and does Dhoni move a fieldsman or try a bowling change? No he doesn't. It's like he is asleep at the wheel. I think a big part of the problem has been Tendulkar. Now Indians will hate me for saying this. When I wrote it back in 2007 they all went berserk saying that I was telling Sachin to retire. I wasn't. All I was saying to him was, 'Mate you need to take a long look in the mirror and ask yourself one question: am I playing for the Indian team or am I playing for the record books?' And I suggested that if he couldn't answer that satisfactorily, he needed to go. Now I'd ask him the same thing again on this trip. Every time he has got to 50 he has started to poke and prod outside the off stump. He is fixated on the numbers, not on the state of the game. I think that has really hurt India and I don't think Dhoni has been a strong enough captain to run the side with Tendulkar there and playing the way he has been playing.'

One of the things I cannot do justice to is just how expressive Ian Chappell is with his hands. He demonstrated Sachin's prodding outside off stump with the casual deftness only a man who has fielded at first slip with aplomb and scored over 5000 Test runs can muster. There is an easy fluidity in his hand gestures that belies his sixty-eight-plus years. It makes him compelling to listen to and watch.

The second hypothesis I wanted to test was about the relative strength of this Australian team compared to the side he took to England in 1972. I ventured, 'Remember when we lost The Ashes in 1970–71, when Dennis Lillee made his debut on this very ground around Australia Day 1971? You could see that out of the rubble that maybe there was a hint of resurgence. Pattinson reminds me a bit of Lillee, and Hilfenhaus and Siddle have never looked better. Do you think it is a stupid proposition that we might be seeing the sort of rebuilding here that started in 1971 and saw your team really fire in 1972, that was the harbinger of a golden age of Australian cricket?'

Again he pondered the question, gaze never leaving the middle. 'I wouldn't say that it is a stupid proposition at all. I can see why you might make it. But I would argue that my team was much stronger than anything we can produce out of the blokes we have seen here. For a start where are the young batsmen to really put pressure on Hussey and Ponting?

They have all been struggling and they might both go to England and they deserve to when you consider what else is on offer.'

'You don't like Usman Khawaja?'

'Mate, haven't you watched him? He's got leaden feet.'

I kept my disagreement with that remark to myself as Chappelli continued. 'Remember in 1972, Ross Edwards had a wonderful series—scored a really big ton at Trent Bridge and got valuable runs at The Oval when it mattered. Now no one had even heard of him in 1971. And my team was much better balanced in terms of slow bowlers. We are weak in that department at the moment and we will need to find a couple of spinners.'

'You don't rate these current blokes?'

'Not really, though Warnie reckons Michael Beer has it. I don't rate him myself, but Shane knows slow bowling so I'd defer to him. But I reckon we are thin in the spin department.'

'What about Xavier Doherty?'

'What about him?'

'Well would you take him to England?'

'Yeah sure—so long as it was to play Lancashire League.'

I burst out laughing at this sardonic remark and Chappelli's face likewise betrayed the hint of a grin. I actually had what I needed for both my magazine and this story. However, one does not often get the undivided attention of an Australian icon and a boyhood hero to boot, so I decided to indulge a few reminiscences.

'Have you stayed in touch with Bob Cowper? He was my absolute hero.'

'Yeah Cowps is around. He works overseas as you know, but I think he has joint at Merimbula these days. He's probably in the phone book. Do you want to talk to him?'

'Given the sort of book I'm writing that would be useful.'

'Give him a crack. Sing out if I can help.'

The glamorous Roz Kelly was gesturing to Chapelli, hinting that it was time to think about getting back behind the microphone. 'One last thing, mate. Remember the Test here in 1966 against the Poms? I was listening to the transistor with my mates in the backyard at home and I think it was McGilvray calling. He thought a snick to slips had gone past you, but you leapt back with both feet off the ground and held it with one hand. He was almost incomprehensible with excitement and said it was one of the finest catches he had seen. We could barely understand what had happened but it turned out to be a wicket. It was one of my earliest memories of Test cricket at the Adelaide Oval. So it is really nice to meet you here so many years on. Thanks for your time.'

'No worries, Malcolm. Good luck with the book. And you know what was so nice about that catch?'

I looked at him quizzically.

'It was bloody Geoffrey Boycott, mate. Doesn't get any better than that.' With that he was gone. And so pretty much was the Adelaide Test match. For most of the last two days I just wanted to spend as much time as possible with my Indian friends and Sam and Jarrod. It felt like the break-up of a high school class and we were all a bit wan as the series wound down to a crushing Indian defeat. I was never able to catch up with Bob Cowper; my phone calls remained unanswered. But, at least I could bear witness to another great batsman's courage and humility. For my part, I knew that I would never see Rahul Dravid bat live again so I made sure that I found a vantage point at ground level and watched every one of the final 71 balls of his Test career intently.

Sam and Jarrod were stunned that Ian Chappell had been so direct in his criticism of Tendulkar, and on the strength of that decided to interview me in the car park outside the Oval as they could not persuade Chappelli to grant them a subsequent interview and reiterate those remarks on camera. As we were outside the ground filming this interview a roar announced to us that yet again the Little Master had been dismissed without reaching that elusive 100th international century. At stumps that night India were in a hopeless position. I walked around the box and made my farewells embracing, in turn, Samip, Abhinav and Mathew. I came to Sam and Jarrod and shook their hands. 'Not here tomorrow?' Sam inquired.

'No. I've seen enough, mate. Time to go home. I have to get a haircut and be soldier again on Monday morning.'

He nodded and smiled. I suspect he found the image of me as a trained killer unconvincing. 'Good luck with the book.'

'And good luck with the film. I've loved your company and you have taught me a lot.'

'It's been fun hasn't it?' With a lump in my throat I departed. I now wanted to just go home and replenish before going back to work on Monday and starting work on this story in earnest.

On the final Saturday morning I walked into the Qantas lounge and was surprised to note that I was not the only one who doubted the capacity of the Indian tail to provide either entertainment or resistance. John Inverarity was boarding a plane to Perth, and my mate Peter Lalor and I were on the same flight to Sydney. We were both tired and slumped into low large armchairs bemoaning how little running we had been able to do while on the road since the Gabba. I pride myself on being in pretty good nick for a man my age, but Lalor is a serious runner and as lean as a greyhound. We soon boarded the flight to Sydney from where I was connecting to Canberra. On the ground in Sydney, as he pulled his cabin luggage from the overhead locker, Peter Lalor looked back at me and winked, 'All out for

201, mate. It's all over'. He had been listening on the in-flight sound system. I had preferred Giselle Scales and classical music.

And it was all over. The Indian tour, which had portended such tantalising prospects, had ended in an ignominious whitewash. I was tired and more than a little homesick. Yes it was all over. Time to go home.

He was a much loved and admired commandant of Duntroon during my graduating year ...

Major General Alan Lindsay (Alby) Morrison AO, DSO, MBE.

11. *Last of the Summer Wine*

I carried the enormous weight of two men whom I barely knew ...

I suspect that many Australians project their hopes and ideals on to our soldiers and our cricketers.

Jim Maxwell suggested that in the season just gone we may be imbibing the last of the summer wine. I fear he is correct.

And so the summer came to an end. For me it had been an amazing adventure, but it had also been punctuated by significant grief and loss. Even the elements appeared to conspire in this. It had been unseasonably wet and cool seeming to mock my nostalgic, idyllic memories of summers past, especially those during my childhood in balmy Queensland when my love of cricket was spawned.

At the outset of this story I invoked Jung's assertion that what was true in the morning becomes a lie in life's afternoon, and so it turned out to be for me. Much that I believed in or held dear when the idea for this story was born, turned out to be a lie or was lost to me in the wake of that Indian summer. It was a period of momentous and unprecedented change in my life. The summer was punctuated by too much personal loss, notably the deaths of friends and the death of some cherished illusions. Perhaps my sense that the game was losing something, was changing irrevocably for the worse, was merely my internal turmoil projected outwards.

Despite being a cool summer, it had also been a long summer on account of the leap year. On the very last day of summer I encountered the Indian team for the final time. Jung would have assured me that this was not a coincidence. It seemed so fitting that I should have assumed that this would happen. Here is what transpired.

On the previous evening, the 28th of February 2012, my boss, the Chief of the Army, had delivered a landmark address at The Sydney Institute about the future of the Army after the withdrawal from Afghanistan. The Sydney Institute, which thrives under the leadership of my friends Gerard and Anne Henderson, is a splendid forum for the serious discussion of ideas. To be invited to address the Institute is an honour. In the years since its inception, every prime minister and anybody with a serious book or idea to discuss eventually attends one of its events. The cast of luminaries who have passed through the beautifully restored terrace in Phillip Street is imposing.

The Chief of the Army, Lieutenant General David Morrison, is a serious thinker and a gifted writer. He excels in addressing large audiences and this was his second major set piece address for the year. He had performed superbly at the Institute the previous evening and had impressed a gathering of senior business and media figures whom Gerard and Anne had assembled for a private dinner after his speech. The next morning his duties took him north to where the real Army is based in the major hubs of Brisbane, Townsville and Darwin. I was heading back to my desk job in Canberra feeling satisfied that the themes the boss was amplifying were impressing his audiences and setting up the Army for success during his term. I had treated myself to a sleep in and a leisurely cup of coffee at the Bambini Trust cafe, which I always like to visit whenever I am in Sydney. War is hell.

At the airport, as I headed to the gate lounge to board the Canberra shuttle I heard a voice to my right: 'Malcolm!' I looked around and quickly fastened on a beaming Harini Rana. Readers have probably become either bored by my references to the slender threads of synchronicity, or will conclude that I am a New Age crank who invests excessive meaning in the routine coincidences of life, but this was a very special surprise. I had been instinctively drawn to Harini ever since I had met her in that rudimentary, poorly sited media box at Manuka Oval in December. Her quiet, unassuming presence in the commentary box over the summer had always acted as a soothing balm. I instinctively gravitated to her and enjoyed our companionable silences as much as our numerous chats. She emanated an appealing reserve, but when she spoke her passion for cricket and her shrewd insights were worth waiting for. It was she who spotted the five-ball over delivered by Sri Lanka against India in the limited over match in Adelaide, much to the admiration of every cricket writer watching. The Twittersphere lit up when Harini noted that the over was one ball short.

One of my favourite memories of the summer was a lengthy chat with her on the final day of the Sydney Test. Sachin Tendulkar seemed to be marching inexorably to his 100th international century in defiant partnership with Laxman during India's second innings. Harini was attempting to get pre-records from eminent past players to prudently cover this eventuality in order to get these to air without delay should the Little Master attain the milestone. She was especially keen to interview Steve Waugh who was a guest of Rodney Cavalier for lunch in the SCG Trust dining room. We failed to inveigle our way past security despite my most persuasive efforts with Terry, one of the attendants whom I had befriended over the preceding three days. There was nothing left to do but await the great man's emergence, so we sat on a brick ledge adjacent to the practice nets where we could maintain unobtrusive surveillance. It was during the ensuing conversation that Harini told me of her fascinating path to esteemed cricket writer and broadcaster, having flirted briefly with the idea of becoming a commercial pilot. She also shed light on the disrupted career of the talented all-rounder Irfan Pathan whom I thought had looked like an heir to the great Kapil Dev when he toured here in 2007–08.

By the tender age of twenty-six, Harini had already achieved an enormous amount and I am confident that she will be a fixture of international cricket commentary for decades to come, should she decide to persist with it. Her insights into the Indian players were always very helpful and I was deeply touched by the extraordinary effort she made to try to arrange a meeting for me with Rahul Dravid after the media conference at the end of the second day in Sydney.

I had chatted briefly to her at the day–night game at the SCG on the 26th of February, but she had gone on to the news conference at the end of play while I left at the fall of the eighth Indian wicket as the match petered out in desultory fashion. I felt a twinge of regret at not having bid her a proper farewell, although we had said goodbye in Adelaide when she had assumed she would be going straight home after the Test series. As it turned out, her employer assigned her to cover the limited over matches; the slender threads of chance rectified the lost opportunity for a proper farewell. Here she was in the midst of Team India awaiting their flight to Brisbane on the very last day of the Indian summer. I have described the camaraderie that had developed over the summer among the media contingent and it was always a thrill to run into someone with whom I had shared my initial summer as a writer.

'Ah Malcolm! It is splendid to see you in your uniform', she said with her wry smile. I chuckled as I suspect that my unmilitary appearance over the summer must have cast doubt on the authenticity of my claims to be an Army officer. Invariably, when Harini introduced me to her Indian colleagues she would embellish the exchange by adding, 'Malcolm is a serving colonel'. The respect for the military among the Indians was quite marked and I knew from Boria Majumdar's *Twenty-Two Yards to Freedom* that on numerous occasions in the past, serving and retired officers had managed Indian touring teams.

My friend Sally Warhaft, an anthropologist and writer who speaks Hindi and has lived in India explained this to me. 'The Army is ubiquitous in India. You see soldiers everywhere and they look very impressive and enjoy considerable social standing.' I am not entirely sure of my social standing, but hoped that on this occasion I looked sufficiently impressive in my full dress uniform and medals. In any event, it managed to impress Harini who generously introduced me to a number of the players with whom she was engaged in a convivial chat. They were clearly pleased to be heading home. As I glanced around the group I observed M.S. Dhoni, Sachin Tendulkar, Virat Kholi, Suresh Raina, Praveen Kumar and Irfan Pathan. Where was that digital camera when I needed it? Then again, based on my performance with V.V.S. Laxman back at that Manuka net session, I may have disgraced the uniform through my ineptitude in nervously failing to secure the shot. We exchanged grins and warm greetings before I was summoned to the departure lounge. I felt a pang of sadness as I looked back over my shoulder with a parting wave to Harini and the guys. Yes, the Indian summer was now really over, though I was thrilled to receive a parting call from her as she

244 OF THE SUMMER WINE

boarded her flight the following Saturday. A trip to India is now at the top
of my bucket list as I am determined to see Harini, Boria, Mathew George,
Samip and Abhinav again.

The tone of this story has been unabashedly nostalgic. In
the afternoon of my life I have indulged memories of cricket and
occasionally my experiences as a soldier and political warrior.
Encountering Team India as I returned from the address by the Chief
of the Army inevitably inspired reminiscences and represented a
confluence of two of the major trends in my life—love of cricket, and
service as an officer in the Australian Army.

I had enlisted in the Australian Army on the 14th of January 1974,
straight from school. The Army I joined was bruised and introspective
returning from Vietnam, refusing to concede that it had been defeated
and subscribing to a more moderate version of the 'stab in the back'
theory that some German officers concocted to salve the pain of their
defeat in 1918. The end of National Service had seriously diminished
its strength. The Army I joined collectively despised the Whitlam
government, some of whose ministers had marched in demonstrations
at which the enemy flag had been defiantly waved in a display of
jejune rebellion.

My boss David Morrison's dad had commanded the 9th Battalion,
The Royal Australian Regiment, which had lost more men killed in its one-
year tour of Vietnam than we have lost in over ten years in Afghanistan.
David remembered his father's troops being jeered at as they marched
through Adelaide before they embarked on their tour. He and I bonded
when we graduated as young officers to the 8/9th Battalion—the successor
to his dad's unit formed through the amalgamation of 8 and 9 RAR
necessitated by the end of conscription and the reduction of the Army

from nine to six battalions by the Whitlam government. I had admired his dad who was a fine and chivalrous man. He was incongruously kind and understated in an era when several generals literally made me tremble at the knees on account of their fearsome reputations as martinets. He was a much loved and admired commandant of Duntroon during my graduating year and I cherish the memory of marching alongside him and David on Anzac Day in 2004—the only occasion I have marched with my Regimental association.

With hindsight I find it remarkable that I thrived at Duntroon, even though I had never considered any other career from my earliest conscious thoughts. Like my love of cricket, I suspect it was an unconscious way of earning the approval of the father I barely knew. He was veteran of Kokoda and he considered himself a soldier first, regardless of his subsequent civilian employment. His service in the AIF was the defining experience of his life and dominated his discussions to the exclusion of the subsequent achievements of the remaining twenty years of his all too short life.

The Royal Military College was a harsh, uncompromising place when I arrived. It maintained an intense focus on preparing officers for war. The emphasis on physical fitness and warrior qualities was relentless, and the vast majority of my class dropped out. Of the 115 young men who marched in with me that January when New Zealand were touring Australia at cricket, a mere 42 originals graduated within the appointed four years. The Army had been on operations without respite since Korea, and our instructors assumed that the withdrawal from Vietnam was a strategic comma rather than a full stop. I entered Duntroon as a shy, fatherless boy predominantly raised by a doting mother and struggling, perhaps too hard, to exhibit the trappings of hyper-masculinity that I believed represented the soldierly ideal. I topped my academic classes and shone on the sports field. I affected toughness and ruthlessness, which I recognise with hindsight was a maladroit way of convincing myself that I was an authentic Australian soldier in the mould of my father, and his father before him. I carried the enormous weight of two men whom I barely knew, and who had both been wounded in combat—one in New Guinea and the other at Fromelles.

I graduated to infantry and was educated rapidly in the school of hard knocks—a fresh-faced boy of twenty-one years old leading thirty-three soldiers, most of whom were older than I and many of whom had been to war. It was a searing crucible in which to learn the rudiments of leadership, but I have never forgotten that period or the sheer exhilaration of leading soldiers for the first time. Other than my independent command of the Australian Army training team in Timor-Leste, it was the best job I have ever had. But at a deeper level, I now realise that I was denying an important part of myself, a part that burst forth some months ago, not to be denied or repressed any longer. More on that later.

But just like cricket, the Army has changed greatly since 1974. Ever since the foundation of the modern Australian Regular Army we have produced excellent individual soldiers and small tactical units through a superb training system. Yet as I mentioned in the previous chapter, we still adhere to the cozy myth of the gifted amateur and the natural soldier—a bit like our romantic notion of what constitutes the ideal Australian cricketer.

Our soldiers are deeply imbued with the Anzac legend, which gives them resilience and sardonic humour in the face of adversity. This is truly impressive and charming. I have deployed with them on operations three times, and their courage and concern for one another has been unfailingly inspirational. Ethos and culture in armies are hard to define, but they are most noticeable in their absence. Our Army is blessed with a strong culture that, in the main, is noble and a source of strength.

But over the past fifteen years there have been thirteen significant inquiries into the culture of the Australian Defence Force or the Army. Too often these arose from the bullying of minorities, especially women. While a deep tribal culture is the foundation of the warrior spirit and contributes enormously to building the 'band of brothers' who can withstand the shock and horror of battle, it can become too exclusive and it can be perverted by those who need to define themselves by what they are not. In their world, these outsiders are to be shunned. As strong as the Anzac myth is, it has to adapt to modern realities. Increasingly we send bands of brothers *and* sisters to war. And the number of women we recruit simply must increase. The current Chief is deeply committed to achieving this and has bravely nominated a target against which his term will be judged.

On a gloomy Canberra winter night in 2011, when he was a freshly minted lieutenant general yet to formally assume command of the Army, we ruminated on the long journey we began as subalterns back in the late 1970s. We concluded that the greatest challenge that the Army would face over the course of his tenure as Chief would be to avoid the same loss of relevance that occurred when we came home from Vietnam as operations in Afghanistan inevitably scaled down. The parallels between the two eras were uncanny. He had read and been impressed by a scholarly paper that I had presented at a conference in 2009 which described the deterioration of the Army's capability following Vietnam in the name of a 'peace dividend'. The political and strategic class had piously resolved that the era of forward defence was over and concluded, not for the first time in our history, that the Army would never again leave Australia's shores. We should in future rely on our geography to defend us.

This insularity looked increasingly absurd as successive Australian governments preached the virtues of globalisation and sought to extend our influence into regional and global forums. How an isolationist defence policy was to support an expansive trade and foreign policy was never explained. Moreover, the Australian scholar Mike Evans revealed the chasm between our declaratory policy and our strategic practice in a superb monograph titled *The Tyranny of Dissonance*. Through the period of alleged continental defence the Army sent troops to Rhodesia, Namibia, Somalia, Rwanda and Bougainville.

In a shameless play on Rick Atkinson's *An Army at Dawn*—his masterful study of US Army operations in North Africa as the precursor to the liberation of Europe—I titled my study of the post-Vietnam Army 'An Army at Dusk: The Vietnam Army Comes Home'. David Morrison was passionately committed to avoiding a repetition of this syndrome whereby the Army was scaled down at the end of a major conflict—which was flattered by the anodyne, but misleading appellation of the 'Defence of Australia'. This was essentially a fanciful exercise in wishful thinking propagated by a group of retired bureaucrats and mediocre scholars from the Australian National University, and abetted by their lickspittles in the Fairfax Media, most notably Geoffrey Barker. The withdrawal from Afghanistan convinced them that, like the Bourbons, their time had come again. Hence David Morrison asked me to serve on as his speech-writer and to help him resist the lapse back into this complacent, intellectually bankrupt Micawberism. I had always liked him, and after some agonising decided to serve on. I had resigned to go and work for Barry O'Farrell as his speech-writer, but felt an obligation to David and the Army as it entered this perilous period.

After the end of unpopular overseas wars, the temptation is always to fondly imagine that Australian soldiers will never again need to serve overseas and that we will deny enemy access to our continent primarily through the use of planes and submarines. It is nonsense on stilts, and conveniently ignores every act of Australian statecraft since the end of the Cold War, as well as the exigencies of our role as a significant medium power in an unstable neigbourhood. All the deployments that I outlined earlier make this point.

Yet as daunting as this challenge appeared last year, much of David Morrison's work has been focused on changing Army's culture. How does this relate to cricket? Well, first and foremost I suspect that many Australians project their hopes and ideals on to our soldiers and our cricketers. And I think both cricket and the Army face huge challenges if they are to continue to represent the full gamut of the Australia of the twenty-first century. I am biased, but I think the Army is handling this better than Australian cricket, which still looks very white and very much like the Australia of my youth. The women's game is a poor relation. I believe that whatever our faults, the Army is shattering the glass ceiling for female soldiers and looks more like contemporary Australia than does our Test team.

But perhaps the deeper challenge for both the Army and Australian cricket comes from the venality and commercialisation of the *Zeitgeist*. Can the appeal of duty bring the best young Australians into the Army when such extraordinary rewards lie elsewhere, and when individualism trumps collectivism in every field of endeavour? This is also especially threatening to cricket. Why play for your country when you can make much more money playing for an Indian Premier League franchise? Why risk injury in state-level cricket and Tests when the real money is in the shorter forms of the game that so accurately epitomises the era through which we are living? Do not get me wrong, I am not grieving for the usual panaceas: 'Just bring back school milk! All will be well'; 'Let's bring the MCC back for a long tour and let them come by steamer. That will bring back the golden age!' I accept where the era of globalisation has taken us, especially the shift in financial power to India. While I have sympathy for Carmen Lawrence's arguments about peak oil and sustainability that have been eloquently corroborated by recent events in Europe, I do not see the march of globalisation slowing in the foreseeable future where cricket is concerned.

We must squarely face reality. The shorter forms of the game are here to stay. So is commercialisation, and so is corruption. But how do we give content to the pieties uttered by the greats past and present that Test cricket is the soul of the game and must be preserved? I agree with Rahul Dravid that there are too many meaningless 50-over fixtures unrelated to Test series—they need to be reduced. Moreover, we need to move some Tests to smaller venues to reconnect the people to the game. This is a lesser problem in Australia where we still fill the main venues if the opposition is of sufficient quality. But surely the odd Test in a major regional centre could ensure packed grounds and help breathe life into the game. Nor am I arguing for a fixture against Bangladesh in Darwin in July.

In the earliest days of planning when I was inspired to write this book, Jim Maxwell suggested that in the season just gone we may be imbibing the last of the summer wine. I fear he is correct. Yet perhaps in the words of Zhou Enlai on the French Revolution, 'It is too early to tell'. Though the failure of Ed Cowan to secure a Cricket Australia contract for the coming summer sends an ominous message about where the traditional game may be heading.

On a crisp, clear, Sydney autumn day, reminiscent of the day when I met Jim Maxwell at Ultimo last August, I asked Gideon Haigh for his thoughts on the future of Test cricket. As is his wont, he was measured and thoughtful, but he is not encouraged at the haste with which the main Test series later this year will be conducted. South Africa will play three Tests against Australia before Christmas and return home, leaving the entertaining, but not lavishly talented, Sri Lankans the Boxing Day Test. This is not a summer to set traditionalists' blood racing.

Moreover, as he noted, 'Two of the best series recently have been screaming for a five Test format to really resolve the issue—Australia in South Africa and India in South Africa the year before'. He despairs of the two and three match format that is becoming the norm. Likewise the constant travel and lack of serious warm-up fixtures are rendering the game homogenous. He recalled a chat with Ed Cowan on his return from the West Indies earlier this year: 'He thinks the Windies are intentionally preparing poor tracks to bring everyone back to the field. And the lack of mid-week fixtures makes it hard to acclimatise. Everywhere feels like home these days. He says it is really strange'.

Have we drunk the last of the summer wine? Will I ever spend the Australia Day weekend switching between the Australian Open Tennis on television while listening to the hum of ABC radio describing a cricket Test match? I fear not. What is true in the morning becomes a lie in the afternoon—and I am living proof.

Over the course of this summer some deep and troubling psychiatric issues returned with an alarming intensity. I had actually been diagnosed as transgendered in 1985, but resolved to repress it and 'man up'. In the light of its recurrence I frankly do not know how I completed this manuscript. The summer sped past me in a disorientating blur of panic attacks and lack of sleep that fuelled thoughts of suicide. Eventually I decided to end the agony the only way that seemed to offer peace and fulfilment in my remaining years. By the time this book is launched I expect to be living permanently as a woman. This will shock many, but hopefully offend fewer. It is, however, a story for another book, and another day.

This book remains dedicated to the beautiful wife who actually inspired it. She is the only person who is entitled to be aggrieved by this painful decision, which has harmed her deeply and robbed her of a husband. We continue to love one another and I hope we always will. Husbands and wives separate, but I do not think soulmates ever do. I was blissfully unaware at the time that the sudden outburst of creativity that spawned this work in August 2011 was the harbinger of the effervescent resurgence of an old ambiguity about my gender, something I thought I had left behind along with my alcoholism over two decades ago. I now believe I was medicating deep existential grief at being in the wrong body. Words fail to describe this agony, so I will not bother trying in this work. Suffice it to say, I think I became a soldier to bury my own doubts about my maleness. But a day comes in every life when the fundamental question of 'Who am I?' must be answered. I have suffered a great deal in grappling with this issue. But in the words of Aeschylus, 'He who learns must suffer, and, even in our sleep, pain that cannot forget falls drop by drop upon the heart, and in our despair, against our will, comes wisdom to us by the awful grace of God.'

Some hard days lie ahead. But I have been deeply moved by the support of many people, none more so than the Chief of the Army who has insisted that I should continue to serve in the Army, which has been my family on and off for nearly four decades, despite my transition.

He has the toughness, courage and integrity to effect the change to the Army that he insists it needs, while inheriting the compassion of his dad. I have faith in him and confidence in the benign nature of the universe. In the words of Sonny Kapoor, the charming host of *The Best Exotic Marigold Hotel*, 'Everything will be all right in the end. So if it is not all right, then it is not yet the end'.

'... Adelaide evokes more than cricket for me.'
Catherine at the Adelaide Oval

12.   *Following On*

It's all now you see. Yesterday won't be over until tomorrow and tomorrow
began ten thousand years ago.

William Faulkner

Adelaide Oval is my favourite cricket venue anywhere in the world. I adore Lord's. Who doesn't? And Trent Bridge, in Nottingham is an intimate, pretty and evocative ground. Among my most cherished memories of cricket is that epic, fluctuating Ashes Test Match of July 2013 when Ashton Agar made 98 upon debut. I love the place nearly as much as did Cardus.

But Adelaide evokes more than cricket for me. As the fictional detective, Inspector Morse said of Wagner 'It is about important things. Life and death and regret.' To me Adelaide came to signify life and death. And regret. In Adelaide, I made a conscious decision to live, after taking deliberate steps towards taking an overdose of sleeping pills on the evening of 25 January 2012.

When I say that I decided to live, that confers clarity definition, and an element of agency entirely absent from my life at that time. I never resolved it as emphatically as that. I did entertain ideas of dying to simply to turn off the incessant, insistent and agonizing thinking about my gender several more times before June 2012. But I never acquired the means and motivation to do so with as much calculation as I did during the final Test Match for the

Border-Gavaskar Trophy. And in June 2012 I made the irrevocable decision to begin gender transition and live the remainder of my life as a trans woman.

Nowadays, my heart sings as I walk towards the Adelaide Oval. It has a dreamy rhythm that reminds me of Trent Bridge, especially on Friday afternoons when fans stream in from the City, stealing an early mark to watch play. After play, I invariably find a spot somewhere at the River Torrens end to sit alone. Then do I indulge my memories of that summer of 2011-2012.

Eventually, I stroll through Adelaide's ethereal twilight to Cucina on O'Connell Street, where Sam Collins and Jarrod Kimber literally saved my life. Neither will accept how pivotal was that sliding doors moment when they insisted that I joint them at dinner. But I suspect that, had I gone back to my hotel room alone that evening, my head swirling with lurid terrors, shame and remorse, that I would have taken the sleeping pills and sedatives I had stockpiled.

Words cannot describe what the medical profession classifies as 'gender dysphoria'. Like most medical terms it is accurate but anodyne. Like a scalpel it is precise but lacks empathy. Whatever talents I claim as a writer, they do not extend to describing what disparity between one's birth gender and one's psychological and emotional gender feels like.

My feelings of turmoil and acute distress at being male had surfaced without warning in October 2011. Then again, is that really true? I had been in therapy for anxiety and depression since July 2010, had grappled with cross gender feelings at intervals in my past and had sought professional help in 1985 and 1992 when they had taken on an immobilizing quality. On each occasion they rendered me incapable of work or normal social function. Each time I experienced this I wanted to die.

Gender Dysphoria—the feeling that one should be living and functioning in the opposite gender—is overpowering. It is incessant. What gives the condition such intensity is that, try as one might, the feelings cannot be expelled. They do not abate. They run repetitiously through the mind of the sufferer like a high rotation rock video of just one song. Or like one line from the same song. In my case, I was anxious, depressed and sleep deprived. I could barely eat and was drinking huge amounts of caffeine. That merely contributed to a vicious cycle of insomnia and panic attacks. In August 2011, I weighed 85 kilograms. In February 2012 I weighed 63 kilograms.

People at work were speculating that I was dying. There was more than a grain of truth to that. Only my wife and my therapist knew what was bothering me over that endless tortuous summer, which in memory's eye assumes the quality of a slow motion nightmare played out under a blazing relentlessly clear azure sky rather than in darkness. My abiding memory of that summer was of lonely, sleepless nights in cramped hotel rooms and seemingly endless days of blinding light. I felt as though was like trudging through a desert without even the fantasy of an oasis to sustain me.

I had confided that I believed I was a transexual to my therapist during a session in the first week of November 2011. Through November I felt growing despair and a strange sense of dissociation. I felt that I had ceased to be and was merely watching the events around me on a screen. The death of Peter Roebuck by his own hand that month pressed in on me as well. He had perished amid the torment and shame of being unable to present to the world without deception.

My therapist believed that I needed to confide in my wife Tritia, who was becoming alarmed at my dramatic weight loss and manifest depression. She could feel me lying beside her awake through the night and sensed that something was deeply wrong. She hoped that my demons were have been related to some form of past trauma of which she was unaware, and that she would steadfastly comfort me through its resolution when I took her into my confidence.

Ultimately, I told her what was bothering me, on the 9th of December. What followed makes a mockery of 'A problem shared is problem halved.' I watched her face drain of colour, then fill with bewilderment giving way to rage, followed by inconsolable sadness.

We both regard that as the worst day of our lives. Neither of us can recall with any clarity the next few months. Grief applies its own healing balm to the psyche. We both know it was a hideous period. Yet whenever we discuss it we each agree that it has become something of a blur. Neither of us can recall large slabs of it with any precision.

Much has since been made about my 'bravery' in ultimately deciding to embark on gender transition. Yet, I still feel remorse at the selfishness that it required for me to pursue my authentic life at the expense of the woman I loved, and still love, like no other. She is the heroine of this story if there is one. That she was able to grieve deeply, to eventually forgive me, then to love me anew is to her enormous credit and to my eternal joy. She has chosen to make no public comment about our life before or since. But as the person most affected by my transition, she has shown a grace and generosity that humbles me. I doubt that I would have survived what followed had she denounced me.

That Indian summer became the summer of final things. I have never again made love. There are places that we frequented as a couple to which neither of us has since been able to since return. Finally, on the day before that Adelaide Test Match, I reported sick to the Duntroon Military Hospital. I told the doctor there that I was transgendered and pleaded with her not to divulge this in the event that I snapped out of it again as I had done twice before. Medical records are confidential but my degree of psychiatric distress could have forced her to involve others.

Despite my defiant prediction to the doctor about normal service eventually resuming, some inner prompting moved me toward the Chapel at Duntroon outside which I had left my car.

I think I knew that this time was going to be different. We had married in that Chapel, promising to love and cherish one another until death. With hindsight, I probably knew that I had arrived at the same point every trans person does. If I was to live at all it would be as the person I felt myself to be or I would die. I lay down on the altar of the empty church and wept. I think I may have even screamed aloud. If there is a God, there was no blinding revelation in the pallid light of my Gethsemane. Mercifully no one intruded on my solitary wailing ritual.

I lay there for some time then went home and packed for the trip to Adelaide. Tritia drove me to see my therapist whom the doctor had called and asked to urgently assess my mental state that afternoon. Although both the doctor and my shrink were concerned at my condition, I disingenuously assured them that I was not a suicide risk. I was terrified that they would admit me to hospital and that I would not get to Adelaide.

In my fatigue and despair, completing the manuscript for the original version of this book became an obsession. Instinct told me that I had to complete this work. Likewise, some residual ember of determination, or perhaps mere egotism demanded that I not allow news of what was going on inside me filter out to the world beyond my home. Eventually, I was able to complete every chapter but the last without disclosing my personal crisis to my publisher Ian Gordon. I could not write about my crisis and he was resigned to the book ending abruptly after the Adelaide Test match.

One morning in May 2012 I encountered him at a newsagent in the pre dawn darkness and he asked me why I could not finish the text. He listened and embraced me. The title was already registered under my old name and we agreed to finish the book and eschew a formal launch. I expected at that stage to be living overseas under another name having abandoned Australia.

But first back to that awful searing January day. Tritia had waited outside the therapist's rooms and then drove me to Canberra Airport for an evening flight to Melbourne with a connection to Adelaide on the morning of the Test Match. I was in shock that I had blurted out my dark secret to an official military doctor. Sensing that my mind was made up, whether I knew it or not, she was trying to spend as much time as possible with the husband she knew was ceasing to exist, wasting away before her eyes.

I did go to Adelaide and I am glad that I did. Rahul Dravid played his last Test Match there and we met fleetingly and discussed staying in touch so that I could include his thoughts on the future of the game in the book. I never sent him the email with the questions about the future of cricket. When I next wrote to him it was to reveal my answers about my own future.

———

India returned to the Adelaide Oval in December 2014. The opening Test Match for the Border-Gavaskar Trophy began on 9 December. On 27 November Phillip Hughes had died, after being struck on the neck and sustaining a catastrophic injury during a Sheffield Shield Match at the Sydney Cricket Ground on 25 November 2014. The cricket world was numbed by the death of the popular young left hander whose lavish talent had not yet secured him a sinecure in the Australian Team.

His flamboyant, though imperfect technique delighted crowds but troubled selectors. He was staking a plausible claim for restoration to the Australian lineup for the scheduled opening Test against India at the Gabba. His death touched the nation deeply. Thousands of grass roots players and supporters left their bats on verandahs or at their front gates.

Social media was swamped with tributes and photographs of the eloquent silent tributes of the cricket tribe.

That spirit of cricket so often discussed, but just as often evading precise definition was vividly displayed in the days following his death. The nation paused as his funeral service was broadcast live from his hometown of Macksville. Behind his casket trod a cavalcade of the legends. Dressed in black rather than white they looked more imposing in their grief than in any moment of triumph. The rich poetic heart of the game was broken. But it never stopped beating. Michael Clarke, whose unabashed tears secured him a place in the nation's heart hitherto denied his talents, led them. Following on were Warne, McGrath, Lara, Lee, Kohli and a deep batting order of current Australians. Those who were out in the middle on the afternoon of 25 November 2014 will never erase the events from their minds. They included key members of the Australian team. No one quite knew what to do next. What was a decent interval between Hughes's death and the resumption of first class fixtures? When would the players be ready to play?

The Brisbane Test was postponed and the First Test moved to Adelaide on 9 December 2014. Three years to the day since that heart-rending conversation with Tritia I was in Adelaide pondering life, death and regret along with the entire cricket road show.

Adelaide sparkled. But the atmosphere at the ground was solemn and a little apprehensive. Play got underway after a poignant film tribute to Phillip Hughes. Adelaide Oval had become his home ground and he was playing for South Australia when he was fatally injured. Christmas trees looked incongruous among shrines to Hughes. Floral tributes, bats, helmets and memorabilia were all around the ground and its approaches.

His friends, especially those who were playing in his final Sheffield Shield Match in Sydney took a long time to grieve Hughes's death and recover their equilibrium. None has entirely dispelled the memory. And the revelations about that final session emanating form the coronial inquiry in October 2016 reopened many wounds and created fresh ones. While not doubting that their stated reasons were true, it struck me that the departures of Michael Clarke, Shane Watson, Ryan Harris, Chris Rogers and Mitchell Johnson over the ensuing year may have been hastened by Hughes's death. The calculus of risk versus reward must have shifted for some of those older players. A successful World Cup campaign and an unsuccessful Ashes series would have clinched the deal.

However, all that lay in an unseen future in December 2014. Eventually, the unfolding contest in the middle of the Adelaide Oval recovered its meaning as part of an ongoing conversation that began with 1877 in the first Test Match. Subtly, gradually, the crowd and the media started to focus on what was about to happen in Adelaide rather than what had happened at the SCG.

There were numerous milestones as Australian Cricket unsteadily returned to its feet. In the fourth over of the Australia's first innings, Indian pace man, Varun Aaron, unleashed a bouncer at David Warner. It punctured the funereal atmosphere at the ground. It gave onlookers a sense that the game could move on. Not until day three, when Mitchell Johnson struck Virat Kohli on the helmet, did the elephant finally leave the room.

Johnson, whose venomous pace, augmented by snarls, glares and grimaces had routed England in fading light here only a year before, looked momentarily stricken. When it was obvious that Kohli had survived, hostilities resumed. It gradually began to feel like any other Test Match. Warner and Varun Aaron exchanged spiteful words on the final day and any sense that the match was taking place in a graveyard was dispelled.

Leaving aside its cathartic, therapeutic significance it was an absorbing Test Match. Nathan Lyon exorcised some personal demons unrelated to the death of his mate. In 2012 Lyon had been unable to steer Australia home against South Africa home in Adelaide when 'Faf' Du Plessis and A.B. de Villiers soaked up nearly 100 overs between them. Lyon, with abundant runs to play with on the final day, bowled 50 overs but could not shut South Africa down. His inability to exploit a game situation and prevailing conditions led many to question Lyon's credentials. He failed singularly to honour the specialist spinner's contract with his team to deliver victory on the final day.

Until that match winning performance, Lyon must have been haunted by memories of Nathan Hauritz, another decent right arm orthodox bowler, who never quite shrugged off the journeyman label and lost his confidence after being defied by England at Cardiff in 2009. That effort against India closed for the time being the revolving door so freely employed by Australian selectors since 2007 when, to their consternation, they discovered that none of the spinners they selected was actually Shane Warne.

Had Hollywood been scripting that Test Match as the sequel to Hughes's death even it would have strained credulity with the Australian first innings. Three Australians, all close friends of Hughes, scored centuries in Australia's gluttonous first innings of 7/517. David Warner led the way, blasting 145 from 163 balls. He paid tribute to Hughes on reaching, 50, 63 and 100, as did Stephen Smith on his way to 162 off 231. Clarke paid homage at 37 to mark Hughes falling short of century by that number in his final innings, then again on reaching 100.

He went on to compile 128 from 145 deliveries. All of them touched the number 408 inscribed on their breasts, and reverently looked skyward on reaching each milestone. That of course was Hughes's number in the Australian Test roll of honour. Likewise, the crowd rose when Australia attained that score. At the time it seemed necessary to the collective healing, though a little mawkish with hindsight.

Yet the Test Match did live up to cricket's self-valuation that it is about continuity rather than full stops. It is a never-ending story. And no one, no matter how illustrious, is bigger than the game nor leaves more than a footprint in its history. Life. Death. Regret. Adelaide invited reflection upon them all. Life prevailed.

Apart from the grand narrative Adelaide represented a deeply personal celebration of life for me. I was part of ABC Grandstand Broadcast team. Much of the inspiration for writing this book came from my memories of long summer days with the crackle of transistor radios on beaches or in lush back yards where it provided a serenade to my youthful infatuation with cricket.

No one had a greater influence on the development of this manuscript, nor on my decision to pursue cricket writing than Jim Maxwell of the ABC. Since that startlingly beautiful Sydney winter day in 2011 a wonderful friendship has grown between us. He is incredibly special to me. Discussions with him helped me to impose some coherence on my vague sense that we had arrived at a moment when it could be no longer assumed that Test Cricket would survive in its existing form. Ultimately, of course, that summer posed the same question to me. Could I survive in my existing form? I did not see it in that light at the time. But how much do we really understand our subconscious motives? A shrink may well conclude that my evasion of my gender variance for decades was why I ended up in an Adelaide hotel room on 25 January 2012 planning my death.

Test cricket has changed since that summer when Jim Maxwell wondered whether we had tasted the last of the summer wine. Adelaide was the venue for the first day-night Test match between Australia and New Zealand in November 2015. More are scheduled including in England in 2017. That format, and the pink ball seem to be here to stay. Four day Test matches seem set to inevitably follow on. The West Indies will oppose that plan no doubt. They are currently making the two and half day test match their own genre.

So on 9 December 2014 I sat with Jim Maxwell in the ABC broadcast booth at the Adelaide. New name. Alive, it felt for the very first time. Given my respect for Jim and the iconic status of the cricket broadcast it was a wonderful experience. It was an experience for that compendiously named bucket list.

Jim was one of the few people in whom I confided about my decision to transition gender during the winter of 2012. Although I knew I could continue to serve in the Army I was pessimistic that cricket would accept me. I was certain that I would be the butt of jokes and shunned as simply too strange. In those early days I was braced for a hostile reaction whenever I ventured out, though mercifully those were few. I was far more fortunate than many other trans women. I sent the final chapter of this book to Jim, to Ian Chappell, Gideon Haigh and Rahul Dravid. In Dravid's case I also attached the Chapter about his Bradman Oration, which had unexpectedly provided the through line for the book.

Jim's prompt response reduced me to tears in my dark lonely apartment one morning. I logged in to find his message: 'Dear Cate, Thank you for sharing such an incredibly personal revelation with me. You must have been through an ordeal. Of course there will always be a place for you in Australian Cricket. The motto of my old school was 'It Is Better to Be

Than To Seem.' I have waited a very long time to see someone live that. See you at the Gabba. We will talk about your love of our game over summer. Hope you sell a million books.'

I did not expect Dravid to reply but wanted to express my gratitude to him for the inspiration he had unknowingly offered to me. Most nights in cramped hotel rooms over that summer I replayed his Bradman Oration. There was something luminous about his gentle humility. I always wept as he described the way he occasionally felt unbidden transcendence while he was out in the middle. His words and demeanour soothed me. It never occurred to me that he would reply or that over time we would meet and work together.

He did reply. Some weeks after I wrote to him I found an email from him upon awakening in the frigid gloom of late winter in Canberra. He offered warm support and thanked me for my gracious words about him, which, he believed, had been too generous. He expressed relief that I had not chosen to end my life and deprived cricket of 'your beautiful book.' He urged me to stay involved in cricket and warned me 'your story will touch people with pain in their lives not just about their gender.' His was the most prescient and touching that I received.

After *Australian Story* featured my transition in February 2014 my life changed considerably. I receive enormous amounts of mail from people questioning their assigned gender but also from people who have felt trapped in their lives. It is a privilege. On occasions I have not been able to emulate Dravid's steel, dignity and restraint in triumph and defeat.

But his example did teach me that no sincere correspondence is too insignificant to warrant a reply. I can never know what impact my story has had on a total stranger whom I will never meet. I try to reply to every person who writes to me. If I can ever offer someone the same hope that Rahul Dravid gave me I will be incredibly pleased and will feel worthy of his gift to me when I was desperate.

I tried to convey this to him when we met at Trent Bridge in Nottingham in July 2014. Dravid was covering India's tour of England for a range of media outlets. I saw him eating alone in the media lunch-room after coming off air. I was at a lunch hosted by Colin Gibson the jovial, bluff, Communications Director of the England Cricket Board. Lunch had become an informal celebration of Sunil Gavaskar's 65th birthday. Indian cricket royalty Kapil Dev, Sourav Ganguly and Sunil Gavaskar had been dropping into the hospitality boxes in the corridor adjacent to the media box throughout lunch. I was a guest of the England Cricket Board and was accompanied by my beautiful English friend Ayla Holdom. I had asked Colin to arrange a pass for Ayla so that she could join me in the media box during play. But he insisted that he could do better than that and organized lavish hospitality for us as official guests of the ECB. I got a mild bollocking from my colleagues for shamelessly taking my thirty pieces of silver. Ayla had never been to a cricket match much less a Test Match and I was touched at what Colin did to make it a memorable day for us.

Ayla knows nothing about cricket and was blissfully unaware both of the score and of the current of male admiration that surged through the room when she entered. She is a true English Rose, beautiful and brilliant with a wicked sense of humour. I burst out laughing when I noticed her Twitter feed. She had posted a shot of our view of Trent Bridge to the great envy of her mates from the RAF Search and Rescue Squadron in which she flew helicopters. One asked her which team was batting and she ventured 'England I think?'

On my way from the commentary position to join my luncheon companions I saw Rahul Dravid alone at a table. The sight of him alone, rather than surrounded by a crush of fans snapping selfies, stopped me in my tracks. As Ed Smith observed of him, Dravid can look shy, boyish and vulnerable away from the square. I was anxious not to intrude as another gushing admirer but felt that I was meant to say something meaningful to him. He looked up and nodded then looked away. Tentatively I approached him, merely hoping to thank him for what his message had meant to me.

'Rahul'

'Yes' He looked at me apprehensively.

'I'm Catherine McGregor'

He took a few seconds to process this. The last time we had chatted I had been male.

His face relaxed. 'Yes. Yes of course. Please join me.'

'No. I must not intrude. I just wanted to thank you for your message. It meant so much during an awful time in my life.'

'That was a beautiful book. My words were nothing. '

'Well to me they were. They meant a very great deal.'

'Please join me. Your transformation is remarkable. Forgive me for not recognizing you'

We chatted briefly and before I returned to lunch. At Southampton and again in Adelaide I enjoyed brief encounters with him. Rotating through the commentary box in Adelaide after him was my most treasured memory of covering cricket.

Rahul Dravid occupies much more bandwidth in my consciousness than I do in his and I do not wish to claim an intimacy to the friendship that is not there. But he had a disproportionate impact on my life. Every minute I have spent with Dravid has been a joy because he is a good man, and an inspiration, because he is also a great man. I hope that our passion for the game will ensure that we cross paths again.

'Every minute I have spent with Dravid has been a joy ...'

As this manuscript was being updated, Jim Maxwell was in St Vincent's hospital recovering from a stroke that occurred while he was covering an Olympic Sailing event from a studio. Jim believes that only the swift response of our friend Tim Gavel, of ABC Sport in Canberra, prevented permanent brain damage. When he heard Jim slurring his words Gavel rapidly assessed that he was having a stroke. He called an Ambulance, which was on the scene in minutes and rushed Jim to St. Vincent's.

That Golden Voice of our summers is unimpaired though he loses some precision in diction as he tires. He was obliged to sit out the 2016-17 but believes that he will return to the microphone. Jim Maxwell has become our most loved sports broadcaster. His style is distinctive, authentically Australian and intimate. Listeners finds him accessible and his appeal extends far beyond those purists who still eschew of television's wizardry and ball tracking gadgetry to listen to the ABC. An Australian summer without Jim Maxwell would definitely be missing the summer wine.

When I visited him, in September, he was in terrific humour. Former Prime Minister John Howard had visited him along with a steady stream of cricketing greats. I arrived late one Friday just as his wife Jen was leaving. He mischievously suggested that he would like to stay longer in hospital as it was easier to host his army of visitors there than at home. Raising her eyebrows Jen left to be replaced like a departing batsman by Barry Knight. Or, as an adoring childhood fan of Bob Cowper should I say The Barry Knight?

After Jim made the introductions I ventured 'Barry Knight? Cowper bowled Knight 307 at the Melbourne Cricket Ground in February 1966?' He beamed and bowed deeply.

'At your service my dear.'

Knight seemed cheerfully oblivious to how much pain he had inflicted on me at the age of 9 by abruptly bowling my idol Bob Cowper for 307 when he was on track to overtake Bradman's record score of 334. A mere fifty years had not assuaged my desire for vengeance. But Knight is a brilliant raconteur with an engaging sense of humour. I achieved 'closure' on my desolate childhood as our conversation unfolded. I hope if Bob Cowper reads this he can forgive me for unilaterally implementing a truce with his nemesis. His wounds are apparently fresh.

'He still brings it up whenever I see him. He never forgave Bradman for dropping him for the Adelaide Test you know. He is still quite cross about it, especially if he has had a drink. Did you ever see the ball?'

'No' I replied swallowing hard. I did not add that I had deliberately spared myself the trauma. They clearly did not have trigger warnings in M.J.K Smith's team.

'It went straight along the ground. Poor bugger. It was unplayable. The bails actually flew off forward over his head. You must see it some time.'

'Yes I must.'

'Goodness surely you are too young to remember that series.'

The Fatwa was lifted at that moment. I am a sucker for a compliment. 'Aren't you sweet. I am sixty actually.' I gushed. Sorry Bob. I know that was pathetic and fickle. But five decades is a long time and he was terribly nice fellow. And I am a cheap drunk on cricket stardom. I soon bid them both farewell and returned Jim's chivalrous military salute as I made my way downstairs to hail a cab to the airport.

The Two Chucks completed *Death of a Gentleman*. It was a powerful film worthy of the toil and love they poured into it. During the English summer of 2014 I had spent an afternoon in Sam's Fulham home watching very rough cuts of the extraordinary interviews he had secured. I was jarred to hear my voice and to see myself outside the Adelaide Oval on 25 January 2012 speaking about cricket to the camera. For a time Sam thought about

With Ed Cowan. 'I fear that I was present for the first and last balls of Ed's career'

using interviews three years apart on the same spot in Adelaide to use a my transformation to dramatize his theme of change and renewal. But I did not make the final version.

On 21 December 2015 I had the honour of introducing the film to Australia when I hosted its launch at the Chauvel Cinema in Paddington. I chaired a panel comprising Ed Cowan and Gideon Haigh and we discussed the film and fielded questions from passionate lovers of traditional cricket. I fear that I was present for the first and last balls of Ed's career. He was treated shabbily by the selectors, and the recent woes of the batting order may yet revive his career. But it seems likely Trent Bridge in 2013 was his Swan song. Sam joined us on skype. It was a marvelous evening. The cast of legends in the audience rivaled that on the screen. Cricket's tribe was at its convivial best.

I left the function with Ed and Gideon who were heading to the pub with a group of animated purists. Gideon had kindly asked me to spend Christmas with his family. I was thrilled as I am really fond of his wife Charlotte and his daughter Cecilia. Moreover, that honour is customarily extended to one of the cricket orphans spending Christmas alone in Melbourne before the Boxing Day Test. Some illustrious names had occupied the crease before me, most notably Mike Atherton, the former England Captain and opening batsman. Atherton is one of the world's finest cricket writers. He is also a consummate gentleman and working along side him for News Limited has been both illuminating and very agreeable.

Knowing that I would see him in a few days I bid Gideon goodnight and headed down Oxford Street to my hotel. I craved solitude. It had been a long year, with an Ashes series in England in July and August. Boxing Day would be the fifth Test since the First against New Zealand in the first week in November. I was already exhausted.

It was also the anniversary of my father's death. My friend and mentor, Chris Mitchell whose legendary tenure as Editor in Chief of *The Australian* is the subject of his book *Making Headlines*, lost his father on precisely the same day. Both our fathers died on 21 December 1964 within a couple of hours of one another.

Every year we exchange messages on the anniversary. More often than not we meet to mark the occasion. On the 50th anniversary in 2014 we met for a long lunch with Paul Kelly, the best writer on politics this nation has ever produced. In 2015, we postponed the annual dinner until the 22nd, to allow me to attend the film launch. I wanted to send him a message and to spend some time alone reflecting on life, love and regret.

It was an unseasonably cool night like the night that Dravid had delivered his Bradman Oration four years before. It seemed so much longer. So much had happened. Serious things. Life, love and regret. The American writer William Faulkner, whom I only resemble in having used alcohol too liberally to quell inner demons, wrote in *Intruder in the Dust*, 'It's all now you see. Yesterday won't end until tomorrow and tomorrow began ten thousand years ago.'

What would my father, a Kokoda veteran, have felt about his son now living as woman? Just a week before the launch of Sam and Jarrod's film my first bat and my last team cap had been placed on display in the National Museum of Australia. Regrettably they were deemed remarkable only for belonging to a transsexual rather than to a left handed prodigy who had glided past Cowper and Bradman and Hayden to claim an Australian Test record. Such had been my childish fantasy, just as I had dreamt of being a woman. Well I got to achieve the latter even if it took longer than a Boycott innings.

Dad knew that he was not coming for home for Christmas in 1964 and had insisted that my mother procure an imported bat worthy of the talent he had discerned in the frail blonde boy who had demanded to play for a team as soon as he had heard the radio descriptions of the Test Matches against Ted Dexter's 1962-63 touring team. That was the only item that I had kept from my childhood though a life of chaotic drug abuse, military transfers and shared accommodation. It is nearly as battered as its owner though it does not have recourse to Botox.

For years after his death, whenever I batted things around me would sometimes seem to disappear. When Rahul Dravid closed his Bradman Oration with his revelation that this had also happened to him tears streamed down my face. I had experienced the same transcendence.

When I had discussed it with my therapist during that excruciating internal battle with gender dysphoria, she speculated that I may have been traumatized by dad's death at such a young age and used cricket as a haven, an escape. That made as much sense as any other explanation.

As Gideon Haigh noted in his moving foreword, the love of cricket embraces both love and cricket. Indeed, he and I have been brought together by the love of the game. The game has loved me back. Amid a welter of change and challenge in my life it has always been there, providing the same haven that I found as a bewildered fatherless child of 8.

My first innings was patchy. Following on is always tough. It tests endurance and courage and belief. Following on is the consequence of initial failure. But in cricket as in life redemption is always an option. Desperate survival, followed by unexpected triumph against the odds provides the greatest allure of this, the very greatest game.

Index of Names